Alexander Janda • Norbert Leitner • Mathias Vogl

Chechens in the European Union

IMPRINT

Publishers:
Alexander Janda, Austrian Integration Fund
Schlachthausgasse 30, 1030 Vienna, Austria

Norbert Leitner, Federal Ministry of the Interior
Sicherheitsakademie
Herrengasse 7, 1014 Vienna, Austria

Mathias Vogl, Federal Ministry of the Interior
Herrengasse 7, 1014 Vienna, Austria

Edited by:
Alexander Schahbasi, Austrian Integration Fund

In Collaboration with:
Jan Kreisky, Simone Ludwig, Johanna Weberhofer, Katarzyna Jackowska

Translation and Editing
Doris Tempfer-Naar

Layout and Print
AV+ Astoria Druckzentrum, cover illustration: © iStockphoto / ann triling

Table of Contents

Preface

In numerous European countries, Chechen refugees have become a group of major importance in terms of integration work. Since the year 2002 the number of asylum applications submitted by individuals from the Russian Federation in Austria exceeded the amount of 2,000 p. a. and has remained at this high level. The recognition quota for asylum seekers with Russian nationality – mainly Chechens – reached more than 70% in the period between 2003 and 2007, and in 2004 this quota even exceeded 93%. In 2007, 2,633 refugees from the Russian Federation were recognized by the Austrian authorities as Convention refugees.

Although the challenges regarding the integration of Chechens have clearly emerged from the high percentage of recognized refugees, the knowledge about their concrete needs and conflict situations was at first insufficient. Furthermore, we know from our practical experience that the attitudes towards Chechens are often determined by superficial clichés spread by the media, by prejudices, and distorted views. It is for this reason that differentiated knowledge about life patterns and cultural particularities of Chechen refugees is needed.

The present anthology, which includes contributions by international experts, attempts to respond to the increased need for information that exists in several European countries regarding this target group. Experts are given an opportunity to present their experiences and insights into the different aspects of the challenge, providing an improved matter-of-fact and well-founded basis for future integration work.

The Austrian Integration Fund has been able to gain substantial expertise and knowledge about this group of refugees in the course of its work experience and in dealing with Chechen refugees. The scientific analysis of the phenomenon of Chechen migration to Europe complements our daily operative refugee work, which aims at harmonizing theory and practice.

Alexander Janda
Director of the Austrian Integration Fund

Preface

Considering that the ethnic group of the Chechens plays a significant role among asylum seekers and recognized refugees in Austria and the number of Chechens seeking asylum or being entitled to asylum is large, it is necessary to pay particular attention to this issue.

It is therefore important, in view of achieving a successful integration, to improve the status of research concerning the Chechen population group. This knowledge is targeted at providing support to the asylum and security authorities, the authorities at provincial, district and municipal levels, and also to NGO's.

The results gained from this research will be critical in promoting the understanding of this issue. In addition, they bring us one step closer to coping with the multitude of challenges.

On behalf of the SIAK, I would like to give my most sincere thanks to all those who participated in this project and to the authors of the publication, for their excellent work.

Norbert Leitner
Director of the Security Academy
Austrian Federal Ministry of the Interior

Preface

In numerous areas of politics and administration there is an ongoing exchange with science and research. Largely differing disciplines are asked for in this interaction between political and administrative practice on the one hand and science on the other. This need for profound scientific support is particularly necessary in the complex field of integration politics. The present anthology reflects this interaction of integration-related politics, administration, and research.

For the Ministry of the Interior, the comprehensive support and integration of recognized refugees is an issue of high priority. Over the past few years, refugees from Chechnya were granted international protection in Austria, as well as in other European countries. In addition to the important concrete practical support, we also see the necessity of a scientific approach to the challenges arising among this target group, especially in connection with the integration process.

It is a major concern to us to learn more about the backgrounds of these refugees to be able to back our integration measures with well-founded scientific findings, and on this basis, to evaluate them and develop them further. Since it combines practical experience and scientific expertise, the Austrian Integration Fund has developed into a pivotal competence centre on issues of migration and integration. Therefore the Austrian Integration Fund is predestinated to enter unknown territory in this field of research and to make European integration experiences accessible to scientific discourse.

Mathias Vogl
Director-General for Legal Affairs (DG III)
Austrian Federal Ministry of the Interior

8

Chechen Migration Flows to Europe – a Statistical Perspective

Martin Hofmann and David Reichel

Introduction

The present article aims at analysing the present size, structure and dynamics of Chechen migration flows to Europe from a statistical perspective. The analysis of quantitative trends and developments of related flows has to come up against a number of methodological limitations. A first problem arises from the fact that the statistical methods used for collecting migration data refer to citizenship and not to the ethnicity of migrants. As regards the subject of this article, the European countries under investigation register ethnic Chechen as nationals from the Russian Federation. Thus, in a first step it was assessed to which extent statistics on Russian migrants referred to ethnic Chechens. A second problem lies in the fact that migration statistics in general cover events on an annual basis and are not suited to record contemporary migration. In addition, migration statistics basically provide information on the size and nationality of migrant populations counted per year but not on the country of previous residence of these migrants. Consequently, an analysis of secondary migration movements of Chechens within Europe is possible only to a very limited extent. However, within these inherent limitations, the available statistics do allow for an identification of main trends, an assessment of the size and a description of main patterns of Chechen migration to Europe over the recent past.

A first analysis of quantitative and qualitative sources allows for narrowing the scope of the subject. First, Chechen migration to European countries is a comparatively recent phenomenon. Significant inflows date back only to the second half of the 1990s. Second, Chechen migration to Europe almost exclusively refers to flight migration. Third, Chechen migration also includes irregular movements but the vast majority of Chechen migrants apply for asylum in a European country in the course of individual migration processes. Thus, European asylum statistics provide not only the only really accessible data sources but also a widely comprehensive overview of Chechen migration flows to Europe. The analysis of annual application figures in European countries confirms a tendency towards a concentration of Chechen asylum seekers in certain main countries of destination. Asylum migration flows constitute heterogeneous phenomena, which are influenced by a variety of determining factors. Migrants from a given country or region of origin do not necessarily constitute a homogenous group when it comes to motivations or migration patterns, a fact that refers to flight migrants as well (Papadopoulou 2002: 1). Individual decisions to leave their home country or country of current residence and to move to a specific destination country are based on a variety of factors that can be summarised along the following dimensions: Overall living conditions in the home country or country of residence, perceptions on existing opportunities in destination countries and/or transit countries of migration flows, and personal motivations, such as partners, family members or friends, who have already settled in a specific country. These conditions become decisive for the development of specific countries into "potentially attractive" or "unattractive" destination countries for asylum migration flows from certain countries or regions of origin. More specifically, such factors comprise political and economic developments in countries of origin and the resulting potential of refugees, the proximity or distance of countries of origin and destination, the geographical position of a destination country on prevailing regular and irregular migration routes, the existence of ethnic communities and networks in the country of destination and/or en route, potential job opportunities on formal and informal labour markets, but also legal and practical aspects of the specific asylum systems and recognition rates. The quantitative impact of these individual factors and/or their interplay on the total amount of asylum applications submitted in a country is difficult to measure. As a matter of fact, only limited research has been conducted so far on the concrete motives and reasoning of refugees to choose a specific country of destination – assuming that they are in a position to actually make such a choice (Neumayer 2005: 15). However, based on the review of the limited number of case studies that have been carried out on the topic as well as on the analysis of asylum and alien statistics, certain factors that influence the size and distribution of asylum migration flows can be identified and shall be outlined in the following as basic hypotheses:

1. In general, asylum migration has to be perceived as the result of so-called "push factors" (war, political crisis, state or quasi-state persecution, threats to personal freedom and security, economic dislocation, poverty, famine, population pressure or natural disaster). So-called "pull factors" (job opportunities, higher wages, better overall living conditions) are of lesser importance in decision-making processes of flight migrants.
2. In the beginning, the immediate need to reach a country that can provide protection constitutes the overriding motive for flight migrants. After reaching a safe country, refugees might develop additional or different aspirations with regard to their individual life-situation, aspirations they expect to better fulfil in a country other than the one which granted them protection in the first place. Subsequent "secondary migration" of refugees can be the result of such considerations (Middleton 2005: 33).
3. The emergence and existence of migrant networks is considered to rank among the most important explanatory factors of migration today. In a simplified version, the contemporary nature of migration could be perceived as a form of "chain migration", with migrant networks developing into "autonomous social structures", becoming institutionally stable and continuously "feeding the very migrations that initially produced them" (Light 2004: 2). The importance of migrant networks is not limited to labour migration flows, established migrant communities in certain destination countries and functioning migrant networks in these countries and along migration routes play an important role in shaping the size and direction of flight migration flows as well. They provide vital information in the preparation and carrying out of the flight, provide financial and emotional support, and assist in integration processes after arrival.
4. Migrant communities and networks not only have "multiplier" but also "channelling effects" in directing asylum migration flows from a certain country or region of origin to specific destination countries. The "channelling effects" result in the so-called "clustering" of asylum migration flows, i.e. the concen-

tration of asylum seekers from a certain country or region of origin in specific destination countries or destination regions (Neumayer 2005: 9).

5. The "clustering" of asylum seekers is reinforced by the evolvement of an "illegal migration industry", i.e. the increasingly dense networks of professional human smugglers. It is a well-observed fact that smuggling networks not only play a key role in facilitating irregular migration movements but also in channelling these movements by directing migration towards or away from particular transit and destination countries (Bilger et al 2006: 74).

The Conflict in Chechnya

The yearly developments with regard to asylum applications submitted by ethnic Chechens in European Union Member States is closely linked to the ongoing conflict between Russian federal forces and rebel fighters in the secessionist North Caucasus Republic of Chechnya. There are varying estimates on the total amount of persons, who had to flee from the conflict zone. Some sources indicate an estimated 500,000 people to have fled Chechnya during the first period of the conflict between 1994 and 1996 (Cutler 2008: 1). The intensification of the conflict in 1999, following an incursion by Chechen-based militants into the neighbouring Russian republic of Dagestan, led to a second wave of flight migration inside and out from Chechnya (Youngs 2000: 15). Between 1999 and 2002, a total of 310,000 persons were registered as internally displaced, inside Chechnya and on the territories of Ingushetia, Dagestan, other North Caucasus republics or urban areas of the Russian Federation (ECRE 2005: 6). In the course of the second phase of the conflict, flight migrants from Chechnya increasingly tried to reach the territories of the EU-15, Switzerland and Norway or – to a lesser degree – the then candidate countries of Central and Eastern Europe. Related figures support the assumption that acute crisis situations in countries of origin in fact regularly result in a significant increase of asylum applications by nationals of the affected countries. Similar trends were observed with regard to asylum seekers from the former Yugoslavia in 1998/1999, from Afghanistan in 2000/2001 or from Iraq in 2002/2003. Experience also shows that the mobilising effects of crisis situations in a country of origin are reflected in asylum statistics of European countries only with a certain delay. Refugees who find themselves in the midst of an acute political or military crisis situation are mostly not immediately in a position to move to a European country, which might guarantee protection, due to the simple fact that they do neither have the financial means nor the access to supporting structures to organise a journey to these countries. It takes a while to build up the necessary support, be it by way of ethnic or family networks or by way of professional human smugglers, who need some time to organise their business as well. The extent to which an acute political crisis situation leads to an increased refugee or migration flow to European countries also depends on the distance that has to be covered. While the Kosovo crisis resulted in a large increase in asylum applications in European countries[1] (compared to the total number of people fleeing Kosovo), the relative share of displaced people from the Afghanistan or Iraq crisis who made their way to Europe was much smaller. Such diverging developments are owed to the fact that larger distances to overcome also entail higher costs to be borne, and flight migrants who had to flee from immediate threat often do not dispose of the necessary financial means for that. Graph 1 shows the yearly development of total asylum applications submitted by Russian Federation nationals in European countries[2].

Between 1997 and 2006, Russian Federation citizens submitted a total of 170,649 asylum applications in European countries. New applications reached their peak in 2003 with a total of 33,906 applications. The sharpest increases in relative terms took place between the years 1999/2000 (plus 79.2% in total applications) and 2002/2003 (plus 75.4% in total applications). The year 2003 saw the biggest jump in total figures with an increase of 14,576 new applications compared to the previous year. After 2003, the number of new applications decreased significantly at a Europe-wide level. Between 2003 and 2006, the total values of annual applications have more than halved (minus 56.2%). This development cannot necessarily be explained by an easing of the crisis situation in Chechnya. On the one hand, a better part of Chechens who had to flee from the intensified conflict after 1999 had made their way to European countries by that time. On the other hand, the entering into force of the "Dublin II Regulation" (determining which EU Member State is responsible for examining an asylum application) and the implementation of the EURODAC system (to collect and exchange finger-print data of asylum applicants) in 2003 had brought about

1 EU-27 plus Norway and Switzerland

2 If not quoted otherwise, all data presented in this article were extracted from: UNHCR Statistical Online Database, United Nations High Commissioner for Refugees (UNHCR), data extracted from 16/01/2008 to 25/03/2008.

Graph 1: Asylum applications lodged by Russian Federation citizens in European States 1997 – 2006

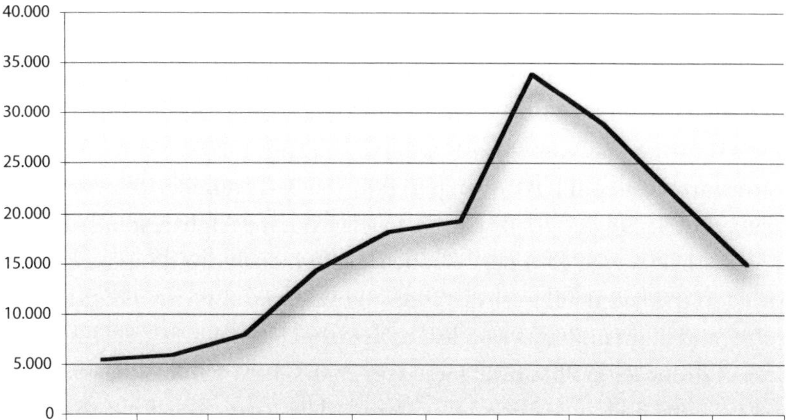

	1997	1998	1999	2000	2001	2002	2003	2004	2005	2006
Total	5.480	5.842	7.990	14.315	18.176	19.330	33.906	28.980	21.763	14.867

Source: UNHCR Statistical Online Database, United Nations High Commissioner for Refugees (UNHCR), Data extracted: 19/03/2008 and authors' calculations

changes in migration decisions and strategies of asylum seekers. Since the Dublin regime became fully operational, asylum seekers increasingly try to avoid applying for asylum in EU Member States along the route before they have reached their aspired target country. Before 2003, a significant share of asylum seekers applied repeatedly in several EU Member States, moving through the respective asylum systems to their final destination (Jandl 2004: 806). This strategy was reflected in asylum statistics as well, since, in case of repeated applications, one and the same individual was counted several times in the statistics of different countries. Thus, the decline in Europe-wide asylum statistics in the years after 2004 at least partly reflects adjusted statistics, the real decline in Chechen flight migrants coming to Europe is less significant than overall application figures would suggest.

The Clustering of Asylum Seekers in Specific European Countries

The analysis of related statistics makes evident that in most cases international migration flows are not distributed evenly across prospective target countries. Emigration flows from a specific country or region of origin tend to concentrate on one or several target country(ies), "immigrants tend to cluster spatially in order to lower the costs of migration" (Neumayer 2005: 10). With certain reservations, this observation also applies to asylum migration. As regards the subject of this article, the question is whether such a "clustering" of asylum applicants from the Russian Federation can be identified from a Europe-wide perspective. The answer has to be yes, the development of annual application figures clearly supports the hypothesis of a "clustering" of asylum seekers from the Russian Federation. From 1997 to 2006, the five most important receiving countries were Poland (a total of 28,906 applications), Germany (24,796), Austria (22,771), France (17,302) and Belgium (15,111). Other European countries with significant numbers of asylum

Graph 2: Asylum applications submitted by Russian citizens in European countries 2000 – 2006

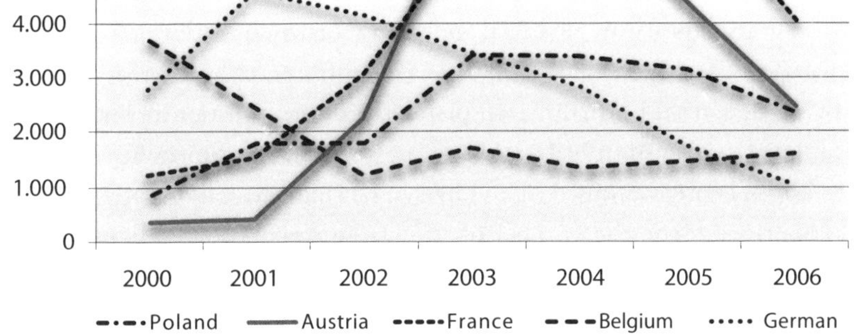

Source: UNHCR Statistical Online Database, United Nations High Commissioner for Refugees (UNHCR), Data extracted: 19/03/2008 and authors' calculations

Graph 3: Total applications by Russian Federation asylum seekers in top 5 European countries compared to other European countries 2000 – 2006

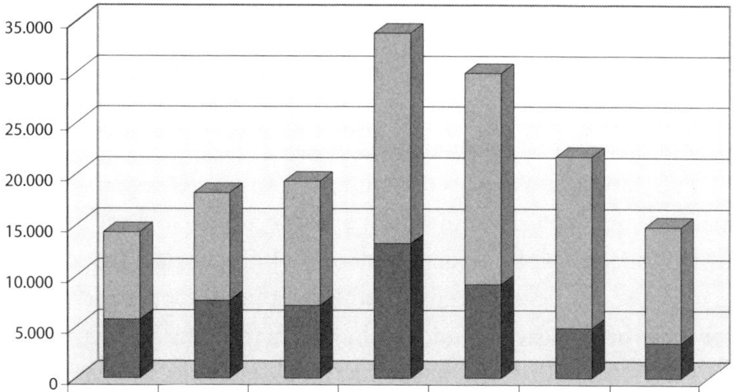

	2000	2001	2002	2003	2004	2005	2006
Top 5 countries	8.598	10.586	12.224	20.700	20.803	16.836	11.378
Other	5.717	7.590	7.106	13.206	9.177	4.927	3.489

Source: UNHCR Statistical Online Database, United Nations High Commissioner for Refugees (UNHCR), Data extracted: 19/03/2008 and authors' calculations

applications lodged by Russian Federation citizens were the United Kingdom (a total of 9,675 applications), the Czech Republic (9,034), Sweden (8,298), Norway (7,949) and Slovakia (7,305). The developments in Russian asylum migration to Europe showed analogies as well as discrepancies. In most European countries, the number of new applications peaked in 2003, namely in Austria, the Czech Republic, France, Norway, Slovakia, and several other countries with lower rates of applications, and decreased afterwards. By contrast, applications reached their peak in Sweden in the year 2002. In Poland, the European country with the most applications from Russian Federation citizens, the maximum value was reached only in 2004. Moreover, the development in Germany differs greatly from most other countries. Here, the number of applications peaked already in 2001 and decreased steadily afterwards. Other discrepancies are observable when examining the further developments of the applications after 2003. The numbers in all countries went down after the year 2003, except in Poland where the number increased further until 2004 and dropped afterwards.

Graph 4: Total applications by Russian Federation asylum seekers in top 5 European countries 2000 – 2006

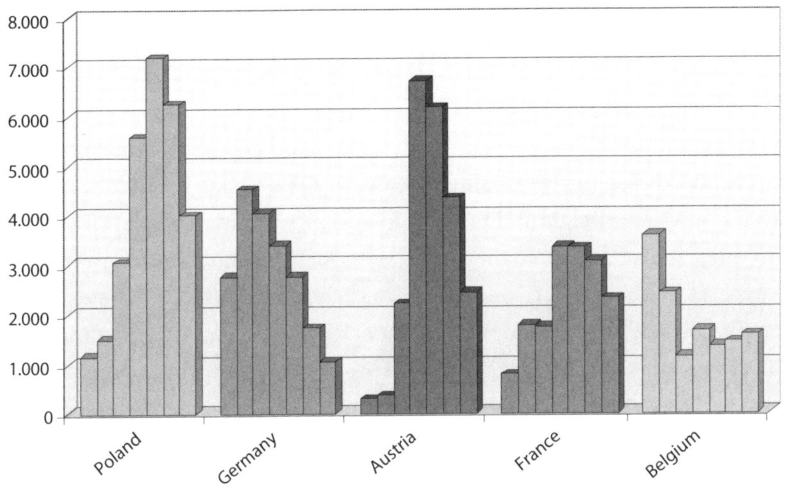

Source: UNHCR Statistical Online Database, United Nations High Commissioner for Refugees (UNHCR), Data extracted: 19/03/2008 and authors' calculations

What is striking, however, is that regardless of the developments in total applications after 1999, asylum migration flows from the Russian Federation increasingly concentrated on specific European target countries. In 1999, 52% of all asylum applications lodged by citizens from the Russian Federation had been submitted in the top-five European countries[3]; in 2006, this value amounted up to 77%. Graph 3 illustrates the trend towards an ongoing "clustering" of asylum applicants from the Russian Federation after 1999.

Graph 4 takes a closer look at the annual developments of applications submitted by Russian Federation citizens in the top-five European countries. The years after 1999 not only brought a steep increase in annual applications, but also turned two European countries into main destination countries of Russian asylum migration that had not been affected by related flows in the years before. Between 1994 and 2004, the total number of asylum applications received in Poland multiplied 65 times (from 109 to 7,182 new applications), in Austria 50 times

3 Poland, Germany, Austria, France and Belgium over the period 1997 to 2006.

(from 120 to 6,172 new applications). Though figures in other European countries rose during that period as well, the annual increases showed comparatively stable developments.

Size and Structure of Chechen Asylum Migration

In the section above it was shown that Russian Federation citizens predominantly apply for asylum in five European countries, that is Poland, Germany, Austria, France and Belgium. For these five countries a more in-depth analysis of related quantitative developments was undertaken by conducting short interviews with experts on the respective situation in their home country. As stated before, one main obstacle to a thorough assessment of the real size of asylum migration of Chechens is the fact that related statistics are based on the citizenship of applicants and thus show Chechen applicants together with all other asylum seekers originating from the Russian Federation.

The actual share of ethnic Chechens in the total of asylum seekers from the Russian Federation varies significantly between European countries. For Austria, migration experts estimate that the share of Chechen asylum seekers in all applicants from the Russian Federation is almost 100%. Although there are no official data on the issue, there are no known cases of Russian asylum seekers who had not originated from Chechnya. In Poland, the exact share of Chechen asylum seekers among Russian applicants has not been officially established. However, migration researchers estimate that the vast majority of Russian asylum seekers in Poland are ethnic Chechens. The same refers to France, experts estimate the share of Chechens to be almost 100% of all Russian applicants. For Germany, where exact data are available, the average share of Chechen asylum seekers in all applicants from the Russian Federation was 43.8% in the period between 2000 and 2006. In total, 9,051 Chechens applied for asylum in Germany during this period. From available information it can be concluded that Russian asylum migration to Europe in fact largely refers to ethnic Chechens with the notable exception of Germany, where less than half of all Russian asylum seekers originate from Chechnya.

Recognition Rates for Chechen Asylum Seekers in European Countries

It is often assumed that there is a link between high recognition rates for certain nationalities of asylum seekers in a country and a corresponding "attractiveness" of this country for follow-up asylum migration. As a matter of fact, recognition rates for Chechen asylum seekers vary significantly among European countries. It is difficult to really compare the respective figures provided by asylum statistics, since countries apply different calculation methods depending on whether they include appeal and review decisions or other forms of protection in their statistics or not. But under the restriction of limited comparability, it is safe to say that Chechen asylum seekers do face different chances of getting protection granted in European countries. On basis of available data and in a rough classification, countries with comparatively high recognition rates comprise Austria, Belgium and France, whereas the Czech Republic, Finland, Germany, Poland, Sweden and the Slovak Republic show lower recognition rates (UNHCR 2006). With an average of 74.8% (between 2002 and 2006)[4] Austria had by far the highest recognition rate among the main receiving countries of Chechen asylum seekers in Europe. The highest value was recorded in 2004 with a recognition rate of 94%, practically implying that in this year, nine out of ten decisions on Chechen asylum applications were positive. The other main receiving countries in Europe had significantly lower recognition rates over the reference period. In Belgium[5], on average 28.3% of all decisions on Chechen cases were positive (between 2004 and 2006), in France[6] 26.2% (between 2000 and 2007), in Germany[7] 23.2% (between 2000 and 2007). Between 2003 and 2006, Poland[8] on average granted refugee status to only 5.2% of all Chechen asylum seekers who had applied during this period. Despite of the low recognition rates, a large number of Chechen asylum seekers found protection in Poland. In 2003, new legislation introduced the possibility to grant "tolerated status", a form of subsidiary protection for asylum seekers in Poland. In 2006, 46.3% of Chechen asylum seekers were granted "tolerated

4 Authors' calculations.

5 Commissariaat Generaal voor de vluchtelingen en de staatlozen (CGVS), Asylum Statistics and authors' calculations.

6 Office français de protection des réfugiés et apatrides (OFPRA) and authors' calculations.

7 Bundesamt für Migration und Flüchtlinge (BAMF), Referat 224

8 UNHCR 2008 and Bureau for Informatics, Documentation and Statistics, Office for Repatriation and Aliens

status" on basis of the new law. However, the "tolerated status" started to show considerable effects only after 2005, in 2004 only 10.1% of Chechen asylum seekers had benefited from this form of protection. Thus, the granting of "tolerated status" cannot be perceived as creating an incentive that would explain the high numbers of Chechens applying for asylum in Poland during the years before (2002: a total of 3,048 Chechen applicants; 2003: 5,581; 2004: 7,182; 2005: 6,244). Noticeably, Austria and Poland, the two countries which have witnessed the biggest increases in Chechen asylum migration after 2000, showed widely different developments in annual recognition rates for this group of asylum seekers. The steep increase in applications in Austria, where Chechen asylum seekers could hope for being granted refugee status more than in any other European country, would support the hypothesis that high recognition rates for citizens from a certain country of origin attract follow-up asylum migration from their co-nationals. However, this hypothesis is contradicted by the developments in Poland, where apparently no correlation existed between the low recognition rates for and the continuously growing number of applications lodged by Chechen asylum seekers.

Destination and Transit Countries of Chechen Asylum Migration

The comparison of application figures and recognition rates in the main target countries of Chechen asylum migration to Europe leads to the assumption that these countries have different roles in related migration processes. It is a phenomenon observed Europe-wide among asylum authorities that a big part of asylum proceedings has to be dismissed due to the fact that applicants have disappeared before a decision on the application has been made – often only a few days after the applications has been lodged. In many cases entering the asylum procedure functions as part of an overall migration strategy. Lodging an application in a European country provides migrants with a limited possibility for legal residence, to take a short break and to organise the onward journey to the aspired country of final destination. Traditionally, it is the EU Member States with external Schengen borders that are affected the most by the disappearance of asylum seekers. First, overcoming the tight controls at Schengen borders is the biggest obstacle for both asylum seekers and irregular migrants on their way to Europe. Second, applying for asylum within the Schengen zone is the main objective of flight migrants as they regard EU Member States as the only countries to offer them real protection. In this regard and in the context of the present article, the developments in Poland before and after EU enlargement are of special interest. After applying for asylum in Poland, a high percentage of applicants from Chechnya did not and do not wait for a first-instance decision. On average more than 66% of all cases involving Chechens had to be discontinued between 2003 and 2006, corresponding to a total of more than 23,000 dismissed asylum procedures of Chechen applicants. This number also represents the potential of onward migration to Western European countries by Chechens, who initially applied for asylum in Poland as well as a strong indicator for the outflow of asylum seekers. The target countries of this supposed onward migration are not officially established, however, based on quantitative and qualitative information, it can be assumed that these secondary flows to a large extent moved to other main receiving countries in Europe, specifically Austria, France and Belgium. This assumption is supported by the requests submitted by other EU Member States after the entering into force of the Dublin II Regulation in Poland in May 2004. Out of 1,052 EURODAC requests addressed to Poland in the second half of the year 2004, the vast majority came from Germany, Austria, the Czech Republic, Belgium and France[9]. Based on these data it can be assumed that Poland and – to a lesser degree – the Czech Republic rather represent transit countries for Chechen asylum seekers, whereas Austria, France and Belgium represent the aspired countries of destination of these migration flows.

Chechen Refugee Populations in European Countries

Available data on stocks of asylum seekers in European countries confirm the overall trends in Chechen asylum migration as outlined in the previous sections with the reservation that these figures have to be looked at with caution. The data on stocks of refugees recorded are less reliable than application figures; they partly over- and partly underestimate the real size of refugee populations residing in European countries. Nevertheless, apart from Germany where figures on stocks of the refugee population originating from Russia relate neither to application

9 ECRE 2006: 185

figures nor to numbers of recognized refugees, data on the respective sizes of refugee populations correspond quite accurately to the developments in asylum migration flows from Chechnya as described above. The total size of the Chechen refugee population residing in European countries in 2006 amounted to a total of 37,132[10] with a total of 29,151 Chechen refugees being hosted by five receiving countries, Austria, Poland, France, Belgium and Norway. In 2006, Austria hosted the largest Chechen refugee population in Europe with a total of 8,723 recognized refugees, followed by Poland with a total of 6,024[11], France with a total of 5,945, Belgium with a total of 5,425 and Norway with a total of 3,034. These figures also imply that in 2006, more than 78% of all Chechen refugees recognized in Europe resided on the territory of the top-five receiving countries.

The Role of Networks in Chechen Asylum Migration

In the previous sections Chechen asylum migration to Europe was described as a comparatively recent phenomenon on the one hand as well as a development increasingly concentrating in a set of target countries on the other. The latter is closely linked to the emergence and maintenance of migrant communities and networks in the main transit and target countries of Chechen asylum migration. Migrant networks are attributed a "multiplier effect", triggering migrants to move "because others with whom they are connected have migrated before" (Arango 2004: 28). Massey et al. define migrant networks as "sets of interpersonal ties that connect migrants, former migrants, and non-migrants in origin and destination areas through ties of kinship, friendship, and shared community origin" (Massey et al 1996: 198). These networks play an important role not only in regular or irregular migration but in asylum migration as well (Middleton 2005: 10). Though from the perspective of asylum seekers the choice of a destination country is primarily determined by the necessity to reach a safe country that can offer protection, there is oftentimes still some room to make choices with regard to an aspired destination country. Migrant networks (relatives, friends as well as other migrants encountered en route) play a crucial role in a manifold manner. It is these networks that can above all provide the information needed to carry out a migration project,

10 Data on EU-26 (excluding Germany) plus Norway and Switzerland.

11 The Polish figure also includes individuals with "tolerated status".

to mobilize the financial resources required for a person to leave a crisis-ridden country and to move to a safe country (Crisp 1999: 6), and can provide the necessary support in all matters of insertion and integration (e.g. accommodation, income opportunities, health care etc.) along the route and after arrival (Jordan/Düvell 2002: 150).

Though comprehensive research on Chechen communities is largely missing, the analysis of the quantitative developments in European countries allows conclusions to be drawn on their influence on the continuation and distribution of migration flows from Chechnya to Europe. In principle, the interplay of three factors impact on the significance of ethnic communities and migrant networks for the stimulation and "channelling" of migration flows: the level of social and economic integration in a country of destination and the resulting support capacity for follow-up migrants; the level of identity and solidarity within a community; and the density of communication and interaction between "migrant diasporas" and their home countries (Crisp 1999: 4). Chechen communities are to be characterised as so-called "new migrant diasporas", i.e. migrant populations, which have no strong historical ties to the societies of receiving countries. Only in France and Belgium smaller communities of ethnic Chechens had already established themselves at the time when significant migration movements set in from Chechnya to European countries. However, the lack of larger, economically and socially integrated communities also meant that newly arrived migrants from Chechnya could not rely on the support of fully functioning ethnic communities and networks once they had reached the territories of European states. This fact also implied that factual support by other actors than ethnic communities and migrant networks, i.e. the asylum systems of receiving countries, was of overriding importance in the early phases of Chechen asylum migration to Europe. In a first step, a small number of European countries developed into main target countries of Chechen asylum migration not because of having close ties to Chechen communities before but because of being in reach of Chechen flight migrants and for offering protection to them. Austria serves as an example for this pattern. In a second step, social networks started to build around the first arrivals, and the traditionally strong role of kinship and shared identity among Chechens strengthened the concentration trend in the primary target countries of Chechen asylum migration. It remains to be seen if an ongoing integration process of the present migrant population will reinforce the "clustering" of Chechen migration flows even more, or if successful integration will provide

Chechen migrants with the possibility to establish themselves in other European countries and thus lead to secondary migration or the evolvement of new significant Diasporas in other European countries. Based on previous experience with other migrant populations it seems most likely that the migration patterns that have evolved over the last years will continue to prevail in the years to come as well.

When discussing the role of ethnic communities and migrant networks in shaping the size and direction of migration flows, the role of the networks of professional human smugglers must be also mentioned. Today, it is commonly accepted that smuggling networks play a decisive role not only in offering their services on a general level but in channelling irregular migration flows through and to specific countries (Koser 2001: 64). Once smuggling networks have established stable organisational structures and forms of interaction between countries of origin and specific transit and destination countries, these structures increasingly stabilise the direction of migration flows from a country of origin as well. Information gathered by European authorities confirms the strong involvement of highly organised smuggling networks in Chechen migration to and within the territory of the European Union. In a majority of cases the clients of these networks apply for asylum as part of a migration/smuggling strategy or once they have reached their aspired country of destination (Republic of Austria 2004/2005/2006).

Conclusions

Chechen migration to European countries constitutes a comparatively recent phenomenon and mainly comprises asylum migration resulting from the ongoing conflict in the North Caucasus Republic of Chechnya. Between 1997 and 2006, Russian Federation citizens submitted more than 170,000 asylum applications in European countries, peaking in 2003 with nearly 40,000 applications. From available information it can be concluded that Russian asylum migration to Europe in fact largely refers to ethnic Chechens. After 2003, the number of new applications decreased significantly at a Europe-wide level. Over the years, Chechen asylum migration flows increasingly concentrated on specific European target countries. In 1999, 52% of all asylum applications lodged by Chechen migrants had been submitted in the top-five receiving countries Poland, Germany, Austria,

France and Belgium; in 2006, this rate amounted already up to 77%. Throughout this process, Austria and Poland turned into main destination countries of asylum migration from Chechnya, countries that had been widely unaffected by such flows in the years before. However, the comparison of application figures and recognition rates in the main target countries of Chechen asylum migration to Europe leads to the assumption that these countries have different roles in related migration processes. Poland and – to a lesser degree – the Czech Republic rather represent transit countries for Chechen asylum seekers, whereas Austria, France and Belgium represent the aspired countries of destination of these migration flows. The total size of the Chechen refugee population residing in European countries in 2006 amounted to more than 37,000, with nearly 30,000 Chechen refugees being hosted by five receiving countries, Austria, Poland, France, Belgium and Norway. This also implied that in 2006, more than 78% of all Chechen refugees recognized in Europe resided on the territory of the top-five receiving countries. The size, structure and direction of Chechen asylum migration flows have been influenced by the emergence of migrant networks and networks of professional human smugglers and reinforced the trend towards a spatial "clustering" of Chechen migration in specific destination countries. It is to be expected that these networks will continue to impact on migration patterns that have evolved over the last years in the future as well. Based on this assumption it can be concluded that the present receiving countries of Chechen asylum seekers migration will remain the main destinations of related flows in the years to come.

Bibliography

Arango, Joaquin (2004): Theories of International Migration. In: Joly, Daniele: International Migration in the New Millennium. Global Movement and Settlement, Ashgate, 15–35.

Bilger, Veronika/Hofmann, Martin/Jandl, Michael (2006): Human Smuggling as a Transnational Service Industry. Evidence from Austria. In: International Migration, 2006, Vol., 44 (4), 59–93.

Crisp, Jeff (1999): Policy challenges of the new diasporas. Migrant networks and their impact on asylum flows and regimes, 1999. Available at: http://www.transcomm.ox.ac.uk/working%20papers/riia3.pdf (28 January 2005).

Cutler, Robert M. (2008): Chechnya, Available at: http://www.fpif.org/selfdetermination/conflicts/chechen.html (17 March 2008).

European Council on Refugees and Exiles – ECRE (2005): Guidelines on the Treatment of Chechen Internally Displaced Persons (IDPs), Asylum Seekers & Refugees in Europe, June 2005.
European Council on Refugees and Exiles – ECRE (2006): Report on the application of the Dublin II Regulation in Europe. Available at: www.ecre.org/files/ECRE%20Dublin%20Report%2007.03.06%20-%20final.pdf (14 Feb 2008).
Jandl, Michael (2004): The relationship between human smuggling and the asylum system in Austria. In: Journal of Ethnic and Migration Studies (JEMS), 2004, Vol 30, No. 4, 799–806.
Jordan, Bill/Düvell, Franck (2005): Irregular migration. The dilemmas of transnational mobility. Cheltenham.
Koser, Khalid (2001): The Smuggling of Asylum Seekers to Western Europe. Contradictions, Conundrums, and Dilemmas. In: Kyle, David/ Koslowski, Rey (eds.): Global Human Smuggling. Comparative perspective. Baltimore, 58–73.
Light, Ivan, et al (2004): Migration Networks and Immigrant Entrepreneurship. Available at: http://www.sscnet.ucla.edu/issr/paper/issr51.pdf (23. October 2004).
Massey, Douglas S. et al (1996): Theories of International Migration. A Review and Appraisal. In: Cohen, Robin (eds.): Theories of Migration, Cheltenham, 157–181.
Middleton, Darren (2005): Why asylum seekers seek refuge in particular destination countries. An exploration of key determinants. In: Global Commission on International Migration (GCIM), Global Migration Perspectives, No. 34.
Neumayer, Eric (2005): Bogus Refugees? The Determinants of Asylum Migration to Western Europe. London: LSE Research Online. Available at: http://eprints.lse.ac.uk/archive/00000580 (22 February 2008).

Papadopoulou, Aspasia (2002): Kurdish Asylm Seekers in Greece. The Role of Networks in the Migration Process. UNU/WIDER Conference on Poverty, International Migration and Asylum. Available at: http://www.wider.unu.edu/conference/conference-2002-3/conference%20papers/papadopoulou.pdf (18 February 2006).
Republic of Austria, Federal Ministry of the Interior, Federal Criminal Police Office (2004/2005/2006): Various years. Organised THB Crime. Organisierte Schlepperkriminalität. Jahresbericht 2004/2005/2006.
United Nations High Commissioner for Refugees (UNHCR), (2008): Statistical Online Database, Data extracted from 16/01/2008 to 25/03/2008
UNHCR (2006): Statistical Yearbook 2006. Trends in Displacement, Protection and Solutions. Available at: www.unhcr.org/statistics (14 February 2008)
Youngs, Tim (2000): The Conflict in Chechnya. House of Commons Library Research paper 00/14. Available at: http://www.parliament.uk/commons/lib/research/rp2000/rp00-014.pdf (17 March 2008).

Understanding Chechen Culture

Martin Malek

Introduction

Until 1991, outside the USSR only a few scholars and specialists on Soviet affairs knew more about the Chechens than their name and the fact of their deportation in 1944. But it is still difficult not to agree with the Chechen poet and philosopher Apty Bisultanov: "The tragedy of the Chechens is that the world simply does not know us" (Bisultanov 2007). And seemingly, it is very tempting to vilify and demonise the Chechens as "bandits", "cut-throats", "terrorists", "Wahhabis", etc. (Ryklin 2003). However, reality is usually much more complicated than clichés, and the Chechens make no exception. It is the task of this brief account to provide some insights into the difficult and bloody history, the sophisticated social structure and some customs and traditions (some of them in Europe often being considered archaic) of this small, but ancient people, taking into special consideration aspects which might have significance for Chechen refugees in EU countries.

The Name of the People and Their Land

The Chechens refer to themselves as *Nokhchii* (singular *Nokhchi* or *Nokhcho*) and to the Chechen people as *Nokhchiin kam*. They call their country *Nokhchichoe* (literally: "the Chechen home"), *Nokhchiin mokhk* ("The Chechen Country"), or *Daimokhk* ("Fatherland"). Some of these terms have been known (at least) since the 7th century, but have been used very unfrequently until the 18th century. The Chechen term for the Chechen Republic, Ichkeria, is historically the name of a region in the eastern foothill and mid-highland part of Chechnya.

Sometimes it is stated that "Chechen" is a Russian ethnonym taken from the name of a lowlands Chechen village, Chechen-Aul, where the Chechens defeated a Russian army unit in 1732[1]. But Russian sources mentioned "Chechen" (at least) already in 1692, and "Chechnya" was shown on a map of the North Caucasus from 1719. Allegedly, the first official document with the term "Chechen" was a treaty between the Russians and the Kalmyks, signed in 1708 (Jaimoukha 2005: 12).

The Chechens are one of the oldest indigenous ethnic groups of the Caucasus. They are related to other ethnic groups throughout the region, most closely with the neighboring Ingush[2]. Together, the Chechens, the Ingush, the Kist and the Tsova-Tush, or Batsbi (both peoples live in Georgia), are called the *Vainaikh*, which means "Our People".

Main Events of Chechen History since the End of the 18th Century

Czarist Russia

The current conflict, which led to the emergence of a significant Chechen Diaspora in Western und Central European countries, has its roots buried deep in the past. Therefore it is necessary to look at the main events of the history of Chechens since they came in contact with Russia and its military in the 18th century.

An uprising led by Sheikh Mansur (1765–1794) is regarded as the North Caucasian highlander's first organised rebellion against Russian expansion. His struggle from 1785 until his capture in 1791 united not only Chechens, but also other North Caucasians under the green banner of Islam to protect their native soil against the Russian "infidels".

1 According to some Russian sources, at the beginning of the 19th century, there were two villages with "Chechen" in their names: Stary Chechen at the Argun river and Novy Chechen (or Yangi-kend) near the Sunzhi river (Ageeva 2002: 379).

2 "Ingush" is not the self-designation but a Russian ethnonym based on the name of the village Angusht (today in North Ossetia). The Ingush call themselves *Galgai*.

In 1816, Russian Czar Alexander I appointed General Alexei Yermolov (1771–1861) commander-in-chief in Georgia with jurisdicition over the entire Caucasus region. Thus, one of the most horrible phases in the region's history began. Hardliner Yermolov considered Chechens an "insolent and dangerous nation", and he stated that he will "not be satisfied as long as even one Chechen is alive" (cited in: Aydaeva 1996: 229). In his leisure time, Yermolov liked to read poems, but his army terrorised the local population, destroyed villages by heavy bombardments and exercised a concerted policy of hostage-taking and forced resettlement. The Chechens confounded the Russians with unconventional guerrilla warfare, using sudden raids and sniper attacks to confuse troops accustomed to a more ordered form of warfare.

For a long time, Imam Shamil (1797?–1871) successfully fought the Russian invaders, mainly because of the creation of a centralised and military-theocratic state – the first in the history of the nations of the north-eastern Caucasus; prior to the Russian invasion, Chechnya had not known any coherent political structure.

However, in the end the balance of power was too unequal. In 1859, Shamil had to surrender to the Russians. Although he was an ethnic Avar from Dagestan (but with good knowledge of the Chechen language, which he used for his jokes), many Chechens still consider him as a national hero. The Chechen losses were horrible, and as a result of mass expulsions, a sizeable Diaspora came into being in Turkey and the Middle East. But nevertheless, the Chechens managed to keep their traditional domicile in the North Caucasus. And they never reconciled themselves to Russian hegemony and tried to get rid of the occupiers. They initiated uprisings and mutinies against Czarist Russia (1865, 1877–1878, 1879, during the 1890s, 1905 and 1913) and later against Soviet rule (1920–1921, 1922–1924, 1925, 1928, 1930–1936, 1937, 1939, 1940–1943). However, despite obvious opposite facts, some Soviet historians were busy in falsifying the history of the Chechens, stating that they "have dreamt of being connected to Russia since time immemorial" (see especially, Vinogradov 1980; Vinogradov/Umarov 1982).

Stalin's Deportation

The deportation was the most tragic event in the history of the *Vainakh* peoples. On 23 February 1944, special units of the People's Commissariate of the Interior (NKVD) of the USSR and the Soviet Army launched an extensive operation to send over 400,000 Chechens and Ingush to remote regions of Central

Asia. Allegedly, the Chechens had collaborated with the Wehrmacht, but in fact the German advance in the North Caucasus had never reached Chechen soil, and Chechen soldiers had distinguished themselves in the ranks of the Soviet Army.

Thousands perished already during the transport. Until the end of the exile in 1956, at least one third, maybe more than half of the entire Chechen people died. The survivors remained defiant. To illustrate Chechen toughness, sometimes the words of the Russian writer and dissident Alexander Solzhenitsyn in his famous Nobel Prize winning book *The Gulag Archipelago* are quoted: "There was one nation which would not give in, would not acquire the mental habits of submission – and not just individual rebels among them, but the whole nation to a man. These were the Chechens. (...) I would say that of all the special settlers, the Chechens alone showed themselves unbroken in spirit. 'Special settlers' ('spetspereselentsy' in Russian) is a Soviet term, in the given context meaning the deported people from the North Caucasus in Central Asia from 1944 onward. They had been treacherously snatched from their home, and from that day they believed in nothing. (...) The Chechens never sought to please, to ingratiate themselves with the bosses; their attitude was always haughty and indeed openly hostile. (...) And here is one extraordinary thing: everyone was afraid of them. No one could stop them from living as they did. The regime which had ruled the land for thirty years could not force them to respect its laws" (Solzhenitsyn 1992: 401–405).

In 1957, 13 years after its abolishment and division among neighbouring republics, the Chechen-Ingush Autonomous Soviet Socialist Republic (founded in 1936) was restored. But the scars left by the deportation run deep until today.

The Last Decades of Soviet Power

The stability and peaceful life in Chechnya after 1957 prevailed only on the surface. Despite their official rehabilitation, the Chechens very often were branded "bandits" and "counter-revolutionaries" by the Russians. The Chechens saw themselves treated as "unreliable", second-class citizens. It was difficult (or impossible) to enter certain "sensible" faculties of higher educational institutions or to get access to prestigious professions. Chechens were hardly endorsed for jobs in enterprises of the Soviet military-industrial complex, and ethnic Russians and other Slavs occupied most of the senior administrative jobs in Chechnya. The Soviets continued the Czarist policy of removing Chechen and Ingush population from economically important areas and encouraged settlement there by Slavs; hence the mixed population of the cities and lowlands.

The Chechens are the largest North Caucasian nationality. According to the last Soviet census in 1989, 898,999 Chechens lived in Russia. The number of inhabitants of the Chechen-Ingush Autonomy totalled 1,275,000, consisting of 734,500 Chechens, 293,800 Russians, 163,800 Ingush, 14,800 Armenians and 12,600 Ukrainians. Although official statistics about the ethnic make-up of the "Chechen" territories' population do not exist, some scholars have presented the following estimates for 1989: 1,084,000 residents, among them around 715,000 Chechens, 25,000 Ingush, and 269,000 Russians (Cherkasov 2004).

Post-Soviet Events: Chechnya's Abortive Independence and Two Wars

In October 1991, during the disintegration process of the USSR, former Soviet Air Force General Dzhokhar Dudaev was elected President of Chechnya. Shortly afterwards, he declared the independence of his republic.

When the Russian army withdrew from Chechnya in 1992, it left behind a considerable weapons arsenal. In December 1994, Russian President Boris Yeltsin deployed forces to Chechnya, anticipating a "small-scale war" and an easy victory. Dudaev was killed by a Russian missile in April 1996. However, Chechen resistance turned out to be much stronger and more successful than expected: In August 1996, Chechen guerrilla fighters under their chief-of-staff Aslan Maskhadov were able to re-capture the capital Grozny.

On 31 August 1996 Russian General Alexander Lebed, Yeltsin's adviser on security affairs, and Maskhadov signed a ceasefire. This so-called Khasavyurt Accord postponed any decision about Chechnya's future until 31 December 2001, but it was later declared void by the Kremlin. By early 1997 the Russian troops had withdrawn. Soon afterwards, Chechen presidential elections were held under the aegis of the OSCE. Maskhadov was elected with 60 percent of the vote. On 12 May 1997, Yeltsin and Maskhadov signed a Peace Treaty, in which they agreed "to reject forever the use of force or threat of force in resolving all matters of dispute" (Peace Treaty 1997).

The Chechens did not make use of this second possibility to build up a *de facto* independent and functioning state. Many areas of the republic fell into anarchy, factional and clan infighting became the norm, crime rates skyrocketed, the economy collapsed, unemployment was almost total, religious extremism raised its head, and the country remained without a cohesive infrastructure.

In September 1999, Russian armed forces invaded Chechnya for the second time in five years. The official reasons behind this move were the incursion of several hundred Chechen fighters in Dagestan, terrorist bombings of four apartment houses in Southern Russia and Moscow, claiming some 300 lives, and the "export" of religious extremism and crime from Chechnya to the entire North Caucasus. However, several independent Russian and international observers hinted at another background, which had more to do with domestic affairs in Moscow than with the situation in the North Caucasus (Malek 2004).

In both wars since 1994, the Russian Army used heavy weapons like bombers, tanks, artillery, and ballistic missiles. Not astonishingly, the price paid by the civilian population of Chechnya was very high. Figures range to 300,000 killed, which is probably an exaggeration; but doubtlessly the Russian campaign has claimed the lives of tens of thousands of civilians. Hundreds of thousands had to leave their homes or were expelled (Cherkasov 2004, Dunlop 2000, Izmaylov 2003, Serebryannikov 1997: 167–168).

The Chechen Society: Basic Features

Geography and Mentality

About half of the territory of Chechnya is covered by plains, almost a third by hills (300–1,200 m), 11 percent by mountains of medium height (1,200–2,400 m), and 8 percent by high mountains. It is therefore not astonishing that the history of Chechnya is inextricably linked with the mountains. The mountains provided Chechens with pastures for cattle grazing, while the plains were used to cultivate agricultural crops.

The life in the mountains had a fundamental influence on the mentality of the Chechens. This manifested itself, for example, in peculiarities in economic relations. Clashes between neighbouring villages, village alliances and *teips* (clans) over the limited economic resources of the highlands – valuable pastures and soil – were common.

The "Hierarchy" of the Chechen Society

Chechen society has always been egalitarian, unstratified, and classless. There have been neither princes nor serfs among the Chechens, and, as mentioned above, a central authority did not exist for centuries either. But there were deliberate bodies on different levels: Council of the Village (*evla-khell*), Council of the Town (*gala-khell*), Council of the Country (m*ekh-khell*).

A Chechen individual is caught in a web of supra-national, ethnic, national, and a plethora of sub-national identities: Caucasian, North Caucasian, Northeast Caucasian, mountaineer, *Nakh*, *Vainakh*, *Nokhcho*, member of a *tukkhum*, *teip* (the predominant Chechen social organisation), *aul* (village), *gar*, *neqe* and *dooezal*. Historically, the life of the Chechens revolved around village and *teip* structures. *Teips* still determine one's social relationships and social behaviour to a considerable extent. If Chechens want to highlight the lack of any affiliation of a person, they used to say that "this man has neither a *teip* nor a *tukkhum*".

A Chechen has two homes, a private (his regular home) and a public one (the village square). The relatively stable *tukkhum* and *teip* structures have been major formers of the Chechen character and spirit. They have played an important role in the preservation of the Chechen ethnos – with all the ancient customs and traditions regulating social interaction. However, the traditional order of the Chechen society has been heavily damaged by the wars since 1994.

Mentality Differences between Highlanders and Lowlanders

Chechens can be divided into highlanders (*lamanroi* – "mountaineers") and lowlanders (*chekharniakh* – "people of the inner part"). There are significant differences in the ways of thinking between them.

The highlanders, protected by the natural defences of the landscape, have always been more independent, whilst the Chechens in the north of Chechnya have lived for centuries side by side with Russians and Cosacks (Gall/de Waal 1997: 27). In the cities and the lowland, urbanisation, modernisation, and new socio-economic relations have weakened the traditional identification with one's *teip*. Therefore, these people can "permit" themselves not only greater emotionalism and laxness, but also less severity. In the eyes of the inhabitants of the towns and lowlands, highlanders are often regarded as coarse, wild, uneducated, cruel, and arrogant. Hence, locals of the lowlands and towns prefer to keep distance from the mountain dwellers unless they understand their customs and habits. Townspeople who are not sufficiently acquainted with the mentality of traditional highlanders may insult such persons very easily. Conversely, highlanders find certain characteristics of the inhabitants of the towns and lowlands irksome: their morals are too relaxed, their way of thinking is "too rational", they are "cowards", atheists, have worse knowledge of their mother tongue and their country's traditions etc. All this is considered by the highlanders as a regression from "Chechenness".

Men, Women and Family

The Position of the Family in Chechen Societal Structure

The basic social unit of the Chechens is the extended family, called *dooezal*, consisting of the parents and their male offspring. They lived together in a large house or several residences surrounded by a wall with a gate. Married daughters always lived with their husbands, usually in a different village; it was unthinkable for a son-in-law to lodge with his wife's parents.

Usually, married brethren settled in the neighbourhood and cooperated. This extended family is called *tsa* ("men of one house"). The members of a *tsa* cooperated in agriculture and animal husbandry. Affiliated *tsa* make up a *neqe* ("people of one lineage"). Every *neqe* (patronymic family) has a real ancestor. Members of a *neqe* can settle in one hamlet or in one end of a village. They can economically cooperate. The next group of relatives is the *gar* ("people of one branch"). The members of a *gar* consider themselves as affiliated, but this can be a mythological affiliation. The next higher level is the *teip*. The social hierarchy of the Chechens culminates in the *kam* (Chechen for "nation").

The wars after 1994, of course, heavely interfered in family live. Well-known Russian ethnologist Valery Tishkov wrote that "the argument about the defense of the own house and family was crucial in the decision of many to take up arms" (Tishkov 2001: 308).

Relations between Family Members

Chechen families were and are usually big. Several brothers usually live, together with their families, in the same village or even on the same plot of land.

There was a strict hierarchy within the family. Each individual member had its sets of rights and responsibilities, and all treated each other with dignity and respect.

The Chechens are accustomed to putting the merits and shortcomings of an individual on the family bill. Each member of a family had the strict responsibility of upholding family honour, because a *faux pas* by any of them could disgrace them all.

Parents usually live together with one of their sons. A good daughter-in-law kicks off the day tidying up the in-laws' part of the house. Free from this, she may attend to other matters. The first thing the sons do when getting back home in the evening is to go to see the parents, to talk and to share with them the day's joys and sorrows. It is not only their children but all other members of the family who take care of the old couple.

If the parents live separately from their sons, the children are especially attentive to them. The children try to create the most comfortable conditions for the parents and meet all the requirements of the old age: the best food shall, for example, be given to the parents. It is an old tradition of the Chechen countryside that the parents live in a separate small house built for them by their children, right by the wall of the children's house.

The parents must do their best for accord and understanding in their sons' families. They must be very considerate to their daughters-in-law. The father-in-law must avoid hurting his daughters'-in-law feelings: they should not see him undressed and he may not drink alcoholic beverages when either of them is around.

A bridegroom is not permitted to sit in the presence of his father-in-law, a bride in the presence of her father-in-law, and this holds true even decades after the wedding.

In Chechen families there still exists an ages-old custom of mutual avoidance (this is either completely or nearly extinct among other peoples of the Caucasus), according to which, for a period of up to a year after marriage, in the presence of other villagers a husband avoids his wife and her relatives, and a wife avoids her husband's relatives; in some areas a mother-in-law even avoids her son-in-law for the rest of her life.

According to a typical Chechen saying, "A father's word is law", it is generally accepted that a father must not show love and affection to his son once the boy is older than seven years of age. The father also must not display his affection towards those he loves in front of other people – not even towards his wife, his relatives, or his children.

A son may not sit down in the presence of his father unless he has been given explicit permission to do so, and he may not speak in a loud voice, smoke, or drink alcohol in the presence of his parents.

If someone has hurt the feelings of her children, the mother of the family should make no complaint to her husband. She may, under the worst of the circumstances, appeal to either of the husband's relatives, but it is bad manners to pay attention to children's quarrels, grudges and tears.

Status of Women – Men and Women

In some respects, women had a subordinate position in traditional Chechen society, and they did not fully participate in the social life of the *teip* (for example, they were precluded from voting in council meetings).

A man should, in keeping with a western tradition, let a woman go first. In Chechnya, a man goes ahead of a woman. This tradition is rooted in the past. Very dangerous encounters – with a wild beast, a highway robber etc. – might happen on the narrow mountain paths. It was only natural for a man to walk ahead of his female companion and be prepared to defend his wife and the mother of his children from any kind of peril. The prevalence of this custom to this day is an example of a practice losing its utility but preserving its form.

At the same time, a woman is an object of deep respect in Chechen society. Women are socially active – one of the reasons for this is the fact that Chechen *teips* adopted Islam only relatively recently; therefore, many of the rules and standards of Islamic views of the world have not been fully embedded in the Chechen character. A woman is the bearer of higher moral values. She has, from times immemorial, kept the fire at home.

It was considered unseemly for the man of the house to interfere in women's domain. There are relics of ancient matriarchy manifest in the fact that woman enjoy a number of privileges, including a measure of financial independence. And women are very often responsible for the family budget.

Chechen mothers enjoy a special social status. Lack of respect for one's mother and her relatives disgraces a man.

Tradition demands that the man avoids smiling at his wife and holding up his children in the presence of other people. But he ought to make sure that his wife never bears more than the woman's part of the family burden. The use of unprintable words, in particular those that make mention of the woman, revolt the Chechen because a woman of loose morals is a big disgrace of her family.

There are rules and rituals of physical contact that are still in effect. Until recently, touching a girl or woman was strictly forbidden, even when dancing: A man who touched a woman during a dance could immediately end up defending himself against the *kinjals* (daggers) of her conservative male relatives.

Extramarital relations were punished severely by the community. Rape and sexual assault are still taboo subjects in Chechen society. A man known to have committed either of these vile acts was slain instantly by the woman's kin. On top of being traumatised physically and psychologically, married rape victims were likely to be divorced.

The wars since 1994 had a profound effect on gender roles in Chechen society. Many Chechen men took up arms or went into hiding, and therefore women were obliged to act as protectors of and providers for their families and even assumed leading roles in society. This has created severe familial strain and resentment among men, who have become embittered by their diminished roles.

Wedding

A man who touched the palm of a girl had to take her as his bride. This custom was also considered a sign of an informal engagement – if a girl let her palm slip into the hand of a young man, this meant that she was permitting his wooing and would take him as her husband. If, however, the marriage did not take place, this was regarded as a stain and the young woman could actually end up getting killed by her brothers or her father.

In the Caucasus, a violent or, on the contrary, pre-arranged abduction of a bride had a special significance – in the latter case this was done so that the poorer family could offset the financial demands of a wedding and payment of the *kalym* (Turkish for "payment to the bride's family").

Bride-stealing is a Chechen tradition which has been tolerated, though not necessarily approved of, for hundreds of years. The Soviet authorities had tried to stamp out bride-stealing, passing a law that kidnapping must be reported to the militia (police). However, it was generally ignored.

A girl may be abducted against her will or with her consent, if she really wants to marry the man and her parents refuse the marriage. According to the *adat*, a young man who abducted a girl without her permission was obliged to ask her whether there was already somebody else whom she wanted to take as a husband. If there was, the kidnapper was well advised to send a message that said "I have taken your bride for you" without delay to the young man to whom the girl was betrothed. In this case, the kidnapper could avoid a blood feud from both sides and, at the same time, gained the respect of the bridegroom by acting as his intermediary during the courtship.

A Chechen man has every right to take a wife of any nationality but a Chechen woman marrying a foreigner is considered no good at all.

Vainakhs usually held marriages after bringing in crops or before harvest time. The traditional marriage ceremony included horse-riding, bridal introduction into the groom's home, acquaintance with the bride, her movement to a river, and a visit of the future groom to the bride's relatives and others. This was accompanied by dance, music, pantomime, and narration, which altogether produced a whole spectacle. Not astonishingly, the Chechen word for "wedding" is translated as "play".

Respect of Elders

A significant part of Chechen social structure rests on respect and deference to one's elders. Obedience to one's seniors was one of the binding rules of the code of conduct, its contravention being regarded as a grave censurable defect.

Only an ill-mannered person will remain seated in the presence of elder people or will sit down without a repeated request from his seniors. It is inadmissible to drink alcohol or smoke in the presence of one's parents or any other older relatives. One should watch his manners and cannot raise his voice in a conversation with an older person.

Children may sometimes disobey their mothers. But it is inadmissible to disobey the grandparents or some other representative of the older generation of the family members or neighbors. Children referred to their grandfather as "big father" and to their grandmother as "mother". The patriarch of the family (*dooezalan daa*) had the final say in important and contentious issues.

At the same time, the older members of a family feel responsible for the well-being of the younger generation and for the consolidation of family relations. Conflicts and quarrels between their children or women are settled by the eldest male or female member of the family. And the village elders were the ultimate arbiters in all affairs; they played a crucial role in maintaining stability and order in their communities.

The ritual veneration of the elders was closely associated with the cult of ancestors. Traditionally, a Chechen man was expected to know the names and places of origin of his paternal ancestors going back at least seven generations, although among Muslims it has never been a custom to keep registers of births and deaths in mosques.

Teips and Tukkhums

The Teips

A peculiarity of Chechnya is the fact that its society became differentiated not by a hierarchical socio-economic class system, but rather by a regional principle – into *tukkhums* and especially by the family/clan principle – into *teips* (from Arabic *tayfa* = group, circle, community). The *teip* is a group of persons or families cooperating economically and connected by patrilinear consanguineous affiliation.

The *teip* is in Russian and foreign literature often designated as "clan". It constitutes the core of the Chechen society. Many Chechens believe that the *teip* predetermines the characteristics and personalities of its members. The perceived link between clan and character type is so strong that *teips* are considered a key aspect of the region's political life as well.

Since the 16th century, the Chechens have been living in distinct *teips.* After the Bolshevik victory in the Russian Civil War (1920), all traditional laws of the mountaineers were banned and the Soviet legal system was imposed – of course, without taking into consideration any North Caucasian local sensitivities. From the point of view of Soviet Communism, the existence of the *teip* system was unlawful and contradicted the ideology of the state. The relations between the *teip* structure and Communist ideology are clearly underresearched, but there is no doubt that Soviet collectivisation led to Chechen resistance when traditional land tenure became endangered.

Therefore, the Soviets achieved only limited success in transforming traditional Chechen society. The *teips,* to a significant extent, continued functioning at a level beyond officialdom: The Chechens found ways to circumvent Soviet conventions and resorted to the ancient laws to settle disputes and to defend their rights.

Industrialisation led to the growth of cities (Grozny, Gudermes, Argun, Malgobek, Urus-Martan and Shali) and the emergence of sizable industrial areas (Karabulak, Chiri-Yurt, Novogrozny, Garagorsk, etc). Since people of various roots mixed, there was less or no room for *teip* differences. Therefore the significance of *teip* affiliation decreased at least in these urban areas[3].

3 However, the scale of this weakening is disputed among experts on the North Caucasus. And it has to be taken into consideration that the degree of urbanisation among Chechens was comparatively low. According to official data, in 1989 only 39 percent, throughout Russia, lived in towns (the average value

The number of *teips* has been varying. In the early 19th century, there were 59 *teips*, increasing to at least 100 five decades later (Jaimoukha 2005: 86). One mechanism for generating new *teips* was for *gars* and *neqes* to be ambitious enough to break off and claim the title and trappings of a *teip* in order to elevate their status. Some *teips* do not belong to any *tukkhum*, most probably being remnants of extinct tribes.

Younger *teips* are often comprised of people from a single village most of whom are mutually related. In the oldest *teips*, which are usually also the most respected and the most populous, the degree of relationships between members is rather formal due to their frequent migration processes.

Vainakh society was known for its tolerance of foreigners who took refuge or wanted to live in their land. They were allowed to join the existing *teip* system or to form their own *teips*. At the middle of the 19th century, more then 20 *teips* originated from newcomers, in particular Avars, Kumyks, Jews, Georgians, Russians, and Turks. The *teips* descending of non-Chechen ancestors are called "impure". They adopted the Chechen language and the local customs[4]. In 2005, the Chechen historian Mairbek Vachagaev identified 30 *teips* of Dagestani origin, 6 *teips* of Georgian origin, 2 *teips* of Russian origin, and 1 *teip* of Jewish origin etc. (Vachagaev 2005).

There is varying information about the current number of *teips*, ranging from 150 to 170. About 100 live in the mountains, the others are plain *teips* (Jaimoukha 2005: 94)[5]. The traditionally powerful Benoi *teip* (of the Nokhchmekhkakhoi *tukkhum*), to whom the ruling Kadyrov family belongs, deserves special mention. It is probably the largest *teip* with roughly 36,000 members.

Each Chechen *teip* is, in essence, a nation within a nation, with an enviable solidarity and mutual support network. According to Caucasus tradition, a member of a *teip* must not be abandoned in times of trouble. A *teip* acts as a kind of family network that makes sure all members have the support they need. *Teip* members should provide protection for the weak and jobs for the unemployed.

---

for all peoples of Russia was 73 percent). And in Chechnya itself, only 24 percent of the titular nation were city dwellers (the average value for the entire population of the republic was 43 percent); see Tishkov 2001: 302.

4 The last new *teip* was founded by the Russian German M. Weissert in Kazakhstan, where in 1941 the Russian Germans were forcibly exiled to. As mentioned above, the *Vainakh* peoples followed in 1944. Weissert became a respected Chechen elder.

5 Tishkov denied that there are any *teips* which live solely in the mountainous parts of Chechnya (Tishkov 2001: 164).

There was even a common revenge for murder of a *teip* member or insulting of the members of a *teip*. However, the solidarity of the individuals, particularly in larger, thousands-strong teips "should not be overestimated" (Souleimanov 2007: 41). In this context, the notion of *teip* honour is of great importance. According to a traditional Chechen proverb, "The *teip* is the fortress of the *adat*."

An *aul* (their size varied from a few families up to a few dozen) could accommodate a whole *teip* or be one of several settlements belonging to the same *teip*. Membership of the *teip* originally was based on land ownership. Today, the *teips* are no longer tied to land, but spread throughout the country. But almost every Chechen knows his roots and the place from where his *teip* originates. Every *teip* had a traditional mountain, its own tower or another building or natural monument suitable as a shelter, e.g. a fortress, cave or rock, and its own cemetery. Modern Chechen surnames sometimes continue *teip* names, but are often more recent formations based on the name of a recent ancestor or the village from which ancestors emigrated.

Every *teip* had an obligatory ethos. The higher the social standing of a man within his *teip*, the stricter he was supposed to adhere to that ethos.

Every *teip* had its own elected Council of Elders (with equal rights), court of justice and its own version of customs and traditions. The civilian chief (*kh'alkhancha* or *thamda*) chaired the Council of Elders and managed mundane affairs, whereas the military leader (*baechcha*) led the men in military action.

The 1944 deportation of the Chechen people and the two wars since 1994 have undermined some social mechanisms, some say irreparably. One salient feature of this deterioration is that the autority of the *teip* elders is not as binding as it used to be.

The Tukkhums

All Chechen *teips* are parts of bigger social-economic and military-political formations known as *tukkhums* (sometimes translated as "tribes"). There are nine such formations (and according to a legend, the Chechens share a common family ancestry of nine brothers): Aekkkhii (with 7 *teips*), Malkhi (16 *teips*), Nokhchmekhkakhoi (27 *teips*), T'erloi (14 *teips*), Chanti (7 *teips*), Chabarloi (30 *teips*), Sharoi (21 *teips*), Shotoi (17 *teips*), Orstkhoi (17 *teips*). Moreover, there are (at least) ten *teips* which do not belong to any *tukkhum* (Vachagaev 2005).

Taken together, these *tukkhums* embraced all the Chechens and, a long time ago, the Ingush, who split away to form an ethnic community of their own.

Sometimes the entire Ingush people is considered as a single Chechen *tukkhum*.

A *tukkhum* is a public association rather than an administrative unit. Unlike *teips*, the *tukkhums* had no heads and no military leaders. The *tukkhum* had no functions to administrate *teips*. A *tukkhum* consists of a number of *teips* that are either kindred or brought into a union for defence or economic purposes. A *tukkhum* usually had a common dialect and a common territory, consisting of settled lands and surroundings. The *teips* used this territory for hunting, agriculture, and animal husbandry.

The affairs of the *tukkhum* were solved by a deliberate body – the Council of Elders, consisting of representatives of all *teips* of the *tukkhum*. The *tukkhum* Council had the right to declare war and make peace, negotiate through envoys, undersign and denounce treaties.

In the past, *tukkhums* were able to organise military efforts. In *tukkhums* the *teips* resolved quarrels and co-ordinated offensive and defensive actions against their enemies. In recent wartimes, the *tukkhums* have played a role that is more symbolic than military. During Chechnya's military conflicts with Russia from 1994 onwards, the *tukkhums* had little influence over the events (Mereu 2002a).

The Teips and Tukkhums in Post-Soviet Times

Developments since the 1980s, characterised by a process of indigenisation, thus a "return to (ethnic) roots", have led to the renewal of traditionalist organisation in Chechen society, which has especially been manifested in strengthening *teip* identification. This undermined the official administrative bodies of the common (post-) Soviet pattern and was an additional reason for some Chechens to be sceptical about the absence of a central power able to function as an arbiter.

During the latter days of the Soviet period, the plain *teips* virtually enjoyed a monopoly on high positions in the Chechen-Ingush Autonomy. Dudaev and Maskhadov were backed mainly by independent-minded, but poor mountain *teips*, whereas the anti-Dudaev coalition was based on plain *teips*.

There are (at least) two views on the effect of the wars since 1994 on the *tukkhum-teip* social order. According to the first, the mass exodus of city dwellers to the countryside caused them to rediscover ties with their kins in their villages of origin and hence lead to the strengthening of their tribal allegiances. In contrast, some observers argued that the war exposed certain weaknesses within the structure of the *tukkhums*, which diminished their influence on the tide of events.

The Adat

In addition to the absence of state power there was also an absence of state law or an executive in its traditional sense. In formally Muslim Chechnya, Islamic law, or *sharia*, was during most of its history not applied either. The Chechens never acknowledged any kind of higher authority other than the voluntarily recognized authority of the *teip* elders, village and town councils, and the generally binding standards of *adat* (customary) law, an unwritten code of standards and rules, prevented otherwise inevitable chaos in the relations among individual community members over the centuries. *Adat* determines a set of rules for the daily life of the *teip* and its members. It is a compilation of moral norms and traditions and, in fact, a real code of conduct that brings together all the different aspects of communal life in Chechnya.

The most important rules of *adat* were:

- All *teip* members fell under the rules of *adat*.
- They enjoyed the right of collective land tenure.
- Murder and public disparagement demanded that a blood feud be declared by one clan on another. But even blood feuds excluded children, women, and elderly people.
- *Teip* members were obliged to help one another.
- *Teip* members were united in mourning.
- No matter what property one possessed, everyone had the right to be elected to the Council of Elders. All members of this Council enjoyed equal rights, and sessions of the Council were open to all members of the community.
- A military leader was to be elected in case of war.
- Aliens could be adopted into a *teip*.
- *Teips* controlled a certain territory and had ancestral mountains.
- *Teips* celebrated holidays of their own, had their own rites, customs and traditions.
- Hospitality was obligatory.

Adat draws a clear dividing line between "us" and "them": The opinions of one's own people carry considerable weight, whereas the opinions of foreigners, who are not a part of the system of *teips* and *tukkhums*, are worth very little. In the words of the human rights campaigner Alexander Cherkasov, a specialist on Chechnya and the Chechens and representative of the Russian NGO "Memorial": "Subjects of the *adat* (...) are only the 'ours' (russ. *svoi*), members of the community, inhabitants of the same valley or gorge, but no 'aliens' (russ. *chuzhie*). The well-known rules of the hospitality of the mountaineers compensated this feature of the *adat*" (Cherkasov 2007).

The "Chechen Character"

Nokhchallah

Customs and tradition are enshrined in *nokhchallah*, the code of conduct and system of ethnics that regulated Chechen society. Although the *nokhchallah* was updated and developed at certain stages of social history, its core goes back to ancient times.

The word *nokhchallah* does not lend itself to translation and needs an explanation. The above-mentioned term *Nokhcho* can be rendered as "Chechenness" – the quality of being a Chechen. *Nokhchallah* unites all the specific features of the Chechen character. It implies a whole gamut of moral and ethical norms and may be described as the Chechen code of honor, which is rooted in the remote days of Chechen history. It is by their own free will that Chechens obey the rules of *nokhchallah*. This Chechen version of mountain etiquette differs from similar rules of etiquette among other Caucasian ethnic groups by its strictness.

The strenuous conditions of their life taught the highlanders to help and support one another. *Nokhchallah* encompasses hospitality, politeness and willingness to compromise; the ability to deal with people without showing one's privileged position; the conviction that friendship lasts all life, in joy and sorrow; special respect for women; and the refusal of all attempts of subjugation.

The Russian authorities, both Czarist and Soviet, tried hard to undermine the local traditions of the Chechens, including *nokhchallah*. Since the 1920s, the Soviets intended to replace it by "socialist vaules". However, *nokhchallah* continued to play a crucial role in Chechen society – to this day.

Perceptions of Freedom and Honour

Freedom and honour have traditionally been the highest values among the mountain peoples of the Caucasus. Chechen history attests adamant resistance against occupiers and invaders, but there is almost no mention of Chechen forays into foreign lands.

Chechens adore independence and in their personal domains strive to become masters of their own affairs. "Come at liberty" is the oldest of the greetings still used in Chechnya. Two lines of separatist Chechnya's anthem read as follows: "Never will we appear submissive before anyone. Death or freedom – we can choose only one way" (cited in: Jaimoukha 2005: 217). And symptomatic in this context is Dudaev's dictum: "A slave, who has accepted his slavery, deserves double slavery" (cited in: Tishkov 2001: 143).

The concept of honour was perceived in a very broad sense: in addition to keeping his word, a man was expected to support his family or *teip* materially so that its members could enjoy a dignified life. Honour also involved independence, being a faithful friend, nearly irrational courage or rather ostentatious fearlessness, generous hospitality, honesty, and the "purity" of girls and women.

Highlanders were not driven to conduct themselves properly by the fear of punishment from a poorly functioning, at times non-existent, central authority. It was the fear of "dishonouring" their family and *teip* by transgressing *adat* rules. The Chechen make great efforts to avoid "losing face" by striving to surpass other men's courage, strength and self-sacrifice, their ability to act properly and honourably in the face of all life situations, their wisdom, hospitality, and, last but not least, ability to "honourably" avenge an offence. In the words of Chechen writer Sultan Yashurkayev, "the fear of death is inherent to all normal people. The Chechens, however, have yet another fear – that the people from their region may consider them cowards. If a Chechen shows that he is afraid, he is already dead to all who know him. He will never have friends, relatives, the love of a woman – he lives his life in eternal shame" (Yashurkayev 1999).

Yakh is a special term of the Chechen language which is difficult to translate into other languages. It contains heroism, pride, honour, nobility, valour, loyalty, duty, self-sacrifice, spirit, bravery, and boldness. *Yakh*, *ekh* (conscience) and *bekhk* (culpability, responsibility), are the three pillars on which character and spirit of the Chechen nation are based.

The wolf (*borz*) is sometimes used as a national symbol of Chechnya and the Chechens. According to the Chechen ethos, the wolf is the only animal that would enter into an unequal match. This allegory is a depiction of how the Chechens have dealt with outside invaders for centuries. Therefore it was logical for the separatist authorites of Chechnya to make the wolf a part of the coat of arms of the "Republic of Ichkeria". However, the pro-Russian Chechen administration removed the wolf, referring to Muslim tradition, which allegedly prohibits such images.

Blood Feud

Although the blood feud tradition gradually disappeared among most ethnic groups of the Caucasus owing to social developments over the last few decades, it still persists in one way or another in the mountainous areas of Dagestan, several northern areas of Georgia and Azerbaijan, some autonomous republics of the Northern Caucasus, and essentially in Chechnya and Ingushetia.

In order to prevent blood feuds from occurring too frequently, a special set of rules and behavioural standards was established in the Caucasus. Violations could have severe consequences.

A blood feud was usually declared at an extraordinary session of the *teip* elders. They then called on representatives of a neutral *teip* to convey their declaration to the enemy *teip*. Representatives of the "offending" *teip* then had two options – they either had to hand over the offender from their own *teip* with the knowledge that he would be executed, or stand behind him and prepare for a blood feud against all the male members of his *teip* to come into effect immediately. The *adat* rules have traditionally demanded that members of the "offending" *teip* leave their homes within one day after the receipt of the blood feud declaration.

Depending on the historical period, the level of socio-economic development and the size of the *teip*, blood feud could involve *teips*, *dooezals*, *neqe*s, or *gars*. There have been instances when entire families, fearing retribution, have sold their property and possessions at low prices and then swiftly left not just their towns or villages, but even the country. This custom has evolved over the last few centuries in order to limit clashes between enemy clans to a close circle of blood relatives and to prevent entire villages from getting involved in the case of a reprisal of men of the offended *teip* immediately after the offence. At the same time it gave room to so-called "people's diplomacy" – in this case the esteemed representatives of the neutral *teips* could actively apply their influence in order to avoid (or at least mitigate) the conflict. Sometimes, however, these meetings were unsuccessful and the ensuing blood feud lasted for decades, because such disputes have no lapse of time.

Arms and the "Culture of Violence"

The highlanders' mentality became substantially militarised in the day-to-day struggle of survival against the harsh natural conditions of the mountains as well as vicious sneak attacks. However, this was not a distinct feature of the Chechens, but affected all North Caucasian highlanders. The "cult of the bold man", characterised by a demonstrative disdain for fear and danger even in the most critical situations, is an integral part of the ethos of the Caucasian highlands. It strengthened bonds between relatives and neighbours and compelled them to remain alert at all times. Men were armed at least with their *kinjals* everywhere they went, even when working in the fields, at home and in mosques. Chechens were educated as warriors with a sense of duty of protecting their own land at any cost. Since times immemorial, male Chechens have been brought up as protectors and trained to bear arms. The freedom of spirit and readiness to fight to protect is a part of *nokhchallah*. But the Chechens have never sought to invade another country or enslave another people.

The Chechens were known as excellent huntsmen, soldiers, fortification builders, and armourers. Making swords and *kinjals* of Damascus steel (hot-forged steel used in Middle Eastern swordmaking from about 1100 to 1700 AD) used to be a prestigious occupation. The Chechens were (and are) very proud of their weapons. They adorned their houses with sabres and guns, hanging them on a carpeted wall for everyone to see. Even poor men tried to procure high-quality weapons. The Chechen "weapons cult" had consequences even for some masculine first names: *Bulat*, the Chechen word for Damascus steel, is now part of Chechen names such as Shchokbulat (which means "snow leopard bulat", Hasbulat ("beautiful bulat"), Sambulat ("watchful bulat"), Dzambulat ("battle axe bulat"), Arbulat ("black bulat"), Tovbulat ("conspicuous bulat") and Beibulat ("special bulat").

The cult of the "strong man" was – and still is – widespread in the North Caucasus. This is reflected even in sports: Some of the finest wrestlers, who represented the Soviet Union, and later Russia, hailed from the North Caucasus and Chechnya in particular. Wrestling is one of the ancient sports of the *Vainakh*.

Mutual Aid, Assistance, and Charity

The concept of mutual help and charity (*belkhi* in Chechen, from *bolkh* – "work") is one of the oldest Chechen customs. It has always played an important role in Chechen society. The hard living conditions made it imperative for the farmers to join forces. In this respect, helping relatives, neighbours, and other villagers with their work has always been a top priority. The first thing a Chechen asks in a meeting is "How is your family? Are all of them safe and sound?" A well-mannered person will inquire, before taking leave, if there is "anything he could do to help".

The tradition of reciprocal aid and assistance has taught the people to be responsive. The neighbors of an afflicted family hold the gates wide open to show that they share its grief. Should someone die, all the villagers will flock to its house to voice condolences and render moral assistance and, if necessary, material aid to his family. The relatives and neighbors foot all the funeral bills.

Friendship and Enmity

Chechens like to tell and to hear from others that they "are the best friends and the worst enemies" and that "if you have a friend from Chechnya, you will never be in misery." As a matter of fact, friendship was a sacred institution sealed by vows of fidelity for good. A Chechen would stand by his sworn friend in good times as well as in his hours of need.

Conversely, Chechens would become implacable enemies to those who antagonise them. It is to the detriment of both the Chechens and Russians that the latter remain ignorant of the Chechen conception of friendship and enmity.

Hospitality

Hospitality was a sacred institution prevalent all over the Caucasus. Many sayings, legends and fables focus on its sacred rules. It was an important aspect of the social life of the Vainakh, regarded as one of the highest principles of the *adat*. In the severe conditions of bygone years a refusal to open the door to a stranger could lead to lethal frostbites. He could succumb to fatigue or famine, fall prey to a wild beast or highway robbers. Another reason for hospitality was that guests were bearers of news about other villages and sometimes even other peoples and countries (Tishkov 1994: 402).

The villagers are most hospitable. Every countryside family has a special guest room that is always kept clean ready for a visitor. No one makes use of this room. Even the children are forbidden to play or do anything else in this room. Every family must always be ready to offer a guest a meal. Chechens used to set aside a special stock of food supplies for this purpose. Their tradition demands that a stranger has to be welcomed, seated by the fire, offered food and shelter for the night. The guest was always seated in the place of honour (*barch*) in a room or at the table. No questions are to be asked in the first three days of the guest's visit.

He was put up for as long as he wished. Hospitality was not conditional and no compensation was expected, any offer in this regard being considered a grave insult. A guest, however, could present the cildren of his host with gifts. The guest was expected to lodge with the same host on his next visit to the village, failure to do so being considered an indictable breach of etiquette. If one's guest was in danger, then it was the host's duty to protect him with a weapon in hand; otherwise, the host would lose the respect of his fellow villagers.

The ancient rules of hospitality were obeyed regardless of the circumstances. Any good man, no matter of his ethnic origin, merited a warm reception. Refusing to receive a visitor, even a fugitive or inveterate criminal, was a stigma that stuck for life. Chechen hospitality even forbade killing one's enemy in one's home during a blood feud, and, in accordance with *adat* laws, the host was obliged to provide his enemy with refuge, food, and a bed if necessary. Khassan Baiev, a Chechen trauma surgeon who treated a countless number of civilians and combatants during the Chechen wars (including Chechen rebels and Russian soldiers), explained the far-reaching consequences of hospitality as follows: "Our Chechen traditions require that if your enemy comes to your house and you allow him in, you are then responsible for his safety. Probably the best example of that hospitality is that I took in Russians soldiers. They were the enemies of my people; they came to Chechnya armed to fight. But taking them in, I had to protect them. It is typical of Chechens that they are ready to take in strangers, house and feed them. It is one of our finest qualities" (Sackler 2003).

Self-restraint and Modesty

The practice of self-restraint (*özdangalla* in Chechen) is very widespread in the highlands of the Caucasus. A Chechen male is to show utmost restraint under all and any kinds of circumstances. He must suppress his feelings and emotions, including great joy or sorrow. Self-restraint must also be shown when eating, drinking and speaking. That is why highlanders, unlike those dwelling in the plains, irrespective of their natural southern temperament, use only a minimum of facial expressions and gestures and are renowned for their reticence.

In Chechen society, modesty was highly valued and arrogance abhorred. Courtesy and considerateness towards others were institutionalised. It was deemed detestable to flaunt one's superior status. Baiev put this approach in the following words: "We believe that praise weakens you and education is designed to make you resilient to hardship. All of this relates to our history of always being under attack. We rarely express our feelings openly. We never use the word 'love' though that does not mean we do not have those felings. On the contrary, our families and friends are the most precious things in our lives" (Baiev 2003: 21).

Islam, Society, and Identity

It is controversial when Islam started to spread among the *Vainakhs* – in the 13th or only in the 15th to 16th centuries. But it is undisputed that they definitely converted to Islam (and specifically to Sufi, a form of Sunni) only in the 19th century. In 1913, it was reported that there were 806 mosques and 427 medressehs (Islamic schools) (Dunlop 1998: 33) in Chechnya. In Soviet times, Islam – like all the other confessions of the country – was suppressed. Stalin tried to eliminate the country's Islamic traditions. Most mosques were closed and Muslim clerics and believers were arrested, deported, or even killed. By 1985, only three mosques (and three churches) were legally operational in Chechnya. However, more than 200 clandestine places of communal worship existed. The situation changed radically during and after Mikhail Gorbachevs "Perestroika": By 1994, there were already about 400 mosques (and about a dozen churches) in the republic.

Islam plays an indispensable role in Chechen society. During critical moments in the people's history it became a powerful source of social mobilisation. Nevertheless, the impact of Islam on the "Chechen character" is a subject of controversial discussions. One of the most comprehensive books about the Chechen people says that it is "less Islamic and more Caucasian" (Jaimoukha 2005: ix). The religion, as it is practised today, is an amalgam of orthodox Muslim tenets, Sufi rituals, ancient customs and traditions and pre-Islamic beliefs, including vestiges of Christianity and the earlier Zoroastrianism.

Chechen separatism as of 1991 was certainly not motivated by Islam (or even Islamism) but developed on a "purely secular basis of socio-cultural and political protest" (Glinskiy 2002: 14; also cf. Malashenko 1998: 165). Islam was not even mentioned in Chechnya's separatist constitution of 1992. Instead, the first paragraph of article 43 reads: "Freedom of conscience is guaranteed. The citizens of the Chechen Republic have the right to profess any religion or profess none, to execute religious ceremonies and to conduct any other religious activity not contradicting the Law" (Chechnya – Constitution, 1992).

Between 1992 and 1996, "the Chechen struggle was overwhelmingly a national or nationalist one" (Lieven 2000: 155). Nevertheless, at the occasion of the Russian intervention in Chechnya in 1994, Dudaev – initially clearly a secular leader – proclaimed "Holy War" and called on all Muslims in the former USSR, and especially in the North Caucasus, to join him and the Chechen resistance. These calls for Muslim solidarity had limited success, but the war served as a catalyst for the emergence of various Islamist groups, both in Chechnya and elsewhere in the North Caucasus. After Dudaev's assassination in 1996, the influence of Islamic radicals increased considerably. In 1997, Muslim leaders put pressure on President Maskhadov to introduce the *sharia* in Chechnya. After some hesitation, he agreed to this demand.

In the second Chechen war since 1999, the Kremlin labelled all Chechen field commanders as "Wahhabis"[6], but this term was and is routinely applied to any Muslims whose political loyalities are considered suspect; therefore it almost lacks an analytical content. Anyway, an artifical dichotomy between "traditional Islam" (allegedly pro-Russian) and "Wahhabism" (allegedly the basis for terrorism and separatism) came into being. But Chechen field commanders loyal to Maskhadov defended Chechen national traditions and opposed fundamentalist groups like the "Wahhabis", since they believed they will shake Chechen national unity. Another group in the armed Chechen resistance consisted of field commanders like Shamil Basaev and Khattab. They aspired to an Arab-style Islamisation of Chechnya (Mereu 2002b). This was, however, never a serious option – and especially after the de facto victory of the Russian army in Chechnya. Pro-Moscow Chechen President Ramzan Kadyrov has energetically promulgated a revival of popular or "traditional Islam". Today, he claims that each and every one of Chechnya's 423 villages now has a functioning mosque.

The Chechen Language

Classification

The Chechen language belongs linguistically to the Nakh branch of Caucasian languages, which includes Ingush and Batsbi, too. The Chechen language has a complicated grammar and is not similar to any other Caucasus tongue – of course, with the exception of Ingush.

---

6 Actually followers of pure Islam, who oppose all practices not sanctioned by the Koran. The Wahhabis look at Sufi Islam as a deviation from the original Islamic rules.

Alphabet Changes

Chechen and Ingush were not traditionally written languages. Until 1925, it was written in the Arabic script[7]. Then, the Latin alphabet came into use. In 1938, the Kremlin "advised" the peoples of the North Caucasus to replace Latin with Cyrillic. In 1992, the Parliament of separatist Chechnya passed a resolution which instituted a new Latin orthography of the Chechen language. The pro-Russian authorities of Chechnya, however, not surprisingly reinstated the Cyrillic script.

Russification

Almost all Chechen and Ingush claim their mother tongues as their first languages, though most also speak Russian, generally quite fluently. The generation that was of school age during the 1944–56 deportation is often even Russian-dominant.

In Soviet times, Chechen and Ingush were taught in schools as subjects, but the language of instruction was Russian. Baiev complained: "Moscow never thought Chechnya possessed a culture of its own. If you spoke Chechen at school the teachers punished you, which meant that many children, especially in urban areas, did not know their native tongue" (Baiev 2003: 25).

Even in post-Soviet times, the Chechen language was not really able to recover. Joanna Nichols from the University of California at Berkeley, who did linguistic field work on the Chechen and Ingush languages for many years, in 1997 (that is, in the period between the two Russian military campaigns in Chechnya) stated the "danger that Chechen and Ingush will be functionally reduced to household languages and will then yield completely to Russian, with concomitant loss of much of the cultural heritage. (...) Since the language is an important part of customs and traditions, loss of the language will probably mean loss of most of the cultural heritage (though not loss of ethnic identity, clan identity, and ties to the land)" (Nichols 1997). This assessment is even more valid now, after the restauration of pro-Russian authorities in Chechnya.

7 For example, the chronicles of the *teips*, which were only accessible for the judges of the *Mekh-Khell* (the Council of all Chechen *teips*) were written in Arabic letters. After the deportation of the *Vainakh* peoples to Kazakhstan, the Soviet authorities burned many manuscripts.

A Short Remark about Clothing: the Papakha

Traditionally, headgear symbolises dignity. This applies to both sexes in Chechnya. Each Chechen man treasures his *papakha* sheepskin hat. For important social occasions and appearances in town, a man has a particularly smart *papakha*. He takes utmost care to keep his *papakhas* neat and clean. Knocking off the *papakha* from someone's head is a horrible offence. Only a bid to end a vendetta forgives publicly taking off a *papakha*.

Bibliography

Ageeva, R. A. (2002): Kakogo my rodu-plemeni? Narody Rossii: imena i sudby. Moscow.

Akhmadov, Yavus / Edilbek, Khasmagomadov (2005): Istoriya Chechny v XIX – XX vekakh. Moskva.

Aydaeva, Yu. A. (1996): Chechentsy: Istoriya i sovremennost. Moskva.

Baiev, Khassan (2003): The Oath. A Surgeon Under Fire. London et.al.

Bisultanov, Apty (2007): Born to be free. http://www.kavkazcenter.com/eng/content/2007/01/20/7220.shtml (accessed 7 April 2008).

Chechnya – Constitution (1992): http://www.oefre.unibe.ch/law/icl/cc01000_.html (accessed 30 March 2008).

Cherkasov, Aleksandr (2004): Kniga chisel. Kniga utrat. Kniga strashnogo suda. Demografiya, poteri naseleniya i migratsionniye potoki v zone vooruzhennogo konflikta v Chechenskoy respublike. http://www.hro.org/war/2004/02/25-4.php (accessed 6 March 2008).

Cherkasov, Aleksandr (2007): Chernaya metka. Chechentsy: obraz vraga. Polit.ru, 12 December 2007. http://www.polit.ru/research/2007/12/11/enemy_print.html (accessed 14 January 2008).

Clans and clan relations in old and modern Chechnya: http://www.chechnyafree.ru/en/article.php?IBLOCK_ID=364&SECTION_ID=0&ELEMENT_ID=53314 (accessed 4 April 2008).

Dunlop, John (1998): Russia Confronts Chechnya. Cambridge/New York.

Dunlop, John (2000): How many soldiers and civilians died during the Russo-Chechen war of 1994–1996? Central Asian Survey, 3–4/2000, 328–338.

Gall, Carlotta/de Waal, Thomas (1997): Chechnya. A Small Victorius War. London/Basingstoke.

Glinskiy, Dmitriy (2002): Musulmane Rossii: obretenie politicheskoy subektivnosti. Konstitutsionnoe pravo: Vostochnoevropeyskoe Obozrenie, vol. 11, nos. 1–2, Winter/Spring 2002, 12–25.

Hassel, Florian (Ed.) (2003): Der Krieg im Schatten. Russland und Tschetschenien. Frankfurt a.M.

Izmaylov, Vycheslav (2003): Bez vesti pogibshie. Novaya gazeta, 8 September 2003, http://www.novayagazeta.ru/data/2003/66/18.html (accessed 28 April 2008).
Jaimoukha, Amjad (2005): The Chechens. A handbook. London/New York.
Klutschewsky, Alexej (2004): Traditional social organisation of the Chechens. http://www.latautonomy.org/TraditionalSocialOrganisationChechens.pdf (accessed 7 April 2008).
Lieven, Anatol (2000): Nightmare in the Caucasus. The Washington Quarterly, Winter 2000, 145–159.
Malashenko, Aleksej (1998): Islamskoe vozrozhdenie v sovremennoy Rossii. Moskovskiy Tsentr Karnegi. Moskva.
Malek, Martin (2004): Russlands Kriege in Tschetschenien: „Wiederherstellung der verfassungsmäßigen Ordnung", „Antiterror-Operation" oder Völkermord? In: Zeitschrift für Genozidforschung, 1,102–128.
Mereu, Francesca (2002a): Russia: War Destroyed Chechnya's Clan Structure (Part 1). Johnson's Russia List, January 5, 2002, No. 6006.
Mereu, Francesca (2002b): Russia: Islam Plays Fundamental Role In North Caucasus Life (Part 2). Johnson's Russia List, January 5, 2002, No. 6006.
Nichols, Johanna (1997): The Ingush (with notes on the Chechen). Background information. http://ingush.berkeley.edu:7012/ingush_people.html (accessed 15 March 2008).
Peace Treaty and Principles of Interrelation between Russian Federation and Chechen Republic of Ichkeria, Moscow, 12 May 1997. http://www.reliefweb.int/rw/RWB.NSF/db900SID/MHII-65G9TK?OpenDocument (accessed 15 March 2008).
Ryklin, Michail (2003): Das Bild der Tschetschenen in der russischen Kultur. In: Hassel 2003, 204–221.

Sackler, Molly (2003): The Oath. A Doctor Sworn to Know No Borders (interview with Khassan Baiev), http://news.bookweb.org/features/1829.html (accessed 2 April 2008).
Serebryannikov, Vladimir (1997): Sotsiologiya vojny. Moskva.
Solzhenitsyn, Alexander (1992): The Gulag Archipelago. vol. 3. New York.
Souleimanov, Emil (2007): An Endless War. The Russian-Chechen Conflict in Perspective. Frankfurt a.M. et al.
Tishkov, Valery (1994): Narody Rossii. Entsiklopediya. Moskva.
Tishkov, Valery (2001): Obshchestvo v vooruzhennom konflikte. Etnografiya chechenskoy voyny. Moskva.
Vachagaev, Mairbek (2005): Chechenskiy teyp. http://www.chechen.org/content.php?catID=123 (accessed 3 April 2008).
Vinogradov, V. (1980): Vremya, gory, lyudi. Grozny.
Vinogradov, V./Umarov, S. (1982): Vmeste k velikoy tseli. Grozny.
Yashurkayev, Sultan (1999): Yakh'. Dnevnik chechenskogo pisatelya, http://lib.ru/MEMUARY/CHECHNYA/dnewnik.txt (accessed 7 April 2008).

Settling-in – the Chechen Diaspora in Europe

ROBERT CHENCINER

Introduction

This article takes a look at the human side of the Chechen Diaspora. Chechens are not mere statistics but come with their particular history, social structure, customary law, culture, social framework and other sociological "baggage". Since the 1860s there have been several waves into exile as well as some returns. With the exception of the successful Jordanian experience, there are no formal sociological surveys. My aim is to help articulate what Chechens feel about exile. My original sponsor at St. Antony's College Oxford, Theodore Zeldin, asked me a few years ago why so little research had been done or published about asylum seekers *after* they were granted asylum, and his question is relevant up to this day. I hope that this represents a first step.

Chechens, like other aboriginal Caucasian groups, have an immense love and regard for their historical land and villages, both in the mountains and in the plains. The smile upon a Chechen face when they see that I have studied and respect their culture is an indication of their central challenge as a Diaspora. It is true, virtually no one understands their background, but to remedy this, how can they transmit this understanding in, say, English? They appear to be in need of a form of cultural public relations. When I chaired a seminar in Oxford with Ahmad Zakaev and Aleksandr Litvinenko as speakers in 2005, I could not find even a brief background note on Chechnya available in English, so I wrote one.

In a similar approach below, I have written and revised clarifications of topics which, as I am informed by the Chechen refugees with whom I discussed this article, are of great importance to Chechens in exile but rarely understood by their host countries.

Chechen Social History

Chechnya occupies a small diamond-shaped area less than 150 kilometres across, considered to be roughly the size of Belgium. The upper part is plane land, and the lower part, the heartland, comprises the northern Greater Caucasus mountain range. Geography gave rise to a village society. From antiquity, there were localised free settlements called *mekhkkel* (literally "council of the land") in Chechnya, similar to and smaller than ancient Greek city states – *polis*, ruled by a local Council of Elders. There was no slavery or class system. Similar to the Highlands of Scotland, over 130 clans or *teips* with combined clans or *tukkhum* were recorded in the late 19th century (Avioutskii 1998). In spite of several attempts first by Imam Shamil to impose Sharia, the Islamic law, and after him, Tsarist Russian law, the Chechen traditional customary law system called *adat* has survived – until today. The worst aspect was blood feud vendettas that were declared illegal in 1923 but never stopped and openly reappeared after the Soviet period. The Chechens believe that *adat* strengthened intra-*teip* stability and prevented inter-*teip* conflict.

Sunni Islam spread during the 18th and 19th centuries in a predominantly animist society. Membership of Naqshbandi and Kadyriya Sufi *tariqats* ("path") was inherited within families and clans. Fierce Soviet suppression of Islam from 1928 to 1938 was only eased during Glasnost when from around 1988, people were permitted to go on Hajj to Mecca. Young Chechen men were targeted by well-financed Saudi Wahhabis and converted, which split families because Wahhabis ban sheikhs, shrines and revering ancestors, essential parts of Caucasian Sunni Islam. The independent warlords such as Basayev converted to Wahhabism, which he employed as a powerful tool to manipulate young minds, and regularly claimed responsibility for suicide attacks in Russia and Chechnya. My Daghestani academic colleague Dr. Magomedkhanov estimated that by 2002, some 25 percent of fighting young men in Chechnya were Wahhabis, compared to 5 percent in neighbouring Daghestan. By 2007, the figures are likely to be lower, if there has been any change. However, a much higher proportion of the Chechen fighters are religious now (all branded by Russians as Wahhabi), having been radicalised by the continuing conflict.

Mountaineer clan loyalty, Sufism, and survival of both historic persecution and forced transportation and exile of the entire nation have all contributed to the extraordinary resilience of the Chechen people.

Blood Feud – What is Adat Customary Law?

To understand whether *adat* is a threat to the Diaspora host countries' rule of law, or an example of a mild "conflict of laws", it is worth looking at *adat* more closely. Obviously, blood feud killing and physical punishment are out of the question, but many of the positive ethical norms can improve the climate of stability in Chechen Diaspora society. In addition, Aglarov and Magomedkhanov, who are specialists on the issue of mountain village society also consider that the prospect of blood feud killing is taken so seriously that it acts as a deterrent and in general forces the would-be perpetrator to be law- (*adat*-) abiding and to show the greatest respect for human dignity and in particular women's dignity.

Against a background of government corruption and impotence, with a breakdown of confidence in state security and the judiciary, it is not surprising that there has been a return to traditional customary law. Aglarov and Magomedkhanov comment that, in reality, Daghestan and Chechen *adat*s are something different compared with what is usually called "customary law". First of all, these *adat*s are just partly "customary" because they consist both of customary and Sharia norms. Secondly, all articles of *adat*s were publicly formed and confirmed, so we can say that *adat*s are public or communal law. The third reason why we cannot say that *adat* is customary law is that all *adat*s were written down and used as sort of a constitution in certain societies. The other *adat*s (or customs) which were not concerned with crime or civic life and were not written down (like *adat* of hospitality) can be classified as customs or ethical rules, but not as "customary law" (Aglarov 1988: 18, 30, 155–163; Magomedkhanov 2004; Kemper 2004: 115–151; Kemper 2005: 319–340, 410–413).

Customary law has re-appeared in Chechnya, Azerbaijan, Armenia and even Daghestan and the Circassian North-West Caucasus, which are also parts of the Russian Federation.

Customary law or *adat* is unrelated to Sharia or Islamic law or Roman law, but Sharia norms are included in *adats*. *Adat* initially arose in regions such as mountains, steppes or desert where there were strong aboriginal societies and the outside ruler's laws were weakly imposed or regarded as unfair or irrelevant. As *adat* became more developed, it was adopted as a parallel law system especially in areas where there was a power vacuum caused by conflicts and wars, generally in villages and agrarian societies. With urbanisation, *adat* also evolved in the towns. During the 1834–1859 resistance to the Russian conquest of the Caucasus, the mountaineers were led by the charismatic Imam Shamil from Daghestan. Even he was unable to impose Sharia law over customary law (Gammer 1994: 42, 43, 232). After the pacification of the Caucasus, the *adat* customary laws passed down by local Councils of Elders were diligently recorded by scholars of the Imperial Russian Academy of Sciences, under the guidance of a former officer, Baron von Uslar. There are 10 volumes of collected Caucasian "material": *Sbornik svedeniy o kavkazskikh gortsakh*, 1868–1881 followed by about 50 surviving volumes of *Sbornik materialov dlya opisaniya mestnostey i plemen Kavkaza*, from 1881 until the Revolution, with additions until 1929 (Chenciner 1997: 245).

In addition, in English, John Baddeley, who visited the region in 1900, collected *adats* listed in his manuscript *Index Caucasica* in the London Library. There are numerous references in his *The Rugged Flanks of the Caucasus*, 1940 (Baddeley 1940). Later, Louis Luzbetak extensively described *adat* in his *The family in Caucasia,* 1951 (Luzbetak 1951).

Adat is based on honour and applied to a defined kinship group, the sib, which is smaller than a clan but larger than a family. A sib can extend to the seventh cousins and, depending on kinship rules, include members of other clans. The legal framework of *adat* is *lex talionis* or "an eye for an eye", which usually is interpreted as material compensation for damage, for example a cow.

What is Blood-wit?

Accidental death or murder and serious family disgrace such as bride-kidnapping is usually paid for by "blood-wit" – blood for blood – or assassination of the perpetrator or other male members of his sib, without a time limit. The victim's sibs then go after and try to murder a member of the avenging sib. Because of poor communications and the hot-bloodedness of the men, several of them could be after several members of the other sib at the same time and several victims be seriously wounded or killed. This way, large long-term vendettas develop. Most local people and anthropologists regard the blood feud as the most self-destructive activity of traditional societies. Wherever possible and before it is too late, elders negotiate an economic settlement. However, in the turbulence of Chechnya, a peaceful resolution can be difficult if the "targeted victim" or his parents have appealed to the elders but the "potential perpetrator" cannot be found. In contrast, in exile, the communities are smaller and more stable, so intervention would be simpler, and cases are extremely rare.

For Caucasians, other causes of blood feud can be an untoward advance to a woman, disgrace of family honour by (for example) marrying a proscribed ethnicity i.e. a Christian Russian, a scandalous broken wedding agreement, or bride kidnapping, usually by a suitor who could not afford the bride price (*tam mah* in Chechen, also known as *kalym*) or because he was from a different and unacceptable religion or ethnicity. Magomedkhanov added that in fact, bride price was only paid by some North Caucasian ethnic groups, not by the Chechen (such as Chinkhoy, Benoy or Cheberloy) and Daghestani mountaineers (such as Avars, Dargi, Laki, Andi-Didoi and Archi). It is possible that some lowland Chechens paid *kalym* under the influence of Kumyks. Nogays, Azeris and Lezghins also pay *kalym*.

During my ethnographic studies in Daghestan, which covered more than a decade, both during the totalitarian Soviet period and the chaotic conditions afterwards, I was made member of several sibs and discussed the blood feud issue at length with my hosts. The positive aspect of this was that I was always protected in isolated regions (Chenciner 1997).

The most violent aspect of *adat* is the intra-family blood feud or vendetta to avenge serious disgrace, called *ch'ira* in Chechen and *kanly* in different Caucasian languages, which involves male members of the families to the third cousin and could involve clans (Luzbetak 1951: 70, 148). According to *adat*, guilt is bestowed by verbal denouncement as well as by evidence or trial.

A (rare) positive aspect of the Soviet regime was the apparent abolition of the blood feud in the Caucasus. They tried less successfully to eradicate all *adat* (Chenciner 1997: 245). During the late Soviet period, in the Chechen State Film Archive in Grozny, I was shown a Soviet propaganda film of grizzled Chechens handing in their arms in 1923, evidence of the end of the blood feud, which in reality never happened, and which was to openly reappear in the 1990s. During the Tsarist period, Baddeley noted that in the Terek province of northern Daghestan and Chechnya with a population of 930,000, in one year there were 365 cases of homicide or attempted homicide (Luzbetak 1951: 150). As an enthusiastic response to my research I was presented in 1985 with a 16th-century single family blood feud siege/watch tower in the Tazbichi hamlet near Itum-Kale in the mountains of southern Chechnya. The defensive nature of their feuding was evident by the absence of steps to the second-floor outside entrance; inside, only a rope ladder gave access to the fourth floor, dimly lit by slits, or small windows (Chenciner 1997: 149). Shamil was reputed to know of a family that had been involved in a blood feud for 400 years.

The concept of *adat* was not confined to Muslims. Caucasian Christians including Armenians, Georgians and Ossetians also had parallel customary laws, since they share a common heritage (Luzbetak 1951: 192). My editor Nicholas Awde, a Georgian specialist, confirmed that in cosmopolitan Tbilisi and many areas of Georgia, *inter*-clan blood feuding has been dropped because too many people had been killed previously, so that if all the killings were avenged, the whole of society would collapse. However, an *intra*-family avenging punishment for perceived gross dishonour is plausible among conservative patriarchal families. Of course, blood feud vendettas are not confined to the Caucasus. There are well-known examples in Italy, Sicily, Corsica, and Northern Ireland.

A History of Diasporas

The first Diaspora was formed after the Russian subjugation of the North Caucasus in 1859, with the last surrender in Kabardia in 1864. From then until the Russian Revolution, many Chechens sought refuge in the Ottoman Empire – in Turkey, Syria and the Middle East. Many Chechens arrived in the Middle East in large groups and settled in Jordan between 1894 and 1901. The next wave was after the Civil War in 1922, when the "bourgeois" Chechens fled again to Istanbul and the Middle East. The third was the transportation of the entire Chechen and related Ingush peoples to Central Asia in 1944 under Stalin's orders. There was a large-scale but incomplete return from 1957. The fourth migration was after 1994, caused by the two Russian invasions accompanied by destructive bombings.

There is also a long history of economic migration of mountain villagers in Chechnya (and the rest of the Caucasus). Actually, there was little for men to do in the relatively poor villages, outside the relatively short agricultural cycle. In addition, women were largely responsible for the work in the fields and livestock breeding. During Tsarist rule, this migration took the form of raiding, somewhat like the now-celebrated 17th-century "Border Reivers" along the English-Scottish borders. Chechens maintain that this was often to recover property which they considered to have been illegally seized from them by the Tsarist authorities. This can be regarded as a tradition which, in addition to their survival through repeated repression, helped them to develop their entrepreneurial skills, which are so important in exile. During the 19th century, male migrant workers specialised in military, construction and industrial work, comparable to the Irish and Scottish migrants.

As a result of these experiences, Chechen exiles tend to stick together in economically viable groups, where their hard-working skills can be put to use. Furthermore, provided there is no outside prejudice because of their language and professional skills, they are likely to rapidly merge into the economic life of the countries where they have been granted refuge.

The Uncertainty of Exile

One of the best-known Chechen exiles was Abdurakhman Avtorkhanov, the historian whose life reflected a series of reactions to their confused history, the principle of which is relevant for a Chechen exile today.

He was born in 1908 in Chechnya, and he joined the Communist Party in 1927. He wrote two books about Chechnya in 1930 and 1933. He graduated from the Moscow Institute of Red Professors in 1937, specializing in Russian history, and he served as a civil servant in the Grozny office of the propaganda department of the Central Committee of the CPSU. He had steadily worked his way up through the Communist Party apparatus, until his opposition to kolkhozes, or collective farms in non-Russian areas, made him a prime target for the purges. Avtorkhanov was arrested by the NKVD in 1937 and sent without trial to Siberia for five years. He joined the abortive 1943 Chechen uprising, and fled to Germany by the end of that year to found the Institute for the Study of the USSR in Munich. The uprising would later serve as a pretext for forced deportations of most Chechens to Central Asia in February 1944. A fervent anti-communist, Avtorkhanov served as a professor of political science at the U.S. Army Intelligence

Center at Oberammergau, and he helped organise Radio Free Europe/Radio Liberty in 1951.

From 1953 to 1992, he wrote ten books which condemned the Soviet system in various ways. In 1991, just before the collapse of the USSR, he was made an honorary citizen of Chechen-Ingush ASSR. Although his name and legacy had been discredited in the Soviet Union during his exile, Avtorkhanov and his writings drew widespread admiration and sympathies from many Chechen and Ingush people. His most famous book, *Stalin and the Soviet Communist Party* from 1960 is regarded as a primary source for political background information on Stalin's rise to power. During the time of the First Chechen War, he maintained a correspondence with Chechen President Dzhokhar Dudayev. He also called for peace negotiations with the Russians during this time but insisted that Chechnya's political independence was a precondition for the talks. He died in Germany in 1997 without having returned to Chechnya, despite several personal invitations by Dudayev.

Lessons from Avtorkhanov's Life

He represents the life of a member of the Chechen intelligentsia, who was forever viscerally connected to his homeland; generations after most other refugees would have assimilated to their adopted countries. He also represents an articulate Chechen exile, who maintained his equilibrium faced with an endlessly changing set of usually adverse circumstances at home. He reminds me of a Chechen I met in 1985. During a long conversation, I asked him if he was anti-Semitic, and he smiled and presciently responded: "No, because after the Jews have gone, we will be next." There is that Soviet-style Chechen heroic hopelessness, buoyed up with quixotic energy, in a mixture of ability and hard work, ever constrained by the extreme difficulty of finding a consistent direction for their unusually high drive and motivation.

The successful Chechen Diaspora in Jordan

There is much to learn about the Chechen Diaspora in Europe from the experience of the Chechen Diaspora in Jordan, which – because of its longevity and success – has been the subject of more extensive studies. In 2000, Professor Bader Dweik, an ethno-philologist at the University of Amman, reasonably considered it extraordinary that the Chechens have kept their language through four generations in exile, in comparison with the generally recognized limit of three generations before assimilation takes place (Dweik 2000). This happened although the language went through several script changes. Chechen was written in the Arabic script until 1928. The latter was replaced by the Latin script in the period of 1928–1938, which in turn has been replaced by the Cyrillic (Russian) script (Amerah/Daghestani 1992: 29). At the same time, "they have maintained a diglossic use of Arabic, the language of the majority of Jordanians, and Chechen. This is despite the fact that most immigrant communities in the world tend to shift to the language of the majority" (e.g. Chechens in Turkey). It was caused by "the social and cultural isolation of the Chechens from mainstream Jordanian life, fostered by the formation of linguistic and cultural islands".

Chechen Professions and NGOs

While there are no census figures, Lebanese sociologist Al-Bashayer in his master's thesis of 1997 estimated that there were about 9,000 Chechens in Jordan in 1995. He reported that the majority of Chechens worked for the government, the army and public security services (Al-Bashayer 1997: 183). The Chechens established their own cultural centres, magazines, and associations, notably the Chechen Benevolent Association established in Zerka in 1958 with branches in Sweileh, al-Sukhna and al-Azraq. The Association of the Friends of the Chechen Republic was founded in 1989. The first Jordanian sports club, the Caucasian Club, was established in Sweileh in 1932. Furthermore, they established intellectual centres such as the Sultan Murad Center for Chechen Studies founded in Zerka in 1994. From them many writers and columnists emerged who regularly write in Jordanian newspapers such as Taha Murad, Yousef Bilto, Ahmad Adel, Saeed Bino and Hameed Younes (Al-Bashayer 1997: 210–215). In 1998, the respected commentator Anatol Lieven noted that Circassians and Chechens "play an important role in Jordan, where they hold posts in the royal guard and numerous senior ranks in the army. Furthermore, two Jordanian Chechens became the 'foreign ministers' of Dzhokhar Dudayev" (Lieven 1998: 315). They were also prominent throughout the Jordanian security services.

Language Survival

Dweik's study investigated language survival. "A sample of 100 subjects was chosen from the lists of names provided for my assistants by friends and contacts. Data were collected from 73 males and 27 females of which 40 were single, 58 married and 2 engaged. Their ages were between 10 and 59. Most of the respondents were aged between 20 and 39, reflecting the relative youth of the community. They had a high education profile, however while almost all 96 percent could speak and understand Chechen, only 16 percent could write it fluently, so the questionnaires were in Arabic and English."

He found that "there are clear domains where the Chechen language predominates and where the norms are still determined by the Chechen community. The Chechen community is closely-knit, and Chechen is used extensively whenever Chechens meet, except in praying, where Arabic, the language of the Quran, is dominant. Essentially, people in the Chechen community can still safely assume that a person who is Chechen will speak Chechen. The general rule is to speak Chechen to Chechens whenever possible. The rule does not hold when Chechens write personal letters because Chechen is acquired orally. Arabic is dominant in praying, invocation after prayer and in religious meetings." His attitude survey found that "in general, Chechens feel very positive about both languages." They also regarded the knowledge of Chechen as an important component of Chechen identity; a symbol of their heritage and culture. Also, the majority remarked how useful it is to be able to speak Chechen when they do not want others to understand.

Reasons for Success of the Jordan Diaspora

The reasons why Chechens succeeded in Jordan as opposed to other Middle East countries were examined by Al-Shishani ("Shishani" = "Chechen" in Arabic, and therefore a common surname for Chechens in Jordan) and Moore[1] (Al-Shishani/ Moore 2005). They considered the reasons to be "perhaps significantly, the more relaxed approach to politics, the Hashemite system of rule and the tribal structure of Jordanian society provides an important framework which did not force the Chechen community to conform to new socio-political forms of identity." However, it allowed these ethnic groups to assimilate, in part, into pre-existing communities and culture. It has been argued that this has not been the case for other Chechen communities in Iraq or Syria.

"In this way, many Chechens who live in Jordan have maintained a separate identity, retaining their own marriage customs, clothing, economic structures and traditional language. They also continue to produce important figures in both Jordanian and Chechen history and politics. Therefore, the experience of the

1 Al-Shishani is a specialist in Islamic Movements in Chechnya, and Moore is a UK academic, specialised in Chechen terrorism and suicide attacks.

Jordanian Chechens was very different from that of other Chechens in the Middle East. This was due, in part, to the Jordanian regime's attitude according to which Arab nationalism is not motivated by prejudice but by a harmonious combination of Arabism and Islam" (Al-Dajani 1993: 264–265). Over a long period, several Chechens have held high political and military positions in Jordan. As a recent example, in 2002, Abdul Baki-Jamo, 75, an ethnic Chechen who had served as a senator and cabinet minister during his 45-year political career in Jordan, said that he urged separatists in Chechnya not to seek independence from Russia. The Chechen war split the Diaspora in Jordan (Working 2002).

Migration History to Jordan

As a background, Dweik described their migration history: "Different sources report different reasons for their migration." Jordanian historian Dr. Taha Murad mentioned that the Chechens were forced to leave their country as a result of the Tsar's Russian occupation wars that started in 1722 and lasted until 1917. The Chechens (alongside the more numerous Circassians, their north-western Caucasian neighbours) were forced to migrate from their country to the Ottoman Empire. The first migration took place in 1865, when 50,000 Chechens migrated to Turkey, Syria and the Golan Heights. The second migration happened in 1877 after their revolt against the Russians. The third migration occurred in 1901, and this time they took refuge in Jordan. The pioneer immigrants settled in Zerka in 1903, and another group settled in the village of Sweileh in 1906. Later in 1911, a new group established the village of al-Sukna near Zerka (Murad 1994).

Other Chechen Communities in the Middle East

Al-Shishani and Moore writing for Prague Watchdog in 2005 as well as my Chechen informants were very cautious about the following estimated figures for the Chechen Diaspora in former Ottoman lands, because there is no census information: Turkey (<100,000), Jordan (8,000>), Egypt (5,000), Syria (4,000), and Iraq (2,500). In addition, significant numbers of Chechens live throughout the Southern Caucasus in Georgia, Azerbaijan and Russia. Furthermore, Chechen groups outside of the North Caucasus have, in some cases, been assimilated into the socio-political systems in the states which host them. From an ethnographic point of view, ethnic communities located outside of the North Caucasus such as the Chechen Diaspora are also labelled more generally as Circassian (Al-Shishani/ Moore 2005). This is also due to the fact that the term Chechen is relatively new in history as it appears first in the mid-19th century after the battle between the Chechens and the Russian army in the village of Chechen-Aul.

Family Structure and Ancestors

Chechens (and other North Caucasians – e.g. Georgians, Daghestanis, Circassians, Azeris) live in a traditionally structured patriarchal family society. Like the Scots, their complicated clan system of villages, *teips* and *tukkhum* or groups of *teips*, are focal points for kinship loyalties, which on the positive side have ensured survival over many centuries. On the negative side they have also provided a structural framework for feuding – as with the Scottish clans. Even in speech, there are frequently accent variations and different dialects of Chechen language spoken by each group and sub-group which are mutually recognisable. Marriage is prescribed by kinship customs. There are rules both as to how close marriage is permitted, for example with regard to cousins or neighbours from the same village, and as to which villages, *tukkhums* or *teips* are suitable for kinship. There was a limited amount of marrying-out during Soviet times, mainly for men who took Russian or other Caucasian wives. It was far rarer for Chechen girls to marry out as their fathers or brothers would consider it a breach of family honour, and *adat* would apply.

Kinship and Elders

The village and kinship structures are important not only for procreation and social relations but also for economic patronage in jobs or other opportunities. More broadly, the structure provided relative protection against officialdom, known as a *krysha* (Russian for "roof"), which continues to be most important in authoritarian states, though not in most European countries where the Diaspora has found refuge. However, the Soviet mentality persists, and having fled with nothing, a refugee's life is not easy until he/she is economically established in his or her new country. Respect for elders is another important aspect of Chechen life, based on the system of self-governance in the village. The Chechen exile will often lack the opportunity to talk to a respected elder who would give guidance on ethics and behaviour and help resolve and defuse life's problems, especially in a strange society. In UK for example, this has been practically resolved by the appointment of a relatively younger man as "elder" to resolve community issues.

Ancestors and Memorials

Respect for ancestors, who naturally include the most recent generation of deceased, is another key activity, and this involves visiting cemeteries. In Chechnya (Russian) laws to prevent burial of rebel dead have been imposed which intentionally caused great distress to their families (Maskhadova 2006). Of course, a visit to a family cemetery or other memorial is impossible for the Diaspora and it gives rise to deep pain and even guilt.

Isolated from Home – Friendship

Accordingly, one can imagine that without his family, village, clan or cemetery, a Chechen refugee must feel isolated. Some Chechen males also usually have one particularly close male friend called *dwottagh*. Others have several close male friends, in addition to male relatives. Frequently, the exiles' *dwottaghs* and close friends have been killed or "disappeared" in Chechnya. This is an example of how concepts of friendship among Chechens may in some ways be more intense than those in their host countries. Furthermore, Chechens understandably have polarized feelings of friendship, in part because of historical and recent experiences. Because of this, they commit to, and expect total friendship which people in European countries are frequently unwilling to give, even among their own families. This gap between expectation and reality can give rise to unintended disappointments in their relations with people from their new home countries. One way of bridging the gap is through relatively less intense relations, for example in the context of professional and cultural life.

Societal Importance of Marriage for Diaspora Chechens

In Chechnya, as in other Caucasian countries, birth and death are connected with important family and community celebrations. Family weddings are most important to reaffirm the order of society and clan structures as well as inheritance. While marriage can be refused by the prospective bride or groom, in a traditional and conservative society the initial negotiations are controlled by parents and close senior relatives. Wedding festivities can cost a relative fortune of $US 5,000 and last for up to a week. This amount is mainly compensated later on by presents and the financial support a potential couple receives from its extended family members and friends. For example, a bride does not speak to any male during the first days of her life in the new house, and in the presence of grown males in the room stays at her special place so she can be seen and approached by anyone. Almost every male related to the new couple should approach the bride and ask her some questions (i.e. "bring me a cup of water", and when she brings it, ask if she allows him to drink; or "what is your name" and if she likes her new home) and she keeps quiet while the male keeps offering larger amounts of money or naming some presents he is willing to give her in return for her consent to speak. Only when the deal is reached does the bride pronounce her name and starts to talk and answer questions. Another custom is that the bride typically just very quietly utters an answer after a first question and the onus then rests with a male relative/friend to give her as much money as he wishes – obviously, the more money is given, the more prestigious it is for a man concerned. This is carried out with a modesty which rules over all Chechen customs. These types of customs are designed to support newly joined families to start their new lives, as well as to introduce the bride to the new community or neighbourhood, so everyone will recognise her as a one of them and as a married woman.

Sometimes there is also a bride price paid known as *tam mah* or *kalym* mainly among lowland people in the eastern Caucasus. The status and future of both families is linked to a good marriage. Chechens both in Chechnya and in exile are part of a patriarchal society, and if a son or daughter wishes to marry into a customarily not permitted and approved family, the social consequences for both families are shame and disgrace with possible violent reprisals according to the customary law which is based on avenging family honour, as described above. In addition, it is an important aspect of family honour that the bride is a virgin, which is of course rare among other people in Europe. Arranged marriages are rare within Chechen society though parents and relatives may play a significant role in its determination. A male and female can meet and maintain relations as long as they wish, but sexual intercourse is deadly forbidden before their official marriage. Since the end of the Soviet period, bride kidnapping, which can be considered as a demonstration of virility and strength, has reappeared both as an arranged method with the connivance of the bride, of avoidance of payment of *kalym* by a bridegroom who would otherwise be too poor (Chenciner 1997), (but only among some lowland *teips* where *kalym* is customary) as well as an unarranged abduction by an unwelcome suitor, as it was filmed on 18 August 2007 (Liveleak.com 2007).

Single Men

The majority of the recent Diaspora consists of single young men, who often left extended families in Chechnya or other parts of the Russian Federation. It is natural that they want to get married and have children. Because of their traditional upbringing it is also likely that they and their families would like them to get married to Chechen girls from a suitable clan and village and to observe the Chechen traditions of marriage, although Chechens quite often marry non-Chechens, and relatives finally agree to their choice. In some European countries, this imbalance is being resolved by Chechen girls coming there to get married. On the other hand, ironically, in some parts of Chechnya so many men have been killed that there is a surplus of unmarried women.

Work, Aid, Making Ends Meet and Creating Capital

Chechens are quick to learn about their host countries, hard working and capable of both making ends meet and building up capital. There is a Chechen custom that it is a universal manly obligation to assist his extended family which in exile includes the entire community. They may disagree with each other on certain aspects of life but they will always keep in touch and will know about each other's existence. It would be strange for a Chechen not to wish to know about other Chechens residing in the same state or community. Wherever they are, Chechens would seek Chechens just to establish a contact. Unlike the custom in many of their host countries, Chechens always look after their elderly at home.

Chechens with their inherited experience of survival under both Soviet ethnic prejudice and the communist job system are ready to study, train and work. In addition, Chechens would be very willing to undergo military training for special police or other security units and would be quick to learn and very reliable in these spheres. Chechens have a saying: the true man won't desecrate (i.e. not respect) the place where he receives his bread (i.e. is a guest). If they know that they have been put in a position of trust, self-respecting Chechens will try to do everything possible not to disappoint. And they do so with a positive attitude derived from righteous pride and self-respect, coupled with what is in effect a Protestant work ethic.

Cracking the New System

Conditions in Europe really are refreshing for Chechens, who have for so long been largely denied the opportunities to build up a material life. Having come to grips in their previous lives with the Byzantine Russian bureaucracy, they find the systems in most European countries easy to understand and to fit in to. Chechens, like other Caucasian ethnic groups, are natural linguists. Chechen is a difficult language and they also speak Russian and perhaps some Arabic and other Caucasian languages, so they are relatively quick to learn English or other European languages.

A Chechen Voice

Some Chechens in the Diaspora complain that they lack a unified voice. This is partly because they are few in number. Also, as several Russian academics have found, it is much harder to write in an accessible way in English or another European language than to speak it, especially if at best, you were taught to write Soviet-style Russian. Chechens tend to be relatively well-educated compared to other refugees unless the wars have interrupted their education, in which case they have to go back to school or university and catch up in host languages, general school subjects, and further university or technical education. From 1988, Soviet Russian education was interrupted by independence and the wars. Motivation is abundant, but (as in UK) full foreign student fees may be charged.

Survivors' Emotions

Another problem is the clan rivalry among refugees, where old feuds can resurface which result in unwillingness to cooperate. There may still be unresolved disagreements about events and loyalties during the wars in which, contrary to widespread polarized views, many were indeed neutral. Some Chechens feel guilty for even surviving, a misplaced aberration similar to that suffered by some Jews after World War II. These rivalries and feelings of pride and/or guilt can often lead to a diffusion of energies. I have heard that one Chechen's achievements may be greeted with envy instead of being celebrated, due to internal Chechen competition to do better than someone else. Others want to have nothing to do with fellow Chechens and are concerned only with economic advancement and/or total assimilation. While there is an understandable possibility of giving way to bitterness, it is important that these negative feelings are overcome for the benefit of the whole Diaspora community. Similarly, NGOs or host government agencies should be aware of this and take this into consideration when choosing people to be involved in future projects. It is also taken into consideration that the best way to organise and control Chechen society would be an authority of elderly and respected persons within the community. A person cannot be respected among Chechens just for material wealth; he/she must have proven himself in life and be known as a wise person known for his/her honesty and bravery. Religiously educated people are met with high respect within the Chechen community.

Aspects of Chechen Refugee Identity

It is anecdotal that a certain number of non-Chechens have been granted asylum in Europe under the pretext of being Chechens. Chechen refugees feel slighted by this and perceive their tragedy as being hijacked and thus devalued. In addition, Chechen refugees obviously do not want to bear the responsibility for possible crimes that these fraudulent non-Chechens may commit. This begs the question of what is particular about Chechen identity. To summarize, Chechens recognize each other by their ability to speak Chechen, their facial features and their names and clans, and their detailed knowledge of all things Chechen.

Chechen Language

A Chechen speaks Chechen, a difficult north-eastern Caucasian language. The only non-Chechen in Europe who speaks a little Chechen, whom I have heard of, is Dr. Simon Crisp, the British philologist. The English-Chechen phrasebook shows how difficult accurate pronunciation is because of ejectives, stress and vowel range[2] (Awde/Galaev 1997). Chechen is entirely different from Russian, a Slav language; even many of the consonants are completely different, with Chechen having a wide range of ejectives, unlike those in any other languages from outside the North Caucasus. In contrast, Russian is characterized by different multi-consonantal vowel-free sounds, i.e. *Vozvrasheniye* = The Return. As Nicholas Awde has observed, and a British Telecom study has confirmed, in Caucasian, speakers even develop different mouth shapes to accommodate their respective languages (Breen/Bowers/Welsh 1996: 2159–2162).

2 There is also a Chechen-French word list dictionary on www.lexicool.com/online-dictionary; but Chechen-German and other languages are currently unavailable.

Chechen Facial Features, Names and Clans

Most Chechens share facial features, though this is not always the case. Their names are Soviet-Islamic and/or Chechen and not Russian, but Russianized i.e. "Magomedov" for "Magomed" plus "ov". A few Chechens living abroad have deliberately changed their personal name spellings to remove the Russian linguistic connotations and to revert to Chechen originals. In addition, full Chechen names (as Chinese names) are written the other way round, compared with the European tradition, i.e. ancestor's (family) name – father's (middle) name – own name. The rationale behind this is to display respect to one's ancestral lineage and one's own lower position within it. This is linked to their *tukkhum* and *teip* clan systems, and the names of his/her parents' clans, which like the Scottish clans were listed in the 19th century (Avioutskii 1998).

Wahhabis and Sunni Muslims and Sufis in Chechnya and Daghestan

The Chechen Diasporas want the world and especially their host countries to understand that since the time of the second war in 1999, Russia frequently propaganda-labelled all Chechen rebels "Wahhabis" – since 9/11 a derogatory term in the Western media. The following is my layman's view of perceptions of these religions both in the region and in Europe.

Wahhabi Arrival in North Caucasus

Dr. Magomedkhanov and his colleagues, who are devout Sunni Muslims, abhor and fear the divisive and violent activities of the Arab Wahhabis in Daghestan and have been telling me of this for several years. The Wahhabis began converting young Daghestanis and Chechens when the Hajj pilgrimage to Mecca was widely permitted in 1990 – the first time since the 1920s (Chenciner 1997: 215). Several impressionable young Chechen and Daghestani men were converted to Wahhabism in Saudi Arabia. Saudi riches were put into building new mosques and founding religious schools in Chechnya and Daghestan as well as in funding converts' travel and "education". To repeat: an estimated 25 percent of young Chechen rebel males are Wahhabis, as opposed to about 5 percent in Daghestan, Chechnya's eastern neighbour.

Religious Discord

According to Dr. Magomedkhanov, Wahhabis oppose and abhor the following four basic concepts and related activities of the North Caucasian Sufis:

a) The system of sheikhs as teachers. The Sufi *tariqat* (path) is passed from generation to generation by sheikhs who are charismatic wise men, for example Sheikh Jamal ad-Din al-Husayni was Imam Shamil's teacher or spiritual guide (*pir* or *murshid*). Even though he died in prison in 1794, Sheikh Mansur was reputedly also considered by Shamil as his teacher.

b) The veneration of ancestors and respect for elders. Daghestani and Chechen Sunnis also venerate ancestors and deceased relatives at Uraza Bayram (Eid-al-Fitr) festival homages in cemeteries that I attended with my late local friend and informant Laki museum director Ramazan Khappoulaev and his family in Daghestan.

c) The maintenance of and pilgrimage to local shrines. They venerate shrines established near or at the burial places of teachers and wise men, recently alive or legendary *sheikhs, pirs* or *murshids*. The shrine may be a *turba,* a domed chamber tomb or a simple tombstone, or a cairn made of rocks, or a tree, festooned with many-coloured ribbons tied on by pilgrims.

d) The Caucasian Sufi *zikr,* a mystical circular dance, physical or spiritual, loud or silent, depending on the *tariqat.*

As a result of its intolerance, Wahhabism split families along generational divides. In Daghestan, villagers had their recently restored mosques seized by local Wahhabi converts.

Sufis – not Wahhabis

How can you tell if a Chechen is a Wahhabi or one of the numerous societal, non-practising Sunnis? It is inconceivable that someone would lie about this, as Wahhabis are fervent, unquestioning believers and hate non-practising Sunnis, and vice-versa. During the Soviet period, the religious repressions from 1928–1938 resulted in many Chechens becoming societal – rather than practicing – Muslims, and their children often found it safer to not know about Islam. This has changed since the collapse of the USSR in 1991. Some Sunnis are also Sufis. For clarification, it is worth describing Sufis in Daghestan and Chechnya, who are a mystical sect of the Sunnis, where male and female membership is hereditary.

The term Sufism covers a variety of mystic groups, beliefs and practices which Alexandre Bennigsen, the late Western authority on Soviet Islam, described as "parallel Islam". Sheikhs with hermetic knowledge – always anti-violent, aiming at spiritual enlightenment, similar to St. Francis of Assisi – organised *tariqats,* which come close to continual seminaries, where membership is usually passed on by inheritance. Sufism was well developed in Persia by the 10th century, and one of the earliest masters, Al-Hallaj, was martyred in Basra in 922. Sufism can simplistically be characterised by several apparent paradoxes such as being part of the world yet outside of it and thus setting impossible standards for the secular world. Accordingly, Sufis have always threatened political power in the Islamic world, for example in the Ottoman Empire of Turkey or the Safavid Empire in Iran. The two main *tariqats* in the North Caucasus are the Naqshbandi and the Qadiriya, which spread 150 years ago, but over the centuries, charismatic sheikhs such as Deni Arsanov (who somehow became a NKVD colonel in the Soviet Army) formed their own traditions, too. Qadiriya was founded by Abd-ul Qadir Gilani, who was buried in Baghdad in 1166. Naqshbandi Bahauddin al-Bukhari was buried in 1389 near Bukhara.

Chechnya and neighbouring Daghestan were demarcated as administrative areas by Soviet Russia. While the Arabs conquered Derbent in Daghestan during the 8th century and there was limited Islamic conversion in the North Caucasus during the 16th century, Islam spread more widely in this region during the late 18th century. Naqshbandi Sufi missionaries appeared in the North Caucasus to mark the second phase of Islamic expansion under the Russian rule of Catherine II at the end of the 18th century. It was the Sufis, who for a century, from 1784 to 1878, organised and led the resistance of the North Caucasian mountaineers to Russian conquest, known as the Murid movements, first headed by the Chechen hero Ushurma, called Sheikh al Mansur, until his imprisonment in 1791. While the Naqshbandiya doctrine had distinguished followers by 1820, a deeper penetration took place during Imam Shamil's leadership from 1834–1859. Following the defeat of the Naqshbandiya in 1864 and the apparent Russification of their charismatic leader Imam Shamil, another Sufi tariqat, the Qadiriya, took root in the North Caucasus through Kunta Haji, a Kumyk shepherd from Daghestan. This resulted in the conversion to Islam of the Ingush (who live west of the Chechens and are ethnically related to them). During the civil war 1920–1921, the Qadiris actively collaborated with the

Communists whereas the Naqshbandis revolted against the Bolsheviks. Since 1928, both were repressed by the Soviet regime and driven underground.

In the North Caucasus, Naqshbandiya and Qadiriya have long been more or less bitter rivals, Naqshbandiya being favoured by aristocratic circles. President Dudayev's eldest brother joined the most radical and recent of the Qadiri *wirds* (separate group) when he was exiled in Kazakhstan. All the clans that supported Dudayev were Qadiris from the mountain clans in southern Chechnya. (Before the 19th-century war with Russia, the Chechens belonged to more than 135 clans or *teips*, before some went into exile in the Ottoman Empire. Each *teip* is composed of several large families. Before the 1944 transportation, 25 *teips* had eponymous villages. In the 1850s, 75 percent of the *teips* were united in nine military-economic unions called *tukkhums* that spoke the same dialect.)

Since the defeat of Shamil, the Naqshbandi have favoured an accommodation with Russia in return for limited freedoms – mainly to avoid the destruction that was inflicted on Grozny and other Chechen towns. To cite an example: "Typical of the Chechen aristocracy, the Chechen family of the Arsanovs belongs to the Naqshbandis." Ahmed Arsanov, supported by members of the Deni Arsanov Naqshbandi tariqat, was appointed Yeltsin's personal representative in Chechnya in 1991. Chechen Naqshbandi Sufi families have tended to support a peaceful solution with Russia in the Chechen wars. It is therefore not surprising that in Chechnya, anti-Dudayev opposition strongholds in 1992–1995 were located in Naqshbandi areas on the plains and lowlands west of the Grozny-Arsanov country. In response, Chechnya's Council of Elders, which was mainly made up of Qadiri members, stated that the Naqshbandi were a KGB stronghold (Timoschuk c2000; Khan/Mohiuddin 2007; Avioutskii 1998; Bennigsen/Wimbush 1985: 187; Tsolak 2004).

Putting internal divisions aside, the North Caucasian Sufis dislike the Wahhabis. Thus, even their internal enmities played into Russian hands.

Acknowledgements

For this article, a significant part of my non-textual information comes from qualitative interviews with several Chechen Refugees and also from academic collaborators in Daghestan, Chechnya's eastern neighbour. I am deeply grateful for my informants' time and attention.

Bibliography

Aglarov, M.A. (1988): Selskaya obshina v Nagornom Daghestane v XVII- nachale XIX v., (Village society in Mountain regions of Daghestan from 17th -beginning 19th centuries), Moscow.
Al-Bashayer, R. (1997): Mujtama Ash-she-shan fil Urdon. Dirasa Jugraphia. Bashariya WaIjtima'iyya. Master thesis. College of Arts, Geography Department, The Lebanese University, Beirut.
Al-Dajani, M. S./Al-Dajani, M. S. (1993): Introduction to the Jordanian Political System, Amman.
Al-Shishani, M. B./Moore, C. (2005): Jordan and Chechnya – An Unquestioned Relationship. In: Prague Watchdog, 28 December 2005. Amerah, M./Daghestani, F. (1992): Muslims in the Soviet Union, Amman. Avioutskii, V. (1998): Clan's rivalry. In: Chechnya: Towards partition? In: La Tchechenie, No. 3332, Paris.
Awde, N./Galaev, M. (1997): Chechen-English/ English-Chechen Dictionary and Phrasebook, Richmond UK.
Baddeley, J. (1940): The Rugged Flanks of the Caucasus, London.
Bennigsen, A./Wimbush, S. Enders (1985): The Muslims of Transcaucasia and the North Caucasus. In: Muslims of the Soviet Empire, London.
Breen, A.P./Bowers, E./Welsh, W. (1996): An investigation into the generation of mouth shapes for a talkinghead. In: Spoken Language, 1996, Vol. 4, No. 3

Chenciner, Robert (1997, 2006): Daghestan: Tradition and Survival, London and New York.
Dweik, B. S. (2000): Linguistic and Cultural Maintenance Among the Chechens of Jordan. In: Language, Culture and Curriculum Vol. 13, No. 2, 2000, Amman.
Gammer, M. (1994): Muslim resistance to the Tsar, London and Portland.
Jaimoukha, A. M./Awde, N. (ed.) (2005): The Chechens: A Handbook, London.
Kemper, M. (2004): Communal Agreements (ittifaqat) and *adat*-Books from Daghestani villages and Confederacies (18th–19th centuries). In: Der Islam, Vol. 81, Hamburg.
Kemper, M. (2005): Herrschaft, Recht und Islam in Daghestan, (in German), Wiesbaden.
Khan, M. N./ Mohiuddin, G. (2007): Naqshbandi. In: Salaam Knowledge encyclopedia.
Leontyuk, A.M. (2000): "Русское зарубежье" – http://russians.rin.ru .
Lieven, A. (1998): Chechnya: Tombstone of Russian Power, New Haven, London.
Liveleak.com (2007): Bride kidnapping Chechnya, 18 August 2007.
On: www.liveleak.com, US video source.
Luzbetak, L., SJ (1951): The family in Caucasia. In: Studia Instituti Anthropos, 3, Leiden.
Magomedkhanov, M.M. (2004): Adat, Shari'at and Russian Laws in Daghestan.
In: Vestnik Daghestanskogo Nauchnogo Tsentra Rossiyskoi Akademii Nauk. No. 16, (in Russian), Makhachkala.
Maskhadova, K./Maskhadov, A./Maskhadova, F. (2006): Appeal to the heads of state participating in the G8 summit. In: Chechenpress.com, 11 July 2006.
Murad, T. (1994): Summary of the Chechen history (unpublished paper), Sultan Murad Center for Chechen Studies, Amman.

Timoschuk, A. S. (ND, c2000): Chechen Islamic revivalism, Moscow/Vladimir.
Tsolak, N. (ed.) (2004): Al Hajjaj mystic and martyr. In: Khamush.com/Sufism, UK.
Working, R. (2002): Jordan's Chechens divided by war. In: BBC News, 6 February 2002

Ukraine – Immigration and Transit Country for Chechen Refugees

Franck Düvell

Ukraine is to be included in this volume because it is one of the first countries that Chechen refugees enter once they fled from Russia to the West. It could be assumed that Chechens easily integrate into the country because they speak Russian which is also widely used in Ukraine and they share some Soviet cultural traditions. Nevertheless, a considerable number of Chechen refugees, just like refugees from many other countries, do not stay in Ukraine but move further west – often in an irregular manner – until they reach European Union (EU) territory. Subsequently, Ukraine is an important country of transit for Chechen refugees on their way west. Thus, the question arises why so many Chechen refugees decide to move on to Western Europe[1].

Refugees in Ukraine

Ukraine is a country of emigration, immigration and transit migration; due to unfavourable economic conditions, between 2 and 7 million Ukrainian citizens seek to work abroad at least temporarily. Nevertheless, soon after Ukraine became

1 This contribution is part of a research project on "Migration on the Fringes of Europe" which is conducted at the Centre for Migration, Policy and Society (COMPAS), University of Oxford. The first case study is Ukraine; all interviews quoted in this chapter were conducted by the author during five field tips in 2006–2007.

independent in 1991, it began experiencing the arrival of refugees, first from Afghanistan, then from Chechnya and other former Soviet republics (Abkhazia, Uzbekistan) and lately from many other parts of the world. These first arrivals from Afghanistan or Chechnya often had some affiliation to Ukraine dating back to Soviet times, for example they had attended university or military academies or they had some relatives in the country. Later arrivals are often attracted by these already existing communities. Since 1993, 28,000 individuals have applied for asylum, 1,890 in 2005 (1,364 in 2004). So far, about 5,300 asylum seekers have been granted refugee status, 2,350 have settled in Ukraine and of those, 740 have acquired citizenship due to a relatively liberal citizenship law (UNHCR 2006c)[2]. The remaining 3,000 refugees are assumed to have left the country for other destinations. The majority of refugees originate from Afghanistan (1,290), the second major group (700) is from Commonwealth of Independent States (CIS) countries (Russia, Armenia, Georgia, Azerbaijan, and Tajikistan), others (320) are from Africa (e.g. Congo, Sudan, Ethiopia and Angola) and the Middle East (120) (UNHCR 2006c). Around 150 refugees are of Chechen origin (SCNM 2006). At present, asylum seekers come from Afghanistan, Pakistan, Russia, Bangladesh, India, Palestine, Iraq, smaller numbers come from Vietnam, China, Iran, Uzbekistan, Sri Lanka, Syria, Somalia, Nigeria, Sierra Leone, Liberia, Ghana, Zaire, Brazzaville, Sudan and other countries. Altogether, asylum seekers originate from 45 to 50 countries; this demonstrates that Ukraine has become an important country on the map of refugee movements.

Table: Asylum applications from citizens of the Russian Federation (supposedly Chechens)

1997	1998	1999	2000	2001	2002	2003	2004	2005	2006	Total
39	49	240	465	183	n/a	101	236	165	n/a	1478

Source: UNHCR Statistical Yearbooks

Since 1997, at least 1,478 citizens of the Russian Federation have applied for asylum and almost all of these are assumed to be Chechen refugees. But Levin

2 This can be acquired after three years of continuous residence in the country. And because language is the main requirement, Chechens who normally do speak Russian have no problems to satisfy the criteria. But also the first Afghan refugees, who often served in the pro-Soviet government or armed forces often speak Russian and could receive citizenship.

(2006: 33) assumes that "most will not apply for asylum in Ukraine" because of a general mistrust of Ukrainian procedures. Thus, the number of Chechens refugees staying in Ukraine for some time must be higher than figures of registered individuals indicate.

However, all sources agree that Ukraine is a transit country and that migrants as well as refugees and asylum seekers aim to move west. For instance, almost half of all asylum applications are filed in Transcarpathia, the county bordering the European Union. Because most are filed upon apprehension for illegal border crossing, it can be concluded that those refugees (and migrants) are on their way west and file a claim in order to prevent return, or to be released from detention. So far, there are few legal channels for refugees. In 2005, for example, only around 50 individuals (around 100 the year before) legally moved from Ukraine to another safe country in course of international resettlement schemes arranged by UNHCR. Normally, minors, single mothers and young families are favoured over other refugees. But the only countries which accepted resettlement refugees from Ukraine were Finland, Sweden, Norway, Canada and the US.

As a consequence, many turn to irregular strategies. In 2006, 26,000 individuals were apprehended by the State Border Guard Service (SBGS) for illegally crossing a Ukrainian border; of these, 1,100 were Russian citizens and Chechens would be part of this group (Söderköping process 2007). Another 11,000 irregular immigrants were registered by the Ministry of Interior of which about 2,000 were Russian citizens (ibid). Altogether, between 2003 and 2006, 59,000 (2,570 Russian citizens) were apprehended on the border, and 56,000 (10,700 Russian citizens) on the territory. About one third of the total was apprehended whilst crossing the borders with an EU country (Poland, Slovakia, Hungary, and Romania) (SBGS 2005). The number of those who are able to cross a border without being detected is supposedly higher, suggested multipliers range from 1:8 to 1:2, though a ratio of 1:3 to 1:4 seems more plausible. This trend is confirmed by refugee support NGOs who report that they are losing half of their case load supposedly due to irregular on-migration.

Chechen refugees arrived first in 1994/1995, approximately 1,500 to 2,000 between 1995 and 1997 (Levin 2006), and again in 1999/2000. Since then, a constant inflow is noted. Exit from Russia, however, is not straightforward. Legally, Chechens, as citizens of the Russian Federation, are entitled to a passport issued by Russian authorities. This bears no reference to ethnicity, thus Chechens can only be identified by their name and place of birth. However, according to the Institute for War and Peace Reporting (IWPR 2005), authorities normally refuse to issue passports to Chechen citizens, which precludes international travel. And although as citizens of the Russian Federation they should enjoy visa-free travel within the federation and most CIS countries, they are in fact prevented from leaving Chechnya, from legal residence in Russia (Desormeau 2005) and often from leaving Russia altogether. According to official figures, between 2003 and 2005, 2,113 Chechens were refused entry to Ukraine and returned to Russia (Levin 2006: 17). Thus, Chechens, if they wish to leave Russia, are compelled to clandestinely cross the border between Russia and Ukraine. Many only transit Ukraine, but Levin (2006) guesses that between 2,500 and 4,500 are residing in Ukraine.

Meanwhile, a small Diaspora has emerged which is dispersed over various locations, notably Kiev, Bila Tserka, Odessa, Dnipropetrovsk, Zaporizhia and Kherson. According to a non-representative sample (Levin 2006), most Chechen asylum seekers are between the age of 18 and 45. Among this group, single mothers represent a specific clientele and some sources indicate that often their husbands were either killed during the war or disappeared (Chechen refugee community representative, conversation 4/2007; Levin 2006: 30). Finally, many children are recorded among this group.

The Legal and Socio-Economic Conditions of Migrants and Refugees in Ukraine

Ukraine still undergoes a period of political and economic transition, unemployment is high, for many wages are low and poverty is widespread whilst public services can be poor. Situated between Russia and the EU, Ukraine is engaged in a complex set of international relations which is also reflected in its internal affairs. All this also affects migrants and refugees though often on a disproportionate level. The next section describes, summarises and analyses the institutional framework and the legal and social provisions to migrants, refugees and asylum seekers in Ukraine.

Statutory Services and Asylum Procedures

In 2002, Ukraine acceded to the Geneva Convention. A refugee law was introduced in 1993 but only implemented in 1996; initially, Chechen refugees were dealt with separately under a cabinet decree, but this expired in 1997. A new refugee law (Law of Ukraine "On Refugees") came into force in 2001 and was amended in 2003 and again in 2005. This does not yet include any provisions for temporary or subsidiary protection, which is considered the most serious legal shortcoming (UNHCR interview, 9/2006). The State Committee for Nationality and Religion (SCNR), formerly SCNM (State Committee for Nationalities and Migration) and in particular its Refugee Directorate is responsible for the refugee status determination processes (RSD). It also deals with refugee integration, other migration issues, international relations and some policy aspects. Its regional branches, the Migration Service, receives applications, accepts or refuses applications, conducts the first hearing and passes on files to the State Committee for final decision. SCNR and Migration Service have 150 staff members, 20 in Kiev and 130 in the counties. Staffing level is an issue as is language proficiency and interpretation but that will possibly soon change; country of origin information is another area of concern (UNHCR interview, 9/2006). The Migration Service in particular in Transcarpathia (Zakarpattyia), where half of all applications are filed, has a considerable backlog; otherwise, the SCNR normally issues a decision within eight months. Appeals can be filed with local courts, these do not have specialised chambers, and procedures may take several years (HIAS, interview, 4/2007). Altogether, 2,300 asylum seekers were awaiting decision in 2007. Because of constant reforms, the SCRN occasionally stopped functioning, as in 2001/2002 and partially again in 2006/2007 (UNHCR interview, 9/2006).

During the early 1990s and under the 1993/1996 refugee law, many asylum seekers were granted refugee status, notably Afghans and Angolans. Altogether, about 30 percent of applicants were granted refugee status until 2001, but then the previous law ceased (ECRE 2006: 9). Chechens were mostly granted temporary protection, as regulated by a 1995 cabinet decree, but around 1,500 also applied for refugee status. But the new law "On Refugees" which came into force in 2001 introduced some serious obstacles to asylum seekers. Now, refugees had to lodge a claim within three or five working days after arrival, respectively. Thus, most claims were rejected by Migration Services merely on formal grounds, because they were handed in after this period had expired, and only 7 percent of all refugees gained access to RSD procedures (ECRE 2006). As a result, the recognition rate dropped to 0.08 percent (UNHCR 2004). In 2005, this restriction was relaxed, but still a claim should be lodged within 15 days (Migration Service Uzhgorod, interview 8/2007). As a result, the rejection rate by Migration Services has decreased to 10 percent (ECRE 2006). Nevertheless, recognition rates of the State Committee for Nationality and Religion remain low (Andryseck/Rantala 2007: 10), varying from 0.4 to 6 percent. Sometimes, refugees do not even have access to RSD procedures, and a UNHCR source (Polikarpova 2007) states that this affected 350 refugees in 2007. For instance, unaccompanied minors require a state guardian to file their application but such guardians because of administrative complications are by and large unavailable to them; as a consequence, minors have practically no access to RSD procedures (HIAS, interview 4/2007). Despite low recognition rates, NGOs hold the view that only 10 to 15 percent of all asylum claims are 'manifestly unfounded' (HIAS, interview). This is supported by the fact that in 2006, HIAS' (Hebrew Immigration Aid Society) success rate at Kiev local courts of appeal stood at 70 percent, thus the majority of SCNR decisions is overturned in court. This example also illustrates a relatively independent judicial system.

Finally, on application, asylum seekers have to submit their passport to the SCNR but because they are not provided with an alternative Identity Document (ID) they are regular but nevertheless de facto undocumented (also see Uehling 2004).

Since 2004, no Chechen asylum seeker was granted refugee status (ECRE 2006: 9); according to other sources even since 2001 (Chechen refugee community representative, interview 2007). Chechen refugee community representatives have no explanation for this but suspect that "there must be some informal rules, but I don't know what is behind this practice" (interview 2007). Levin (2006: 15), referring to an interview with the SCNM explains that "SCNM maintains that Chechen asylum seekers do not fall under Ukrainian refugee law. Officials argue that Chechens are 'war refugees', victims of indiscriminate violence, and therefore ineligible for protection under Ukrainian refugee legislation."

In particular Chechen refugees are reported to "have a case (but) don't get access to refugee status (determination procedures)", for instance, Chechens who are arrested by border guards can only apply for asylum "if they have a chance to inform a refugee rights protection organisation, but not all have such opportunities" (Chechen refugee community representative, interview 2007). Sometimes, access to RSD procedures is impossible for purely practical reasons, for example a spokesperson talking about Chechen refugees in Odessa explains that "none has a refugee status, they have no papers. They can't even go to UNHCR because the journey is too expensive." Instead, several cases of refoulement have been reported, specifically of Chechens (ECRE 2006) but also of Uzbeks. According to Levin (2006: 17), 2,109 Chechens were deported from Ukraine to Russia between 2003 and 2005.

Reception and Integration

There are only two temporary reception centres for asylum seekers, both mostly for women and families. One is in Odessa, it has a capacity of 250 individuals and is funded by the EU and UNHCR; the other is a much smaller facility in Mukachevo (South West Ukraine) and accommodates only 15–20 women and children. Both seem unpopular among asylum seekers as it is found that residents often prefer to leave and find somewhere else to stay (various interviews and own observations, 2007). This is either because asylum seekers miss support from their communities which are residing in distant cities, as it is the case with Odessa; or because they tend to be overcrowded at times, as it is the case in Mukachevo. For long, another (temporary) reception centre for 80 individuals is planned in Lavritza (western Ukraine). Occasionally, unaccompanied minors are held in an asylum for orphans and street kids in Kiev but given the lack of any integration measures this must be considered an unsuitable solution (HIAS, interview 4/2007). Access to health care is free according to legislation; however, in practice, patients have to pay a fee to general practitioners which normally asylum seekers cannot afford. For asylum seekers in Kiev, UNHCR has an arrangement with a clinic where they can be treated free of charge in case of emergency. By law, refugee children can go to school free of charge, as it is the case in Kiev; in particular Chechen refugee children are more likely to go to school than other refugee children who often do not speak Russian (Levin 2006: 30). However, in other cities and for some nationalities access might be difficult, as reported by Somalis in Vinnitsa. But there are also other obstacles as reported by Chechens:

"(My son) plays football, he is very good, but if there is a competition in another city all the other boys get subsidies but my boy does not get subsidies because he is not Ukrainian. He could play in the national team, his coach says 'I need him, I don't bother about his papers, but he can't play because of his papers, he is not Ukrainian. It is always this problem: If you don't have papers you get no help and you can't work" (Chechen woman, Bila Tserka, interview 4/2007).

Access to housing and employment is another crucial aspect determining the quality life of refugees and asylum seekers. Unfortunately, there are various legal and practical obstacles that prevent them from accessing legal markets. Most asylum seekers lack proper IDs either because they do not have any or because they had to submit their IDs to the SCNR. UNHCR issues a replacement ID-like letter with a photograph which is valid for six months, after which they require extension. But this document is not officially recognized as an ID by the police. Furthermore, landlords frequently refuse to issue tenancy agreements or even rent receipts to foreigners, to evade taxing, as it is said. Therefore migrants and refugees cannot register their residence with local authorities. Subsequently, migrants and refugees normally do not hold a *propisca*, which is *the* vital statutory registration document. Thus, a "vicious circle" emerges (Andrysek/Rantala 2007: 7) and refugees are excluded from several services.

By the law "On refugees", asylum seekers and refugees are entitled to work but so far, the related employment act has not been changed accordingly, and the Employment Law does not list refugees as a category of people who have a right to work (ECRE 2006). Hence, an inconsistency is created between refugee law and employment law, and for asylum seekers and refugees it is almost impossible to find regular employment. The main reason is that in order to employ a foreigner, employers have to pay a considerable fee which acts as a major disincentive for employers. Another obstacle is to obtain a tax number which is impossible because of the lack of an ID.

"I am a doctor, a gynaecologist. I cannot work here even though I was quite famous in my country, because I don't have a refugee status yet. But I go to the elderly here, I give injections and other medical treatment and they pay me for this" (Chechen woman, Bila Tserka, interview 4/2007).

Therefore, only irregular employment, mostly on markets or in construction is available; alternatively, refugees and asylum seekers engage in small-scale self-employment. But for women and specifically for single-mothers, as for asylum seekers who are not living in one of the large cities, not even that seems to be an option.

"I am a single mother, I have three children. (...) I cannot work because of my children. Thank God there are nice people, I take the two children from some rich Ukrainians and they pay me for babysitting, I would not be able to do anything else as I have to watch my kids" (Chechen woman, Bila Tserka, interview 4/2007).

Finally, there are some handicapped individuals among the Chechen refugee population, but no services are provided for them.

"There is a young man, his house was bombed, he wasn't a fighter, just a civilian, but his house was bombed and he was thrown against the wall. Now his spine is injured and he can't move his legs. He is in a wheel chair. He can't go out, he is always at home. So sometimes I go and take him out, bring him food as well. There is another person who is completely blind" (member of a Chechen refugee community organisation, Bila Tserka, 4/2007).

Non-statutory Services

A few international organisations and NGOs provide services to asylum seekers, such as UNHCR and Caritas Austria. But also the Jesuit Refugee Service (JRS), the ECRE and the Danish Refugee Council have some activities in Ukraine. UNHCR (budget $ 2.1 million, UNHCR 2006a) has two implementing partners: HIAS and Rokada, both in Kiev. Since 2002, HIAS, which is a branch of the US American organisation, provides legal assistance to asylum seekers in the Kiev region; in 2006, they had 2,100 clients. HIAS and some other regional NGOs also implement the UNHCR's RSD process parallel to the state. Rokada, set up in 2000, provides some social services to refugees and asylum seekers in the Kiev region. In 2006, they served 1,300 individual clients. To a selection of the most destitute asylum seekers, around 450, they hand out $ 80 per month; others are handed out emergency food packages, second-hand clothes, bedding and some other items. Rokada also runs a refugee integration centre providing language classes, counselling and a crèche.

In Western Ukraine (Transcarpathia), where most asylum seekers file their application, there are two NGOs, Caritas and NEEKA. Caritas is based in Uzhgorod, it is a project of Caritas Austria and funded by the EU. They provide legal aid to asylum seekers, in particular to detainees in the three detention centres in the region. But at the time of writing this chapter, access to the detention centres was suspended. NEEKA, the second NGO, is a Christian faith organisation in Mukachevo, they are implementing partners of UNHCR with some further funding from Caritas Austria, whilst the local Red Cross helps with second-hand clothes. NEEKA provides mostly social services, such as food packages, including health services, but also some legal aid.

Across the country, thirteen other local NGOs, usually partners of UNHCR, provide diverse services, mostly legal aid, such as in Chernihiv, Charkiv, Donetsk, Odessa, Lviv, Luhansk and Vinnitsya. In most cases, funding is scarce and often project-based and the future of many activities hence uncertain. Unfortunately, often NGOs seem to "lack suitably experienced/qualified staff with the desirable level of professionalism" (Andryseck/Rantala 2007:8), even cases of corruption are alleged. It needs to be noted that NGOs have little tradition of being independent from statutory agencies; instead they are interconnected with state agencies and cannot always be considered confident advocates for the rights of refugees. For these and other reasons, asylum seekers and detainees are indeed often very negative about such NGOs and consider them as part of the problem.

Finally, there are a few refugee community organisations, for instance of Afghans, Chechens and Angolans that provide some assistance, mostly of non-material nature. In the Kiev region, only Berkat, a non-funded Chechen aid charity which is supported by just one donor in the US supports asylum seekers of any nationality. They are handing out second-hand clothes, walking aids and stationery for school children. And in Zaporizhia, there is the Chechen cultural centre Voina, which organises support for Chechen refugees. Furthermore, there are a few services available in other cities, and refugees have to travel long distances to obtain support.

Relations between the Chechen refugee community organisations and other NGOs and international organisations display a certain level of frustration.

"The rich organisations don't help us, they have high salaries, big cars, offices, but they don't help us. The International Organisation for Migration (IOM) never gave any help, they have a big office in the centre of town but they don't help. We turned to them but they always refuse. Refugees in need turn to us and not to IOM, because they know that they won't get any help from them. (...) I can't understand how can they pay such salaries and expensive rents for offices in the city centre when there are so many refugees suffering and not getting any help" (member of a Chechen refugee community organisation, Kiev, interview 4/2007).

"We receive acknowledgement letters from UNHCR but that doesn't help us. (...) We are thankful that UNHCR listens but sometimes we feel they do not want certain information" (another member of a Chechen refugee community organisation, Uzhgorod, interview 8/2007).

"A family was stranded at the train station (in Kiev); they actually lived at the train station. But Rokada refused to support them. UNHCR was appalled" (ibid).

Nevertheless, it must be acknowledged that international organisations often have only limited resources and are not meant to step in where statutory services do not exist; subsequently, local NGOs that are usually implementing partners can only offer very limited services whilst refugee community NGOs lack any funding and can do very little to relieve their clients' situation. Thus, blaming international organisations and NGOs as refugees and their representatives sometimes do is understandable but not always fully justified.

Arrest, Detention and Deportation

In legal terms, "illegal immigrants" or migrants attempting to illegally cross the border to the EU are held for up to ten days at the point of arrest, e.g. a border guards' detachment either at the border or an international airport or at a police station. So far, there are only two purpose-build detention centres for illegal immigrants, both in western Ukraine and run by the border guards: Mukachevo for women and children with a capacity of 20, and Pavchino for men with a capacity of 250. Two more EU-funded centres are to be opened soon, Lutsk, which will mostly serve the EU-Ukraine readmission agreement and which will be run by Ukrainian authorities with some participation of the IOM, and Chernihiv, which will possibly facilitate implementation of the new readmission with Russia. In the other regions (*oblasts*) illegal immigrants are held in police cells and prisons. Conditions in detention centres are often critical and the Council of Europe (2007), UNHCR (2007a) and human rights organisations (Human Rights Watch 2006) raise various concerns.

Once the status of suspected illegal immigrants is established, CIS citizens arrested in the country or on the western border would be released but ordered to voluntarily leave the country whereas CIS citizens who are arrested on entry, e.g. on the Russian border will be returned to the country they have entered from, mostly Russia. All other nationalities are detained for a maximum of six month in order to establish identity, nationality and prepare their return. Repeated arrest results in repeated detention. Those who are arrested on entry on the eastern border and who cannot be returned to Russia are transferred to Kiev and referred to the Migration Service for establishing their status (SBGS, interview 4/2007). Immigrants who apply for asylum should normally be released.

Social Conditions, Racism and Skinhead Violence

Asylum seekers are not entitled to any state benefits and because they lack tenancy agreements they cannot register with local authorities and therefore cannot claim access to local social services. Once refugees are recognized they receive a one-off payment of Grivna 17 by the state, the equivalent of two cups of tea, less than $ 200 annually of cash for all refugees (HIAS, interview 4/2007). UNHCR benefits, which are paid only to the neediest, are only half the legal minimum income; the poverty line is defined as $ 5 per day, $ 150 per month. Because of high rents, in particular in the capital, benefits are often not even sufficient to provide for shelter. Occasionally, destitute asylum seekers live in weekend homes (*datchas)* or are referred to a homeless shelter for a few nights and some food. Health and mental problems are reported by several respondents, those who would need hospital treatment cannot afford to lose working days because this is their only source of income. Others are addicted to drugs, e.g. sniffing of glue. A specific cause for concern is the rise of skinhead violence within the past three years (UNHCR 2007). Certain groups of migrants report incidents on a daily basis; other sources report that every three months a black or Asian person is murdered (Pastor Sunday, conversation 10/2007). So far, Chechen refugees do not report such incidents, but complain about racial stereotyping as "terrorists" instead, though this has diminished in recent times, as they noticed.

Administrative Obstacles

Almost all sources report some sort of unduly request for extra fees by civil servants, self-employed interpreters and even NGOs that are to be paid at different stages of the asylum procedure. These are of particular concern to asylum seekers who often have no or very limited sources of income. Another set of problems relates to the lack of appropriate documentation, such as IDs *propiscas* and work permits (as explained above). Often, the police stops migrants on suspicion and if the required documents cannot be produced and on-the spot payment is due. This is perceived as unfair in particular by those who do actually have a regular status and who believe that they cannot be held responsible for lack of papers.

Conclusion

For almost fifteen years, Chechen refugees have arrived in Ukraine. Those who arrived first, during the mid 1990s, found relatively favourable conditions and were able to regularize their status within a reasonable period of time. They managed to secure reliable sources of income, often in small-scale business, and their children go to school and have a chance to integrate into Ukraine society. Provided that these conditions remain stable, they are unlikely to migrate onwards to another country but will permanently settle down. Meanwhile, and due to its complex international relations with Russia, Ukraine seems to disadvantage Chechen and other refugees from the Russian Federation and the CIS. Notably, those asylum seekers who arrived after 2000 met a deteriorated political climate and were often unable to regularize their status and to secure a stable livelihood. Within the Chechen refugee population, specifically vulnerable groups can be identified, notably unaccompanied minors, (widowed) single mothers, and disabled refugees. Due to these conditions, recent Chechen refugees do not feel able or safe to stay in Ukraine.

For the various reasons described in this contribution, diverse European bodies and international organisations are generally critical of the asylum system in Ukraine. For instance, the International Centre for Migration Policy Development (ICMPD 2006: 13) believes there is "a general lack of a human rights culture", staff of the IOM in Kiev in an interview in 2006 did not consider Ukraine a safe country for most refugees whilst UNHCR (2007) recently reaffirmed that "no assurances can be given that the persons in question (...) would have access to a fair and efficient refugee status determination procedure, would be treated in accordance with international refugee standards or that there would be effective protection against *refoulement*" (also see Council of Europe 2007).

So far, there seem to be three alternative responses: measures that are designed to improve conditions of asylum seekers and refugees in Ukraine; resettlement in other safe countries (see for e.g. UNHCR 2004), or return to Chechnya, if feasible at all.

Bibliography

Andrysek, Oldrich/Rantala, Tarja (2007): Local Integration of Refugees in Belarus, Moldova and Ukraine. Interim Report. Presented to the Cross Border Cooperation/ Söderköping Process, Senior Level Review Meeting, 6–7 of September 2007. Stockholm.

Council of Europe (2007): Report by the Commissioner for Human Rights, Mr Thomas Hammarberg on his visit to Ukraine, 10–17 December 2006. Strasbourg.

Desormeau, Kate (2005): The Outside Inside. Chechen IDPs, Identity Documents and the Right to Free Movement in the Russian Federation. Working paper 22. Oxford. Retrieved from: http://www.rsc.ox.ac.uk/PDFs/RSCworkingpaper22.pdf.

ECRE (2006): Ukraine. Situation for refugees and asylum seekers. Country Report 2006. London.

Human Rights Watch (2006): Ukraine: On the Margins Rights Violations against Migrants and Asylum Seekers at the New Eastern Border of the European Union. London.

ICMPD (2006): EU Justice Freedom and Security. Assessment mission to Ukraine. Vienna.
IWPR (Institute for War and Peace Reporting) (2005): Chechnya. The Great Migration. London. Retrieved from: http://iwpr.net/?p=crs&s=f&o=254606&apc_state=henicrs2005.
Levin, Mariah (2006): Chechen migration and integration in Ukraine. Retrieved from: http://www.chechnyaadvocacy.org/refugees/ChechenMigrationinUkraine.pdf, (23/1/08)
Polikarpova, Alina (2007): Refugee resettlement from Ukraine, Belarus and Moldova. Paper presented to European Conference on Models of Integration and Resettlement of Refugees, Madrid, 8–9 November.
Söderköping Process (2007): Ukraine: Illegal Immigration statistics. Kiev. Retrieved from: http://soderkoping.org.ua/page12489.html.
State Border Guard Service (2005): State Border Guard service of Ukraine, presented at Senior Level Review Meeting, 12–13 May 2005:
Retrieved from: http://soderkoping.org.ua/files/presentations/Ukraine/Presentation1.ppt.
SCNM (State Committee on Nationalities and Migration) (2006): Statistics. Kiev. Retrieved from: http://www.scnm.gov.ua/ua/a?migration_stat.
Uehling, Greta (2004): Unwanted migration: combating and unwittingly creating irregular migration in Ukraine. Working paper 109. Geneva.
UNHCR (2004): Country operation plan: Ukraine. Planning year 2004. Kiev.
UNHCR (2006a): UNHCR in Ukraine. Geneva.
UNHCR (2006b): Fortress Europe. The wall is getting higher. UNHCR News story. Kiev/Budapest.
UNHCR (2006c): Refugee statistics in Ukraine. Kiev.
Retrieved from: www.unhcr.org.ua/main.php?article_id=22&view=full.

UNHCR (2007a): UNHCR Position on the Situation of Asylum in Ukraine in the Context of Return of Asylum-Seekers. Kiev.
UNHCR (2007b): Ukraine: UNHCR concerned by rise in attacks on asylum seekers, refugees. Retrieved from: http://www.
alertnet.org/thenews/newsdesk/UNHCR/45ca151baa0d363f5b5b4eba8b25d326.htm.

Settlement and (Re)construction of Gender Relations in Exile: Chechen Refugees in Eastern Europe

Alice Szczepanikova

Introduction

This chapter examines how Chechen refugees in Europe come to terms with displacement by using a gender perspective. I analyse their settlement experiences through the notion of *(re)construction* which indicates that refugees' settlement in a host country involves *reconstruction* of the past conceptions of family and home as well as *construction* of new strategies and patterns of life shaped by pressures and opportunities of the new environment. I show that gender relations are a particularly contested area in this process and constitute a fruitful site for exploring how refugee women and men (re)construct their identities and family lives in exile. This chapter demonstrates how Chechens' notions of family are rooted in patriarchal structures. Although the material basis for patriarchy crumbles in the conditions of war, disruption of social norms and displacement and despite the fact that men have troubles reconstituting their masculinities and women gain new roles in the family, I explain that a radical challenge to patriarchal family relations among Chechens in Europe is unlikely.

Existing literature on the situation of Chechen refugees around the world is scarce. This is especially true for Chechens in Europe. That is despite the fact that the Russian Federation topped the list of countries of origin of asylum seekers in industrialised countries in 2003 and 2004[1]. After a short period of decline, Russia has recently moved up again to occupy the second position with 18,800 asylum claims submitted by citizens of the Russian Federation (most of them being from North Caucasus) and it now ranks right behind Iraq (UNHCR 2008).

Chechens usually figure as Russian nationals in asylum statistics, therefore their movements and characteristics are difficult to grasp by these numbers. Moreover, we know very little about conditions of their stay in Europe. Most ethnic Chechens returned to Chechnya after the first period of the conflict with Russia (1994–1996) and tried to rebuild their lives (Norwegian Refugee Council 2005). Back then, many people still had strong hopes for a better future. Many of today's refugees who are fleeing the second outbreak of war since 1999 and the continuing instability in the region have been less hopeful and less willing to go back despite intensive pressures from Russian and Chechen authorities. Although the country has now turned toward greater stability and the move to "normalcy" has been reasserted many times in recent years, violations of human rights continue and the feelings of insecurity persist among people (Matveeva 2007). Those who have "made it" to Europe are particularly hesitant when considering return. Having experienced much-sought-after stability, security, legal predictability and also greater prospects for their children's development and education, many Chechen refugees continue to invest in their European settlement and (re)construction of life in exile rather than in a permanent return to Chechnya.

It has been widely documented in other contexts that renegotiation of gender relations and identities is an integral part of the process of refugee settlement (e.g. Al-Ali 2002; Buijs 1993; Franz 2003; Kay 1988; Kibria 1993). A number of feminist migration scholars emphasized that gender relations in migration processes represent a dynamic and contested area and require careful contextualisation in order to avoid essentializing and oversimplifications (e.g. Hondagneu-Sotelo 1994; Morokvasic 1983; Pessar/Mahler 2003; Phizacklea 2003). These accounts form a theoretical backbone of this study.

The chapter is structured as follows: first, I introduce the empirical case study carried out in the Czech Republic and explain the methodology used; second, I analyse how the patriarchal structures of Chechen family norms have been sus-

1 Over 35,000 asylum-seekers from the Russian Federation applied for asylum in 43 industrialised countries in 2003 (UNHCR 2008). The numbers of Chechen asylum seekers coming to European countries intensified in early 2003 after Russian authorities had closed the first tent camp in Ingushetia, and announced more closures to follow (Norwegian Refugee Council 2005: 32).

tained and transformed in the times of displacement imposed on Chechens by the 1944 deportation to Central Asia, I look at how the gender structure of Chechen society changed during the times of relative stability under the Soviet rule, and I also discuss changes and challenges to gender relations in families caused by the recent wars. Third, refugees' strategies to (re)construct their gender identities and family lives in European exile are analysed. I show how refugees painfully experience the absence of wider kinship networks, how Chechen men struggle to reconstitute their masculinities in the structures of the Czech asylum system and what new roles women take up to support their families while at the same time carefully preserving the family unity. Finally, I debate what implications these changes have for the patriarchal order of Chechen families and their futures in Europe.

The Case of Chechens in the Czech Republic: Data and Methodology

In 2003, the number of asylum seekers in the Czech Republic increased by more than 30 percent (compared to the previous year) and reached over 11 thousand applications. Most of the applications were launched by citizens of the Russian Federation 93 percent of whom declared Chechen nationality (Government Council for Human Rights 2004: 97). The number of Chechens seeking asylum in the Czech Republic increased even more dramatically as it moved up from 416 applications in 2002 to 4,515 in 2003 (Government Council for Human Rights 2004: 97). The Chechens' share in the total number of asylum applicants grew from 7 to 43 percent. No wonder this sudden inflow was remembered by many employees in refugee accomodation centres as the "Chechen wave". The water metaphor is quite appropriate in this case since the majority of these people did not stay in the country, some left prior to being given a notice in their asylum case, some left after being informed that their decision was postponed (a postponement of one year was not an exception) or rejected. Between 2000 and 2007, 297 asylums were granted to Russian nationals (DAMP 2008)[2]. In the same period of time, 131 Russian nationals were granted some form of subsidiary protection (DAMP 2007)[3].

2 Specific data about how many of them declared Chechen nationality are not available.

3 Until 2006, subsidiary protection was granted on the basis of recognition of an "obstacle to leave". Since September 2006, this category has been substituted by Subsidiary Protection (a requirement of the

This chapter draws on empirical research among Chechen asylum seekers and recognized refugees in the Czech Republic conducted between 2004 and 2007. To account for the complexity of the forced migration process, the research was carried out at various sites and with different actors including: 1) interviews with representatives of the Czech Ministry of the Interior responsible for the refugee status determination and accommodation in refugee centres, 2) interviews and participant observation in non-governmental organisations (NGOs) assisting refugees and 3) in-depth interviews with Chechen asylum seekers and recognized refugees living both in refugee accomodation centres and in private accommodation; most of these interviews were conducted in Russian.

Altogether, 25 Chechens living in 17 separate households were involved in the study (10 men and 15 women). Most of them were coming from urban or semi-urban parts of Chechnya. Men's age ranged from 26 to 52 with an average of 36 years, the average age of women was 32 years (ranging from 15 to 45). Four of the women had finished university, five attended secondary school and six had elementary education. Three male informants had a university degree, four either completed secondary education or had not finished their university studies and three younger men had elementary education. Back in Chechnya, most of the informants either lived in their own house or shared one with their parents. Despite a relatively high level of education, most of the women did not work outside their homes in the last years before their flight from Chechnya. Most men had some form of employment either formal or informal while some had to go into hiding from Russian forces and lived constantly on the move.

While interviews with the state officials and NGO representatives were mostly (but not always) conducted during a single meeting, I met with the Chechen informants for a number of times and some of this research encounters evolved into ongoing relationships which allowed me to follow their lives over a longer period of time. Developing a closer contact with refugees also enabled me to cross the barrier of mistrust and gain a more intimate insight into their personal and family lives. I was determined to make the research process meaningful to the informants; not based solely on me getting information from them but shaped it into a more mutual exchange. Some of our meetings did not match the conventional interviewer-interviewee interaction as I was the one answering questions (e.g. about the asy-

European Union). Although Subsidiary Protection gives more support and better conditions than the "obstacle to leave" status (for example allows for family reunification), support and security provided by this status is still incomparable to the status of people granted asylum.

lum procedure, the State Integration Program, the Czech labour market, NGO programs, Czech society more generally or my personal life). At points, I might have influenced their decisions by an advice or a recommendation.

Chechen informants were mostly contacted in various refugee centres where I conducted fieldwork in 2004, 2006 and 2007. I later followed some of them as they moved to private accommodation or decided to leave the Czech Republic and seek asylum in other parts of Europe. Initially, I was determined to spend equal amounts of time with both men and women knowing that gender is never just about studying women and constructions of femininity. As a growing number of scholars emphasize, gender is always also about masculinity and its relations to femininity as the two are constituted in relation to each other and fundamentally operate through contrast with each other (Salzinger 2003: 23). Although this theoretical perspective has remained a guiding line throughout my research, the actual "doing of gender" (West/Zimmerman 1987) resulted in a situation when my interactions with women were, with a few exceptions, more frequent and more intense than those with men.

I see three possible reasons for this: Firstly, women were usually my entry points to Chechen households. Chechens' informal rules of interpersonal communication with people who are not family members require that gender lines are crossed with caution. This applies especially to women who are restricted in communicating with outside men but also to Chechen men in approaching unfamiliar women. When entering Chechen households it seemed more "comfortable" for everyone that I developed a contact with the women first. Secondly, Chechen men were more restraint when speaking about family and personal matters. Once my conversations with women focused around family relations and other more intimate aspects of life, it became more difficult to reach out to men. As a Chechen surgeon Khassan Baiev describes in the preface to his memoirs, "it is considered improper for a man to talk about his wife and children. We do not keep photographs of them in our wallets or on the wall" (Baiev/Daniloff 2003: 14). Thirdly, I think that Chechen women found it somewhat easier to overcome the convention of emotional restraint and reveal aspects of their private life to me because they painfully experienced abrupt separation from their female relatives and peers back home. I was sometimes told, "you seem like a sister to me". Therefore, it has to be acknowledged from the outset that women's views are privileged in my account because I got to know more about them.

Displacement, War and Everyday Life in Chechnya: Gender Perspective

We can hardly understand how refugees' perceptions of gender and family relations change in exile without knowing something about the way these relations developed throughout their lives in their home country. As Wenona Giles points out, gender relations in migrant households and families are constructed and negotiated in line with particular "remembrance" of home (Giles 1999: 85). This section sets out to analyse the development of gender relations and family norms in the lives of ordinary Chechens from the gruelling experience of deportation in 1944 until the recent wars. It should help us to understand from which positions Chechen women and men negotiate and strategize as they (re)construct their identities and family relations in exile.

This account makes no pretence of providing anything but a few observations based on a combination of scarce secondary resources on the issue of gender relations in Chechnya and the narratives of my informants. It is worth noting that existing research on Chechnya focuses predominantly on the Chechens' struggle for independence, armed conflict with Russia or the country's recent redefinition as a security threat due to concerns with the rise of Islamist terrorism in the region. In contrast, we know very little about past and present lives of ordinary citizens of Chechnya and even less about developments and changes of gender relations. Moreover, there is little information about Chechen society in decades of "relative stability" under Soviet state socialism. Discussions of both recent and more distant history are dominated by male actors: politicians and fighters. With the exception of a handful of journalistic and literary publications (e.g. Brežná 1997; Procházková 2003), the voices of Chechen women are absent. Specific attention to women's agency can be found mostly in relation to female participation in hostage-takings and suicide attacks against Russian targets. Labelled "black widows", these women's acts tend to be presented as an epitome of the "level of desperation and the degree of decimation of the male Chechen population" (Nivat 2005: 419). Thus, women's identities and actions are defined by the men they have lost. This approach risks a number of simplifications and overshadows ordinary women's contributions to developments of Chechen society.

Chechen society is commonly described as Muslim and deeply patriarchal (e.g. Human Rights Watch 2000; Myers 2004; Rousseva 2004). The two features are presented as inextricably linked together. However, such an approach does not encourage further investigation of the dynamics of gender relations and their development over the times marked by dramatic social and economic changes. Treating patriarchal traditions as a synonym for women's subordination in Chechnya or as immutable part and parcel of Chechen culture does not help us understand how the daily operations of both masculinity and femininity shape people's experiences of displacement and settlement.

Already in the late 1980s, Deniz Kandiyoti (1988) called for a more culturally and temporally grounded understanding of patriarchal systems. She introduced the concept of *patriarchal bargains* which raises questions about how women strategize within a set of concrete structural constraints that exert a powerful influence on their gendered subjectivities and how these bargains determine the nature of gender ideologies in different contexts (Kandiyoti 1988: 274–275). She argued that there are different forms of patriarchy that present women with distinct "rules of the game" and "call for different strategies to maximize security and optimize life options with varying potential for active or passive resistance in the face of oppression" (Kandiyoti 1988: 274). Kandiyoti's categorisation of what she calls "classic patriarchy"[4] serves as a useful grid for the analysis of Chechen family relations and for thinking about how they were changing in the past. It also allows us to better contextualise changes in family and gender relations among Chechens during the war and in exile and how individual men and women respond to them.

The key to the reproduction of male dominance through a patriarchal family lies, Kandiyoti argues, in the operations of the patrilocally extended household (Kandiyoti 1988: 278). This means that after marriage, young women move into a household headed by their husband's father where they are subordinate not only to all the men but also and importantly to the more senior women, especially their mother-in-law (Kandiyoti 1988: 278). In the system of patrilineage, the husband's family appropriates both women's labour and children and renders their work and contribution to production invisible (Kandiyoti 1988: 279). Women are subjected to various seclusion and exclusion practices and to extensive control. However, it would be misleading to see women only as victims of the system. Women's compliance with patriarchy is supported by the promise of economic protection and social status on the one hand and is rooted in a specific dynamic of the life cycle in the patriarchal extended family. It is based on the belief that women's

4 According to the author, classic patriarchy is characteristic of South and East Asia (specifically India and China) and the Muslim Middle East (including Turkey, Pakistan, and Iran) (Kandiyoti 1988: 278).

hardships as young brides will eventually be superseded by the control and authority they will gain over their own subservient daughters-in-law. Kandiyoti concludes that this pattern of power circulation in the household "encourages a thorough internalization of this form of patriarchy by the women themselves" (Kandiyoti 1988: 279).

The structures of classic patriarchy underpin what are considered to be the pillars of Chechen traditions and social norms. The accounts of my informants as well as secondary literature corroborate that patrilocality – practiced in line with the above description – constitutes the dominant pattern of family relations in Chechnya. Chechens are characterised and characterise themselves by strong kinship solidarity ties (most prominently the responsibility towards one's elders) and the emphasis on the preservation of individual and family honour (e.g. Brauer 2002; Nichols 1995; M. Pohl 2002). Although women occasionally participate in the public sphere, femininity is constructed as primarily associated with the domestic sphere and the roles of mother, wife and homemaker. Masculinity is defined primarily by man's ability to provide for the family needs but it also stands for more general "human" virtues such as honesty, trustworthiness, or dignity (Szczepanikova 2005: 290). Honour and dignity are praised among Chechens as the most important attributes of one's identity. However, the actual practise of these seemingly gender-neutral values is significantly gendered. Although Chechens referred to men's and women's honour by using the same word *chest'*, it was obvious that in relation to women, honour was perceived in terms of chastity. The imperative of preserving women's (and thus also family's) honour legitimises their exclusion from the public sphere as well as a number of measures to control women's behaviour that would be unprecedented with regard to men's codes of conduct. As I will show below, this idea of femininity is likely to position women in the essentialized roles of biological reproducers and embodied boundaries of ethnic-national collectives (Anthias/Yuval-Davis 1992; Korac 2004). In what follows in this section, I focus on two of the above characteristics: strong family relations and honour. I analyse how they have developed over the time throughout dramatic events in Chechen history.

Family Relations under the 1944 Deportation and Exile

At the times of dramatic changes in people's lives, such as was Chechens' deportation to Central Asia in 1944, preservation of family norms gained new meanings and new importance. Although the material basis of patriarchy was significantly challenged by virtual dispossession of the whole nation and by putting it on the fringe of survival, it seems that strict adherence to traditional family norms and the imperative of honourable conduct were among the key means of preserving Chechens' national identity and their resistance to forces of Soviet assimilation.

In 1944, Chechens were among the thirteen nations which were designated as inherently treasonous and disloyal to the Soviet state and accused of collaborating with the Germans. They were to be "punished" by a complete removal from their traditional areas of settlement. The two largest groups deported were Soviet Germans and North Caucasians, primarily Chechens and Ingushs (M. Pohl 2002: 401). Otto Pohl describes that within a week between 23 and 29 February of 1944, over 387 thousand Chechens were deported to Kazakhstan and Kirgizia (O. Pohl 2000: 284). By 1950, almost 28 percent of the exiled North Caucasians had died and the total number of deaths in this period amounted to 104,903 people (O. Pohl, 2000: 267–268). Since the vast majority of these deaths were the direct result of the poor physical conditions deliberately inflicted upon them by the Stalin regime, the author concludes that "the deportations constituted acts of ethnically motivated mass murder" (O. Pohl 2000: 268). Furthermore, the ultimate goal of these policies was to dissolve the national identities of the Chechens and other deported groups[5].

In her study of Chechens and Ingushs exiled in Kazakhstan, Michaela Pohl (2002) concludes that the exiles managed to find a variety of effective means to remain separate in their refusal to accommodate to the Soviet regime. One of the key concerns was how to keep the women pure, chaste and to shelter them (Brauer 2002: 396). This was to be achieved through strict control of women's sexual and reproductive behaviour and their exclusion from the public sphere. For example, Pohl (2002) cites records of party officials resenting Chechens' antagonistic attitude to the officially propagated emancipation of women. As a result, no Chechen girls participated in the communist youth organisations (while there were over a

5 This strategy was pursued, for example, by elimination of all education and publications in their native languages by the Soviet government (O. Pohl 2000: 288).

hundred of Chechen boys) (M. Pohl 2002: 412). Moreover, no Chechen women took part in lectures on childcare, hygiene and the role of women in Soviet society (M. Pohl 2002: 413). The author quotes the local party official who wrote that "the girls of these nationalities (the Caucasians) are still being held hostage by feudal-religious attitudes, their parents observe old customs and do not allow the girls to take part in public life" (M. Pohl 2002: 413). Young women were carefully guarded from contacts with non-Caucasians, and Chechen men were ready to take revenge if outsiders did not respect their customs (M. Pohl 2002: 413). Another highly gendered strategy of preserving ethnic distinctness was the emphasis on the biological reproduction of the nation. Although in demographic terms, the Chechens and Ingushs never completely recovered, Pohl reports that despite persisting hard living conditions, in the years after 1949 the birth rate of Caucasian "special settlers" in Kazakhstan rose sharply and almost tripled the death rate (M. Pohl 2002: 407). From these scarce accounts, it can be concluded that during the deportation, Chechen women were constructed as reproducers of the boundaries of ethnic and national groups and were assigned a central position in the ideological as well as biological reproduction of the Chechen collectivity.

Since the deportation of Chechens was *total* i.e. all people of Chechen ethnicity were supposed to be deported, the experience of deportation is still very much present among Chechens today. During my research, deportation was often mentioned in my informants' narratives. Some of the older ones were born in exile or had heard a lot about the harshness of deportation from their parents and/or grandparents. The ability to survive and to remain distinct even under extremely difficult living conditions and under intensive pressures to assimilate was recounted with pride and was repeatedly ascribed to the strength of family relations.

The Times of Relative Stability

In 1957, the Presidium of the Supreme Soviet of the USSR restored the Chechen-Ingush autonomous republic and after thirteen years of exile cancelled the ban on Chechens' and Ingushs' return home (Brauer 2002). During the subsequent years of relative stability under the Soviet rule, Chechen society greatly diversified with regard to people living in urban and rural settings, educational and occupational structures. The society underwent substantial changes in line with processes of industrialisation, urbanisation and to an extent also (imposed) secularisation. While many Chechens saw the Soviet rule as refurbished Russian domination, others perceived it also as Chechnya's path to modernity. The Soviet system provided both men and women with professional opportunities and social infrastructure that the strictly patriarchal order could hardly offer (Wood 2004: 12). On the other hand, it must be noted that urban ethnic Russians who represented 24 percent of the republic's total population in 1989 were better positioned to benefit from these developments. They dominated the oil and machine sectors, health, education and social services while predominantly rural Chechens and Ingushs worked in agriculture and construction (Wood 2004: 15). In 1989, only 5 percent of the population of Checheno-Ingushetia had higher education, while 16 percent had no education at all (Wood 2004: 15). Despite ethnic discrimination and the lack of freedom in some areas of life, for those who spent most of their lives in this period of relative stability, it is the key point of reference for what is considered "a normal life". That is how Kheda, a woman in her late thirties, described the time she grew up in:

"Compared with how our parents lived, during the Stalin's regime and the deportation, I and my husband had a very peaceful childhood. Nobody forced us into anything, there was not a single war and then, it was only war. So we could see a bit of that normal life and we think that this life was very beautiful. I never lacked anything at that time" (April 2006, Prague).

After the 1917 October Revolution, it was believed that, if Soviet authorities could challenge the traditional patriarchal family structures, this would provide them with leverage for the disintegration of traditional societal structures and their subsequent reconstitution in a new, Soviet style (Ishkanian 2003: 479). However, after Stalin consolidated his power in the 1930s, some of the initial revolutionary changes in favour of women's equality were abandoned and the emancipation of women was declared achieved. The family was redefined as a place where women share the burden of breadwinning on the one hand, and play the primary role as mothers, wives and homemakers on the other (Ashwin 2000: 9). Sarah Ashwin (2000) summarises state policies regarding women and gender relation in the Soviet society as follows:

"In the case of women, their role was defined as worker-mothers who had a duty to work, to produce future generations of workers, as well as to oversee the running of the household. In return, they were to receive 'protection' from the state in their capacity as mothers, as well as independence through their access to paid work" (Ashwin 2000: 1).

It goes without saying that in such a diverse country as was the USSR, gender policies did not reach and transform the society in a unitary way. Pilkington argues that "the 'Soviet model', if we can talk of such a thing, was experienced very differently by women depending on their ethnic origin and their social and economic background and position" (Pilkington 1992: 188). There is very little specific information available about the socioeconomic characteristic of Chechen population during the Soviet period let alone divided by gender categories. In a report by the United Nations Development Programme, the level of women's economic participation in less urbanized republics of the Northern Caucasus with "traditional national family roles and higher birth rate" was estimated to be the lowest in Russia – less than 15 percent of women from the population aged between 15 and 75 were reported as economically active (Zubarevich 2003: 11). While exact figures for population growth are unknown, Fredholm argues that in the 1970s and 1980s, the Chechen rate of annual population growth was as high as between 31 and 40 per 1000 inhabitants which clearly outnumbered other countries in the region (Fredholm 2000: 322). It is the generation of people who grew up in these large families that are now coming as refugees to Europe.

Despite the diversity of various Soviet societies, one feature was shared throughout the USSR – family's response to Soviet economic conditions commonly defined as a constant shortage. The household, although formally outside the economic planning system, was "the flexible unit that made things work, that compensated for the functional gaps of the plan by developing a counter-system of production and exchange" (Burawoy/Krotov/Lytkina 2000: 60). It was clear from the narratives of my informants that labour-intensive, small-scale agriculture was one of the coping strategies adopted to complement poorly paid jobs together with engaging in informal economy by doing extra jobs besides regular employment. Many people I interviewed described that both of their parents worked outside home with mothers often "helping" their fathers either on a construction site or in a family business while their young children were cared for either by grandparents or by older siblings.

Having experienced attempts of ethnically-based assimilation if not annihilation, Chechens were particularly resistant to the Soviet influence. This was easier in more remote rural areas. Abdurahman, a man in his fifties, commented on the significance of regional differences in Chechnya:

"There are mountain areas and lowlands and in each, people have quite a different upbringing. What is not allowed in the mountains is possible in the lowlands. Mountain people are very strict in keeping their traditions while those in the lowlands live closer to European ways" (January 2007, refugee centre).

Kheda explained how the rural/urban divide was being reinforced by the fact that village girls and in particular those from the mountains, were not allowed by their families to come to study in the cities:

"Usually, their parents would take them out of school after their eighth class; they were not allowed to travel to the city on their own, what would the neighbours say about such a girl?" (September 2007, Prague)

The major fear was that having their reputation and honesty damaged, girls would have problems in getting married into a respectable family. Today, it is estimated that around 67 percent of Chechnya's population live in rural areas (Relief Web 2001).

Kheda, on the other hand, lived in a town near Grozny and travelled thirty kilometres everyday to attend lectures at her university. She proudly describes that she and her sisters had a full support of their father to finish their university studies and to get good jobs which would provide them with a living in case their husbands could not provide for them properly:

"My father always said: if you'll have an irresponsible husband, then I don't want my girl to suffer. Maybe I will not be around at that time to protect you. I want you to have your own head with brain as well as your own copeck. That is how he saw it, he had these modern views" (Kheda, July 2006, Prague).

Nevertheless, she also knew of a number of families in her neighbourhood where women were not encouraged to pursue higher education and she remembered cases of women who dropped out of their studies after they got married. Therefore, although women had access to higher education, their family responsibilities were clearly prioritised over their professional careers.

Also for Kheda, it was not an obvious thing to continue her education after she got married in the fourth year of her studies just one year before completing her degree. Her story illustrates how women who wanted to pursue their careers had to combine their ambitions with demanding family obligations. When I asked her how the decision whether she would continue her studies after marriage and moving into her husband's family was made, she replied:

"There are families where they did not allow girls to study any further. But my husband and his father said: if your father gave you such an opportunity, you can continue with it and finish your fifth year. Well, maybe, if I were somewhere at the beginning, they might have said: It is enough, leave it. But I believed that they would allow me to continue, otherwise I wouldn't get married. It was very important for me to finish that fifth year" (Kheda, July 2006, Prague).

Although her husband and his family allowed her to complete her last year, they nevertheless expected her to help with the household and do all the work a young bride was supposed to do. That is how combining household duties with studies looked like for Kheda:

"According to our customs, I had to get up early in the morning and do all the work. But I also had to study to defend the diploma; the fifth year was particularly difficult. So I did that at night. I got up at four and milked cows, fed them and took them to the pasture on the margins of the town. Later, I also had to clean the cowshed. Then I took a proper shower because I did not want to look like I have just come from the cowshed in front of my schoolmates. Sometimes, I even managed to drop by at a hairdresser to make my hair look better on the way to university. So once I finished my morning duties, I took a taxi to Grozny to attend my lectures which started at 8 am. As a matter of fact, I did everything a normal bride who did not study or work outside would do and I also completed my studies on the side. I did manage somehow, but it was quite difficult. I had to study in the evenings, so if I got to bed around midnight I was lucky" (Kheda, July 2006, Prague).

Kheda's story indicates that despite the official Soviet rhetoric of gender equality, women were still those responsible for doing the household chores. The workload of a young bride in a Chechen family was usually hard enough even for those who were doing it full time. The women I spoke to never complained about their ordeal as newcomers into their husbands' families. However, the weight of this task often became clear from indirect comments. For example, Patimat, a woman in her mid-thirties, who spent a year living with her husband's family, described her feelings when she and her husband moved out after she gave birth to their first child:

"When we started to live separately, everything seemed suddenly so easy to me. I was very happy; There (in his parental house), I had to do the washing for all his brothers; I cooked for them and washed the dishes after them, I did everything. But then, when I was alone, I did only *my* work, and I did it with pleasure. You know, if there are so many people living in one place and you have to take care of them all, you get really tired and you don't have time for anything. So when we had moved away, I could also find time for myself" (April 2004, refugee centre).

If better off, the couple can also move directly into the husband's house, usually built by his parents around the same courtyard. Even in such a case, the bride was expected to come and help her mother-in-law every day. Her workload decreased when she gave birth to the first child or when another son's bride came to the house. It is a pride of the family, I was told by my informants, if the bride is hardworking and dexterous. Kheda explained that, "when a son gets married, all the neighbours are curious what is the bride going to be like, there is always a lot of control." More research is needed to support this claim, but it seems that although women were given more opportunities for professional development during the Soviet times, the basis of the Chechen patriarchal family was not substantially transformed.

Families in the War Zone

During the war times starting from 1994 some women had to become the sole breadwinners in the family and because they were perceived less of a threat, they have become the most mobile members of Chechen society (Conley 2004: 332). It was very dangerous for men to go outside their homes because they could be caught by Russian soldiers, accused of being fighters, tortured or killed and then sold back to their relatives as a number of human right reports describe (Human Rights Watch 2000; IHF 2003). Therefore, Chechen women often had to work and earn money to provide for the family needs. This situation is well illustrated by the story of the "aluminium queen" – a woman who, in the second war, kept her family alive by collecting metals from the rubbles into which Grozny was turned (Procházková 2003). Patimat described how she observed this shift in gender responsibilities:

"You know, before, many women just used to look after their children and stay at home. Now, many men sit at home. Every woman prefers to see her husband at home, because for him, it is more dangerous to go outside than it is for her. Therefore, women do everything, they spend hours and hours in the market place selling whatever they have, they pick dirty aluminium, and they are willing to do anything not to let their men go outside" (April 2004, refugee centre).

Apart from being the primary breadwinners, women are sometimes the only ones allowed to rescue their sons, husbands and brothers from the hands of soldiers. They go through the laborious process of negotiations with human rights lawyers and the military in search of the release of their family members (Procházková 2003). Women could no longer confine themselves to the "domestic" sphere which has been assigned to them by patriarchal family norms – they had to fight for themselves and their families in public. Moreover, they were the ones who raised orphaned children, many of them nephews and nieces or other relatives whose parents died during the war (Bersanova 2004: 3).

Zulfia, a woman in her mid-forties, reflected on how women's perception of men had changed because of the current "shortage" of men in Chechnya caused by the war and emigration:

"Some men who used to drink before and did not care much about their family changed a lot during the war. However, whether he drinks or not, women don't care about it anymore, because there are almost no men in Chechnya at the moment. The entire burden is now on women" (April 2004, refugee centre).

Since marriage still represents a "compulsory" institution without which women are particularly vulnerable and can easily lose their honour and respect in the community, women's position becomes precarious. On the one hand, they have to struggle hard to provide for their families, on the other hand, they have to tolerate basically any kind of behaviour even though men may no longer be the main breadwinners in the household and may not be able to provide the economic protection that constitutes the basis of classic patriarchy (Kandiyoti 1988: 282).

Despite the fact that many Chechens insist that their values and traditions are able to survive even under the hardest conditions, it seems inevitable that family norms and practices are changing in today's Chechnya. For example, there are a number of reports indicating significant increase in the occurrence of polygamous marriages (Isayev 2005; Murtazalieva 2005). The practice which was persecuted as a "savage" tradition during Soviet times is now being revived despite low living standards and the lack of basic necessities (Isayev 2005). The number of polygamous marriages has sharply increased since the beginning of the Second Chechen War in 1999. Although current Russian law forbids polygamy, this can be circumvented by officially declaring only one wife and then living in a de facto religiously sanctioned relationship with the others (Isayev 2005). In 2006, BBC reported that Chechnya's Moscow-backed president Ramzan Kadyrov told Ekho Moskvy radio that women in the Russian republic outnumbered men by 10 percent, and that a man should be able to choose how many wives he had without the state getting involved (BBC 2006).

Some recent reports also indicate that bride abduction is now increasing in Chechnya (Bersanova 2004; Isayev 2007). Bride abductions or kidnappings as they are called are practiced not only in Chechnya, but also in other parts of Caucasus. They range from a prearranged and agreed-upon strategy of a couple to circumvent parents' disagreement with the marriage to instances when a girl is forced into a marriage with a person she hardly knows (sometimes by means of rape). Because many cases go unreported, it is hard to estimate the presence of this practice in Chechen society. During my research, I got to know that four out of fifteen female informants were abducted. Two had agreed to stay and spent their lives with the men, while in the two other cases, relations were very unsatisfactory for the women, and they eventually left the men who abducted them. In the first case, the woman was actually "encouraged" to leave as her mother-in-law was not satisfied with her as daughter-in-law and she later got married to another man, this time of her own choice. In the second case, the story was more tragic, because a child was born out of the relationship which had become unbearable for the woman because her husband was abusing her physically. As she was leaving the husband, she took her small son with her, but he was later abducted and taken away by his father, and she lost contact with him for many years.

Also, the consequences of losses of relatives, painful as they are, are experienced differently by men and women. For widowed women, especially those with children, it may be hard to remarry as well as to stay alone. If they remarry, it is in line with the family norms that their children remain with the husband's family. It is a question of family honour. As Pohl put it, "it would be a dishonour if the deceased's brothers permitted the children to live with a stranger" (M. Pohl 2003). On the other hand, if the women remain alone, not only is their material situation likely to be difficult, but they can also be targeted by both Russian or Chechen forces under the suspicion that their lost husband was a fighter.

It is clear that the experience of wars and over thirteen years of instability and insecurity must have had a dramatic impact on all areas of Chechen society. For example, Patimat described how the experience of war shattered her idea of a family and how closely it was linked with the notion of security:

"This war changed everybody who lived through it. When you are still with your parents, you only think about nice things, you can be certain that your relatives will *never* let you starve, they will *always* protect you. That is how I saw it when I got married. When the war came, I suddenly realised that this certainty simply does not exist. There are forces against which not even your closest relatives can protect you. So you slowly lose faith in all that is good" (October 2006, Austria).

It is yet to be seen what direction these changes will take in the area of family relations. Some indicators, such as the increase in polygamy and bride abductions, show one possible direction is a reinvention and cementation of patriarchal structures to the detriment of women's rights.

Gender and Family Relations in European Exile

The most common reason to flee Chechnya was my informants' determination to bring their families into safety and the vision of a better life for their children. In this section, I discuss that despite significant changes in men's and women's roles in refugee families, radical challenges to patriarchal family norms are hardly to be expected. It is because of the need to regain lost security and familiar patterns of life as well as because the structural position of refugees may not offer viable alternatives to women who seem to be most burdened by the new situation.

As opposed to labour migrants who often migrate as single men or single women, leaving their families behind, the majority of Chechen refugees have been coming to the Czech Republic as nuclear families (although not always complete families). Their goal was to secure a permanent or at least long-term residence. Their destination was either rather general – any European state far enough from Russia – or more specific – mostly some Western European country where they had relatives or which they imagined as a safe and prosperous place to live. The vast majority of Chechen asylum seekers were young people of productive age. In case of the Czech Republic, out of five thousand Russian nationals (above 18 years old), who applied for asylum between 2000 and 2006, 46 percent were below thirty and as many as 78 percent were below forty years old (DAMP 2007). Women represented 44 percent of these asylum seekers (DAMP 2007). With regard to their family status, the majority of "Russians" were married at the time when they applied (78 percent of women and 58 percent of men) (DAMP 2007). The most typical household composition among recognized refugees from Russia living in the Czech Republic was a nuclear family composed of five members: parents and three children (Uherek et al. 2005).

Separation from Kinship Networks

Despite the traditional imperative to take care of one's elderly parents, only a minority of families are actually accompanied by elderly parents and only a few can afford to support them financially by sending money home. Most informants argued that their parents would simply refuse to move away from Chechnya or neighbouring Ingushetia. As Kheda put it:

"They would never move permanently away from Chechnya. It is probably because of the experience of deportation during Stalin that they value our land so much" (July 2006, Prague).

Moreover, most of my informants were born during the years of high birth rates in Chechnya (Fredholm 2000) and they have many siblings (having seven brothers and sisters was not an exception). Since it is very rare that the whole extended family migrates altogether, they know that despite their absence, their parents are taken care of, mostly by their brothers and their wives.

Thus, for the majority of refugee families from Chechnya, reunification with their parents is not an option. Due to the current worldwide perception of Chechnya as a potentially dangerous region breeding Islamic terrorists as well as difficulties Chechen residents face when obtaining travel documents, it is hard to imagine them coming to the Czech Republic to visit their relatives. Throughout my three-year fieldwork, I have not heard of such a case either among my informants or in their social networks. It is important to note that neither asylum seekers nor recognized refugees can travel back to Russia without risking the termination of their asylum procedure or, in the latter case, withdrawal of their asylum status. Thus, obtaining Czech or other citizenship is the only way to be able to travel back home and visit one's family. I have observed that a mental strain caused by the absence of extended family continues to affect the lives of Chechens in exile.

The loss or the long separation from the loved ones represents for many the core of their thoughts and grief in exile and was experienced as a continuous gaping absence. Patimat's expression speaks for many:

"I am very far from my family, I haven't seen them for more than three years and I know that I will not see them in the coming years; that really torments me. As if I lost part of my soul. Ever since I left Chechnya, I feel this emptiness inside me" (October 2006, Austria).

It seems that the situation will not change in the coming years. On the contrary, it will become more painful as their parents will be dying and refugees will, in most cases, not be able to participate in all the rituals of grief back home. I have witnessed a number of these losses among my informants. Usually, they only find out about the death of their parents ex post, their relatives do not want to worry them, so they do not tell them about their parents' illness. Therefore, the news about their death often comes as a great shock. Being more than two thousand kilometres from home and not able to cry on their parents' grave, refugees find it extremely difficult to relief their pain over these losses.

Being separated from their extended family networks, refugees also experience an unprecedented shift towards exclusive reliance on members of the immediate nuclear family. This represents a major rupture to the classic patriarchal arrangement of Chechen families. It also increases the feeling of insecurity and isolation because refugees can no longer draw from the support of kinship networks which was vital in Chechnya. In her study of families and clans in Ingushetia and Chechnya, Ekaterina Sokirianskaia (2005) concludes that:

"One's family is among the primary channels of wealth redistribution and acquiring access to jobs. Most of the respondents either actually found their jobs through relatives or thought this was the way to look for employment (...) if a person gets access to jobs and is able to influence decision making concerning recruitment, he is likely to lobby for his relatives. This is thought to be moral and right and in addition reduces the number of unemployed relatives one has to take care of" (Sorkirianskaia 2005: 461).

Clearly, these networks are no longer available to many refugees and are not yet replaced by other sources of support.

Troubled Masculinities

Displaced and dispossessed Chechen men can no longer offer economic security to their wives and children, and attempts to reconstitute their manly honour are sometimes directed through highly disruptive means. Magomed, a man in his early forties, who has been living in a refugee centre for almost a year at the time of our interview and whose asylum case decision was postponed by a year, explained why, despite all the difficulties, he thought it was easier to be a man back home than in the refugee centre:

"There, I could at least provide for my family, with my own hands, but here, I am doing nothing, I am not at all used to this, it was certainly easier to be a man back home" (April 2004, refugee centre).

Some men also found pride in describing how they were protecting their families. Abdurahman was describing it in great detail:

"I was always protecting my family; we didn't have to run away from home. I built a special shelter in our garden, it was about five meters deep, and that is where we always hid. We even had a TV set there and a tape recorder, I was able to bring electricity there" (January 2007, refugee centre).

While waiting in the asylum procedure, asylum seekers cannot officially work, and working in an informal labour market, they are likely to be exploited and cheated due to their low-rights foreigner status. If living in refugee accomodation, the protection of their families is no longer their essential task as everything "essential" from accommodation to food is provided in the centre. However, sources of dignity and self-esteem are in short supply in this environment of imposed passivity.

Chechens who fled the war zone and felt strongly entitled to receiving a dignified reception in the country they imagined as a part of the "civilised world" felt deeply hurt by instances of discriminatory treatment from local Czechs. This was especially the case in areas around refugee centres where asylum seekers of different nationalities and different patterns of behaviour were moving around. Neighbours of the refugee camp often did not bother differentiating between different groups of refugees and perceived them all as potential thieves and problem-makers. Young men in particular were feared by the locals as aggressors. I witnessed this discrimination first-hand when I tried to go for a drink with Salman, a man in his late twenties, to a bar nearby the refugee centre where he and his family lived.

Salman said he'll show me something but asked me to keep quiet. We entered the bar next to the centre. He was absolutely sober and well dressed when he approached the bartender and politely ordered a beer for the two of us. He spoke Czech with a bit of an accent. The bartender asked him whether he was from the centre and after Salman replied that he was the man said he would not give him anything. Salman politely asked whether he could get at least a glass of limo but the bartender coolly replied: I will not give you anything at all. After we left the building, Salman turned to me and said, "you see, that is how we live here" [field notes, March 2007].

One can easily imagine what impact these interactions have when being experienced on a daily basis. Also women were exposed to similar discriminatory practices, for example in local shops where they were often followed by employees and suspected as potential thieves. However, men were more vocal about these experiences and probably more likely to encounter them as they were perceived as more violent and thus more dangerous.

Ruslan, a man in his mid-thirties, expressed his feelings about the atmosphere in the camp with the following metaphor:

"We live here like parrots in a cage. Sometimes, they want us to sing a bit and if you don't, they won't feed you (...) that's how it is here. Sometimes, I wish I could fight with somebody, but I don't do it" (April 2004, refugee centre).

The association with a parrot in a cage could be interpreted in different ways: Chechens as well as other groups of refugees felt humiliated by "being fed" three times a day with food they were not accustomed to in the centre's canteen without the possibility of consuming their food in the privacy of their rooms[6]; moreover, they were stressed by the requirement to repeat their story of persecution and flight again and again during the interviews with the officials of the Department of Asylum and Migration Policy. Finally, the need to suppress aggression is obvious from Ruslan's account.

Chechen men in refugee centres employed various coping strategies as they were trying to (re)construct their self-esteem and dignity under these difficult conditions. Some participated more in their family life, spent more time with their wives and children. For example, Aslambek, a man in his late twenties, whom I often saw walking around the centre with his two small kids, commented on changes in his relations to his wife:

"We are closer to each other, we are in this one room anyway, we see each other all the time and we talk more. At home, we could not have seen each other for several months; I had to run away all the time" (April 2004, refugee centre).

Others preferred to spend money on alcohol or drugs, started dating other (usually non-Chechen) women or/and occasionally also resorted to physical violence towards their wives and children. It was confirmed by the camp psychologist that there were many instances of domestic violence behind the walls of the centre. He explained it by the following two factors: Firstly, men can no longer fulfil their roles as breadwinners and protectors, "whatever happens to his family, he will hardly know what to do, where to turn to, he does not speak the language, these men often feel totally paralysed here." Secondly, women are usually able to

6 After fifteen years of functioning within the system of refugee centres, most of the canteens had been gradually abandoned by 2007 in favour of what is called "independent cooking" and what in practice means that asylum seekers are given subsistence money to prepare their own food instead of being forced to consume food cooked for them in canteens.

continue fulfilling *their* roles as mothers and take care of their improvised, tiny households in what usually consists of some thirty square meters of privacy and shared kitchen and bathrooms. Some even managed to bring some extra money into the family budget by cleaning the corridors and bathrooms in the centre. Despite this, however, the psychologist argued, men often insist that women keep their submissive roles which causes problems and sometimes leads to women's protests:

"I have seen many men groundlessly punishing their wives after they were trying to tell them: look, you do not fulfil your roles, so you should also listen to me now. But some men do not listen, they do whatever they want and this is when the important aspect of collective consciousness is missing. What he would probably suppress back home, what he wouldn't dare to do in front of his family or neighbourhood, he will freely do here in the centre" (psychologist, April 2004, refugee centre).

Lastly, I have witnessed some Chechen men employing what could be called a "strategy of quick money": *bistrie dengi*. These were the men who engaged in various criminal activities that became readily available in their position as asylum seekers: smuggling people through the borders with Austria or Germany; taking advantage of other asylum seekers in the centre – usually single men from Ukraine and Belarus – and demanding money from them under the threat of violence; providing the so-called *krysha* (Russian word for "roof"), i.e. criminal protection racket to other migrants, etc. Although men of different nationalities engaged in these activities, over the last few years, these acts have become associated primarily with Chechens. Consequently, Chechen men are often a priori perceived as criminals and fighters who always act from the position of power.

Lolita, a woman in her early thirties provided an interesting interpretation of this behaviour when she insisted that also these men's wives play their role in sustaining the "quick money strategy":

"Some women just don't know where to stop; they constantly bug their husbands with complaints that they need this and that, that they need more money. They want to show off in front of the others in the centre and sometimes, they even send things home to present the success they have made abroad, that they are doing better. They don't care where the money comes from" (March 2007, refugee centre).

Although she herself appreciated the money her husband was bringing home from his (irregular) work on construction in a nearby city, she said this was normal, because everybody was doing it. She claimed that she would never let him do real criminal things.

The example "quick money strategy" among Chechen male[7] asylum seekers[8] highlights several important points: 1) male asylum seekers, especially those living in refugee centres, find little non-problematic ways of "restoring" their sense of manhood, 2) the structure of Chechen asylum seekers has been changing with an increasing number of people coming with unrealistically high expectations of improving their economic situation rather than "just" seeking protection. When these high expectations are not satisfied, frustration and alienation emerge. 3) After thirteen years of war, lawlessness and general instability in Chechnya, there are now more young men who have seen little but the war around them and may consider some forms of highly problematic behaviour as normal, 4) many asylum seekers do not see prospects of staying permanently in the Czech Republic; either because they know that the recognition rates are very low or because they ultimately aim for other western European countries and see the Czech Republic as a transit zone where sanctions can be avoided simply by exit.

Changing Positions of Chechen Women

Chechen women, on the other hand, are often better disposed to earn income for the family and work hard to secure the well-being of their children by assisting them in entering Czech kindergartens and schools and looking for leisure-time activities to show them a bit of "normal life" without the war. Many Chechen refugee men have experienced torture and are unable to perform physically demanding jobs that are usually available to migrants with inadequate knowledge of the language of the host society such as construction work. Therefore, it is often women who step in and quickly find some kind of a cleaning job to contribute to their household's income. Indeed, some men make the painful experience that their wives and children were faster in getting oriented within the Czech society and having contacts in the majority population. Abdurahman commented on the passivity of his fellow countrymen:

7 Although I have encountered a case of Chechen women engaging in smuggling (after their male relative was put to custody for this activity), the strategy of "quick money" is a predominantly male strategy.

8 I have heard much less about similar cases among already recognized refugees.

"Women and children can find their ways faster here. This is a fact. I am over fifty but there are young men around and they sometimes behave like old people" (Abdurahman, January 2007, refugee centre).

Moreover, I have also observed that many Chechen women have quickly become the key mediators between NGOs, welfare offices and their households. During my fieldwork in refugee centres, I saw that from the very beginning of the asylum procedure, women were more likely to approach social workers (also mostly women) and discuss issues related to their children's school attendance, healthcare, food and so forth. These actual responsibilities together with internalised expectations of being a good mother in the eyes of "Czech hosts" often compelled women to learn the Czech language more quickly than it was the case for their husbands. This division of labour was reinforced by the attitude present in many refugee families (not only Chechens) i.e. that it is undignified for a man to go and ask for help from strangers (especially if these strangers are mostly young women as is the case in Czech NGOs) and thus to openly acknowledge their position of dependency. This was well expressed by Kheda when I asked her why she is the one who always runs around and arranges things even when her husband is unemployed and spends a lot of time at home.

"A woman, when necessary, is able to lower herself, to ask for something when a man cannot do it. He will, for example, never go somewhere and ask for help; that's not the way we do it. He doesn't abandon his upbringing from home only because he's here now. That is why I can better explain our situation when I go somewhere. I shed a tear, if needed; these are the things that women can do" (December 2006, Prague).

Women are perceived and perceive themselves as more proficient in using emotive strategies and thus gaining access to various forms of goods, even if such behaviour may be interpreted as slightly undignified. Moreover, as Kibria (1993) explains in her study of Vietnamese refugees in the U.S., it is also because of "difficulty of such bridging work, and the feelings of marginality and powerlessness often accompanying it, that men were often willing and even eager to leave these tasks up to women" (Kibria 1993: 126).

NGO workers as well as employees in refugee centres would often speak about refugee men's sense of their manhood being challenged in the process of reception and settlement and they described its negative consequences, such as men's feeling of degradation, alcohol or drug addiction, violence against their family members (Counselling Centre for Refugees 2005). In a number of interviews, NGO social workers presented a simple theory of how gender relations in refugee families are being transformed. Despite small variations, it is best expressed by this account of a female social worker:

"It works like this: women are faster in finding some sort of a position for themselves. Even if they are still at home, but the fact that she takes care of the household makes her feel that she is up and running. It's different with men, if they can't find a job, be it a regular or illicit one, than it is usually pretty bad. I have a lot of female clients who function perfectly, they take care of their families, but their husbands do not function at all" (Anna, June 2007, Prague).

Although social workers repeatedly acknowledged that refugee men may have more difficulties in adapting to a new environment (Roubalová 2007), many acknowledged that they found it extremely difficult to organise some effective support programs for men.

Moreover, I have observed that NGO workers preferred to communicate with women, even over subjects related to their husbands or sons. They found them more communicative, adaptive and less willing to complain or get into conflict. As mentioned before, communication with women was also usually easier because they tended to speak the Czech language better than their husbands. Both in refugee centres and in NGOs, Chechen men have a reputation of claiming services and support in a forceful and demanding manner which is disliked by social workers. This is partly due to the fact that many refugees, especially in the early stages of their stay in the country, do not entirely understand what the capacities of NGOs are, and therefore have unrealistic expectations about what kind of help they can receive from them. On the other hand, Chechens' proud and uncompromising behaviour often irritates social workers who prefer to deal with more submissive and grateful refugee clients. Thus Chechen women appear to be better integrated into these (highly feminised) servicing organisations and thus also able to direct vital resources towards their families.

There is also another side to this integration. In observing the practices of NGOs, I have realised that Chechen women do not only outnumber men when seeking some form of assistance. They (together with women of other nationalities) are also more likely to be expected to contribute to NGO programs, often with implicitly gendered contents. The most typical examples are activities promoting multiculturalism and tolerance coupled with NGO fundraising activities. At these occasions, refugees are given an opportunity to present their "cultural contribution" to Czech society, most commonly by exhibiting tables full of samples of their traditional cuisine for degustation. The important thing is that women are not always adequately remunerated for their work. Often spending long hours preparing and serving the food, they are usually refunded only for the costs of the products or can keep some minor share of the income they raised. After all, it is their opportunity for a positive self-presentation, some NGO people say when justifying these practices. On the other hand, it is almost always NGOs who define the setting and the format of these cultural displays and refugees are invited to "fill up" the predefined framework. It should not be forgotten that such offers are made in a highly unequal set of relations. In other words, many women will be reluctant to decline to participate in such activities, notwithstanding expected benefits. They have, most likely, been helped in the past by those asking them to pitch in or they know that they may need their assistance in the future. Thus, NGO assistance is not void of mechanisms of reciprocity and paying back. Therefore, notwithstanding the essential help they provide to refugees, NGOs may inadvertently contribute to overloading refugee women with responsibilities. Moreover, it is through these practices that women are symbolically constructed as bearers and reproducers of a rigid conception of culture as a set of cuisines, traditions and festivities.

Chechen women sometimes expressed a sense of empowerment stemming from their positions as substantial contributors to the family income as well as mediators with the outside world of institutions. Zulfia, a mother with four daughters of school age who came to Europe hoping to find her husband who fled Chechnya before her, described how she realised her potential when she was suddenly on her own:

"I've understood that I'm responsible for everything, when there was my husband besides me, I did not feel it that way, I have become both a father and a mother to my daughters" (April 2004, refugee centre).

This new position is sometimes interpreted as a space for women's emancipation from the patriarchal structures of their families in migration studies (Kosack 1976). While I agree that for many women, new horizons opened in the course of their asylum journey, I have observed that this new situation also has another side which is often not fully acknowledged in the literature. Some of my female informants perceived their situation in exile as a potential threat to their family's unity which, in the insecure time of refugees' early settlement, seemed to be more valued than Western-style independence and freedom.

Some women, especially those who were already recognized as refugees and allowed to stay, engaged in the following strategy in order to create the impression that even as they were the ones in charge of arranging essential resources for the family, their husbands should not lose their position as the key decision-makers. Kheda showed particular sophistication in this sphere. Although she was the one who managed the household's tight budget and constantly mobilized her social networks to find a job for her husband Aslan, she was careful not to make him feel detached and powerless. She would not make a single decision on her own, such as taking part in an integration program, weekend activities for their children or her acceptance of a short-term job, without asking him for approval first. This seemed to be a typical pattern that irritated many social workers. It went against their idea of social work based on the personal autonomy of their client. As a female NGO social worker explained to me:

"When communicating with us, some women are not able to decide for themselves, their activities and plans. They always ask for some time to consult it with their husband, or to ask for his approval. It is a typical attempt to keep the family patterns and family cohesion intact, but it complicates our work with them a lot" (Petra, September 2006, Prague).

Here, we see a clear conflict between the idea of a refugee woman as an individual to be activated by NGO services and the woman herself, who is embedded in a number of social relations of which family hierarchies seem to have key importance. Women's strategy to prevent their husbands from feeling alienated from family decision-making was not employed as an act of submission or out of the lack of an independent mind. As the example of Kheda demonstrates, there can be a clearly thought-through rationale behind this behaviour:

"It is a problem when a woman starts to be active and she, sort of (...) starts to move away from her husband. Because you always have to take him with you (...) if I leave him at home then he starts to think all day while I am running around some offices and kids are at school and for him, one day is like a month and then he starts looking for something. Some men start to drink, some leave the family altogether. I think that it really depends on women" (November 2006, Prague).

This dynamic of gender relations has been poignantly demonstrated in Kibria's study of Vietnamese refugees settling down in Philadelphia, U.S. (1993) where she proposed the concept of *ideological tightrope* to highlight how refugee families cope with changes that have seriously affected the norms of the traditional Vietnamese family system. Due to a decline in men's earning power and other socioeconomic forces, refugee women found themselves exercising greater influence in their families in the U.S. as a result of their greater control over resources in comparison to the past. However, they did not use their enhanced powers to directly challenge traditional conceptions of gender relations and family life. Instead, Kibria describes them as walking an *ideological tightrope.*

"Vietnamese American women worked hard to incorporate the new realities of their lives into the ideological confines of the traditional family system (...) struggling to take advantage of their new resources but also to protect the structure and sanctity of the traditional family system" (Kibria 1993, 109).

Her account is important because it shows that patriarchal relations, albeit often seriously affected by conditions of displacement, are not transformed in any straightforward way. In other words, despite their paid employment and their ability to better negotiate with welfare institutions and NGOs, Chechen women may not be willing to demand more influence at home.

Conclusions

This chapter demonstrated how gender norms and relations are being (re)constructed in Chechen families as they struggle to regain their lost secure and familiar patterns of life while adapting to new conditions of the host country. I have argued that even when Chechnya-style classic patriarchy enters a crisis in exile, many women will not be willing to step out from the position of submissiveness and propriety. I agree with Kandiyoti who argues that:

"Despite the obstacles that classic patriarchy puts in women's way, which may far outweigh any actual economic and emotional security, women often resist the process of transition because they see the old normative order slipping away from them without any empowering alternatives" (Kandiyoti 1988, 282).

This argument also helps to explain a somewhat paradoxical situation I encountered when interviewing Chechen women. While acknowledging that Czech women are better off in many aspects of life, Chechen women continued to praise their system of traditions and hierarchies upon which family relations are built. It gives them the sense of security when what they see as a possible substitute does not seem an attractive option to them. For example, both Chechen men and women often spoke about the lack of respect for elders they observed and disliked in Czech society. Ending up in an old-people's home seemed like the worst nightmare to them and was presented as something unimaginable in Chechen society.

They also disliked instances of Czech children circumventing or even openly despising their parents' authority. Chechen parents were often worried that their children may get under the wrong influence of their Czech peers and lose their code of good behaviour and respect for the parents. Girls, in particular, were to be protected from the influence of loose sexual behaviour prevalent among the Czech youth. When asked about potential partners for their growing-up daughters, Chechen women insisted that the only acceptable partner would be a Chechen man. Should their daughters find themselves Czech partners their choice would not be respected.

However, I have also shown that while Chechens may be able to preserve some aspects of their traditional family relations, some changes seem to be inevitable. For example, adult Chechen women are likely to experience the breakdown of the cyclical fluctuations of women's power in the family as it seems unlikely that they will be surrounded by subservient daughters-in-law who will work in their households. Cohabitation of multigenerational families is hard to imagine as the majority of refugee families already live in overcrowded apartments. Moreover, it is questionable whether young Chechen women brought up in the Czech Republic or elsewhere in Europe would be willing and able to assume such roles given increased opportunities for education and employment.

It seems that in the short or even medium-term, Chechen women are likely to take over many new family responsibilities while not openly challenging their husband's patriarchal authority. But it has to be acknowledged that at the same time, they gain stronger ground in the public sphere which predisposes them to use it for their own self-fulfilment and self-realisation in the future. Then, they might decide to seriously redesign their position in the family as they will no longer be willing to combine their extensive household and childcare responsibilities with paid employment. For this, however, certain structural conditions in host societies are required providing a non-discriminatory environment for refugee women's and men's education, retraining, and employment. The support of refugees' integration which has recently been amplified at the EU level and promised by a number of national policy documents needs to take seriously the fact that gender is a crucial structuring force in refugee settlement and if ignored can lead to undesired effects of social exclusion and marginalisation of both refugee men and women.

Bibliography

Al-Ali, N. S. (2002): Gender relations, transnational ties and rituals among Bosnian refugees. In: Global Networks, *2*(3), 249–262.
Anthias, F./Yuval-Davis, N. (1989): Introduction. In: Anthias, F./Yuval-Davis, N. (eds.): Women-nation-state. London, 1–15.
Anthias, F./Yuval-Davis, N. (1992): Racialized boundaries: Race, nation, gender, colour and class and the anti-racist struggle. London/New York/Routledge.
Ashwin, S. (2000): Introduction. Gender, state and society in Soviet and Post-Soviet Russia. In: Ashwin, S. (ed.). Gender, state and society in Soviet and Post-Soviet Russia. London/New York/Routledge, 1–29.
Baiev, K./Daniloff, R. (2003): Grief of my heart: Memoirs of a Chechen surgeon. New York.
BBC (2006): Polygamy proposal for Chechen men.
Bersanova, Z. (2004): Values stronger than war: Islam and the struggle for meaning in Chechnya today. Retrieved March, 2008, from: http://www.chechnyaadvocacy.org/Zalpa/research%20presentation.pdf.
Brauer, B. (2002): Chechens and the survival of their cultural identity in exile. In: Journal of Genocide Research, 4(3), 387–400.
Brežná, I. (1997): Die Wölfinnen von Sernowodsk. Reportagen aus Tschetschenien (The she-wolves of Sernowodsk: Reports from Chechnya). Stuttgart.
Buijs, G. (ed.) (1993): Migrant women: Crossing boundaries and changing identities. Oxford.
Burawoy, M./Krotov, P./Lytkina, T. (2000): Involution and destitution in capitalist Russia. Ethnography, 1(1), 43–65.
Conley, B. (2004): For the women of Chechnya, hope dies last. In: Journal of Human Rights, 3(3), 331–342.
Counselling Centre for Refugees (2005): Annual Report 2004. Retrieved from: http://www.uprchlici.cz/ppu/docs/PPU_VZ_2004.pdf.
DAMP (Department of Asylum and Migration Policy, Ministry of Interior of the Czech Republic) (2007): Requested statistics about Russian asylum seekers. Prague.
DAMP (2008): Azyl udělen – počet rozhodnutí obou instancí v jednotlivých letech 1990 – únor 2008 (Asylum granted – both instances: 1990-February 2008). Retrieved March, 2008, from: http://www.mvcr.cz/statistiky/2008/uprch02/6pr_02.html.
Franz, B. (2003): Transplanted or uprooted? Integration efforts of Bosnian refugees based upon gender, class and ethnic differences. In: The European Journal of Women's Studies, 10(2), 135–157.
Fredholm, M. (2000): The prospects for genocide in Chechnya and extremist retaliation against the West. In: Central Asian Survey, 19(3/4), 315–327.
Giles, W. (1999): Gendered violence in war: Reflections on transnationalist and comparative frameworks in militarized conflict zones. In: Indra, D. M. (ed.): Engendering forced migration: theory and practice. New York/London, 83–93.
Government Council for Human Rights (2004): 2003 Report on the state of human rights in the Czech Republic. Prague.
Hondagneu-Sotelo, P. (1994): Gendered transitions. Berkeley.

Human Rights Watch. (2000): Welcome to hell. Arbitrary detention, torture, and extortion in Chechnya. New York/ Washington/London/Brussels.

IHF (International Helsinki Federation for Human Rights) (2003). Chechnya. Impunity, disappearances, torture, and the denial of political rights. Retrieved December 1, 2003, from: http://www.reliefweb.int/w/rwb.nsf/0/ca01862b2f36182bc1256df60054499f?Open Document.

Isayev, R. (2005): Polygamy in present day Chechnya. Prague Watchdog, Retrieved from: http://www.watchdog.cz/?show=000000-000015-000006-000013&lang=1.

Isayev, R. (2007): In Chechnya, attempts to eradicate bride abduction. Retrieved from: http://www.watchdog.cz/?show=000000-000015-000006-000024&lang=1.

Ishkanian, A. (2003): Gendered transitions: The impact of the post-Soviet transition on women in Central Asia and the Caucasus. In: Perspectives on Global Development and Technology, 2(3–4), 475–496.

Kandiyoti, D. (1988): Bargaining with patriarchy. In: Gender and Society, *2,* 274–290.

Kay, D. (1988): The politics of gender in exile. In: Sociology, 22(1), 1–21.

Kibria, N. (1993): Family tightrope. Princeton.

Korac, M. (2004): War, flight, and exile: Gendered violence among refugee women from post-Yugoslav states. In: Giles W./Hyndman, J. (eds.): Sites of violence: Gender and conflict zones. Berkeley/Los Angeles/London.

Kosack, G. (1976): Migrant women: The move to Western Europe. A step towards emancipation? In: Race and Class, 17(4), 370–379.

Matveeva, A. (2007): Chechnya. Dynamics of war and peace. In: Problems of Post-Communism, 54(3), 3–17.

Morokvasic, M. (1983). Women in migration: Beyond the reductionist outlook. In: Phizacklea, A. (ed.): One way ticket. Migration and female labour. London/Boston/ Melbourne/Henley, 13–31.

Murtazalieva, A. (2005): Chechnya. Chechens consider reviving polygamy. Publication from Women Living Under Muslim Law. Retrieved from: http://www.wluml.org/english/newsfulltxt.shtml?cmd[157]=x-157-306033.

Myers, S. L. (2004): From dismal Chechnya, women turn to bombs. In: The New York Times. Retrieved from: http://www.nytimes.com/2004/09/10/international/europe/10chechnya.html

Nichols, J. (1995): Who are the Chechen? Retrieved March, 2008, from: http://socrates.berkeley.edu/~bsp/caucasus/articles/nichols_1995-chechen.pdf.

Nivat, A. (2005): The black widows. Chechen women join the fight for independence and Allah. In: Studies in Conflict & Terrorism, 28, 413–419.

Norwegian Refugee Council (2005): Whose responsibility? Protection of Chechen internally displaced persons, asylum seekers and refugees. Retrieved 2005, December, from: http://www.nrc.no/Whose_responsibility_Chechnya.pdf.

Pessar, P. R./Mahler, S. J. (2003): Transnational migration. Bringing gender. In: International Migration Review, 37(3), 812–846.

Phizacklea, A. (2003): Gendered actors in Migration. In: Andal, J. (ed.): Gender and ethnicity in contemporary Europe. Oxford, 23–40.

Pilkington, H. (1992): Russia and the former Soviet republics. Behind the mask of Soviet unity. Realities of women's lives. In: Corrin, C. (ed.): Superwomen and the double burden: Women's experience of change in Central and Eastern Europe and the former Soviet Union. London, 180–235.
Pohl, M. (2002): "It cannot be that our graves will be here." The survival of Chechen and Ingush deportees in Kazakhstan 1944–1957. In: Journal of Genocide Research, 4(3), 401–430.
Pohl, M. (2003). Entre libre! The special energy and passion of Chechen culture. In: Marx, Frederique L. (ed.):La guerre jusque'au dernier? Paris, 204 pp., map, bibliography.
Pohl, O. J. (2000): Stalin's genocide against the "repressed peoples". In: Journal of Genocide Research, 2(2), 267–293.
Procházková, P. (2003): The aluminium queen. The Russian-Chechen conflict through the eyes of women. Praha.
Relief Web (2001): Northern Caucasus (Russian Federation). Retrieved March, 2008, from: http://www.reliefweb.int/rw/rwb.nsf/AllDocsByUNID/e1b34d469444d379c1256a88004a549f.
Roubalová, V. (2007): Multikulturní skupiny jsou vstřícné, stát je nevstřícný (Multicultural groups are welcoming, the state is not welcoming). In: Přes: uprchlický čtvrtletník Nesehnutí, 4(12), 9–10.
Rousseva, V. (2004): Rape and sexual assault in Chechnya. In: Culture, Society & Praxis, 3(1), 64–67.
Salzinger, L. (2003): Genders in production: Making workers in Mexico's global factories. Berkeley/Los Angeles/London.
Sokirianskaia, E. (2005). Families and clans in Ingushetia and Chechnya. A fieldwork report. In: Central Asian Survey, 24(4), 453–467.
Szczepanikova, A. (2005): Gender relations in a refugee camp. A case of Chechens seeking asylum in the Czech Republic. In: Journal of Refugee Studies, 18(3), 281–298.
Uherek, Z./Černík, J./Grohmannová, J./Hyánková, T./Korecká, Z./Plochová, K.(et al.) (2005): Integrace azylantů a efektivita státního integračního programu (Integration of recognized refugees and effectiveness of the State Integration Program). Praha: Etnologický ústav AV ČR.
UNHCR (United Nations High Commissioner for Refugees) (2008): Asylum levels and trends in industrialised countries, 2007. Geneva.
West, C./Zimmerman, D. H. (1987): Doing gender. In: Gender and Society, 1(2), 125–151.
Wood, T. (2004). The case for Chechnya. In: New Left Review(30), 5–36.
Zubarevich, N. (2003): Russia: Case study on human development progress toward the MDGs at the sub-national level. Moscow. United Nations Development Programme.

Chechen Youth in the Diaspora – the Austrian Case

EDITH VASILYEV

Introduction

According to UNHCR reports since 2003, Chechens count as the largest group of new asylum seekers in Europe. Austria besides Belgium and France belongs to the main target and also host countries. Life in Austria offers young Chechens not just chances and possibilities for further development in a peaceful environment, but also confronts them with problems and challenges that have to be coped with. The new living conditions and altered cultural requirements in the Diaspora put the juveniles despite their flexibility to new tasks.

For the purpose of closer definition and limiting of the said target group of juveniles, some statistic data allows us the framework within which we move. In lectures and further-education training on the topic of "Chechnya", the talk is repeatedly about approximately 20,000–25,000 Chechens within the entire Austrian federal territory. However, the exact numerical ascertainment of ethnic groups of peoples is very difficult. Both during asylum proceedings in the Federal Asylum Office and within the censuses of the Statistics Austria only the question of the applicants nationalities is raised, not the ethnic affiliation. Similar to the case of Palestinians or also Kurds, no accurate information is possible about the number of Chechens living in Austria. Talks with employees from social facilities show that a majority of the Chechens they deal with arrives in Austria through an asylum application. The asylum statistics of the Federal Ministry for the Interior can therefore most likely provide an overview of the approximate dimensions:

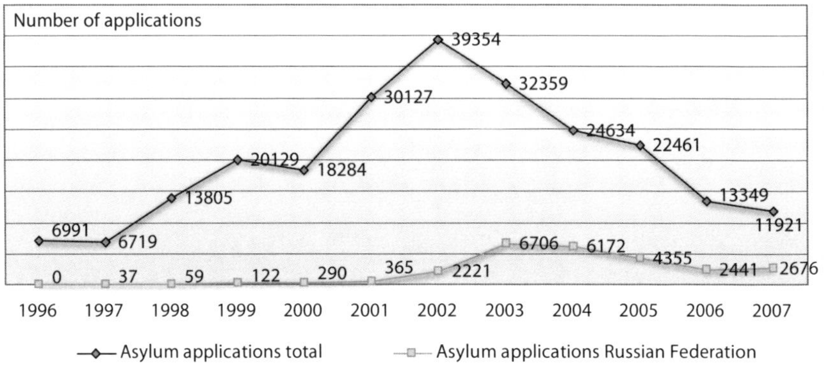

(cf. http://www.bmi.gv.at/downloadarea/asyl_fremdenwesen_statistik, updated 13.04.2008).

The statistic shows that starting from the year 2002 there was a salient rise of asylum seekers from the Russian Federation. Altogether, from 2002 to 2007 there were 24,571 applications from this country, which in these years is the nation with most applications in Austria. Interviews with those concerned, as well as empiric reports from social facilities show that to a very high percentage it involves members of the Chechen group of peoples. Contrary to other European countries, which refer again and again to the domestic resettlement possibilities of Chechens, Austria recognizes, like other countries e.g. Belgium and France, numerous Chechens (see acknowledgment ratio) as persecuted according to the Geneva Refugee Convention and issues positive asylum rulings in these cases.

It is clearly recognisable in this statistic that in the years 2002 to 2007 considerably more positive than negative rulings were made concerning asylum applications of persons from the Russian Federation. The acknowledgment rate ranges on average around 70%, in the year 2004 at over 90%. From the beginning of 2002 to end of 2007, 11,001 people from the Russian Federation received a positive asylum ruling, therefore authorized to future residency within the federal territory. In comparison, merely 1726 negative rulings were passed. Analysis of the asylum statistics from the Federal Asylum Office concerning unaccompa-

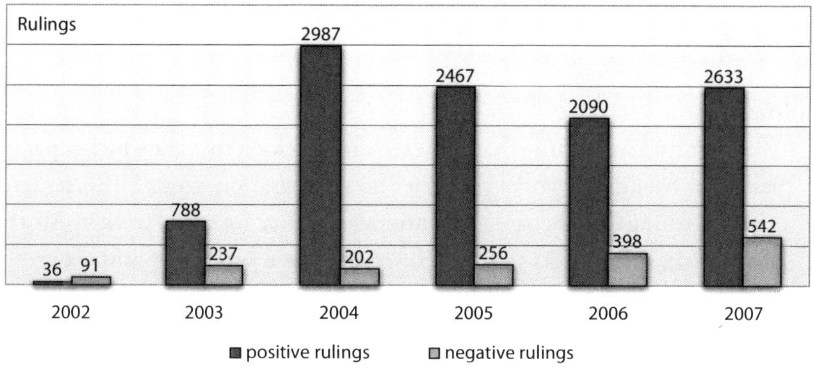

(cf. http://www.bmi.gv.at/downloadarea/asyl_fremdenwesen_statistik, updated 13.04.2008)

nied refugee minors shows a comparatively small number of applicants from the Russian Federation. This allows the conclusion – which is confirmed also by reports from practice – that Chechens tend, almost exclusively, to flee together with the closer family, the so-called nuclear family. A more exact classification of age structure and therefore more detailed information about the number of the juvenile Chechens in Austria is not possible because of the reasons mentioned above. However, the families with many children allow us to conclude that we can reckon with a large, and in the coming years still larger target group, the closer observation of which, by all means, lies within the interest of society as a whole.

The absence of exact statistic data and information concerning the number, as well as the socio-graphic composition of Chechens in Austria, should not, however, prevent the pointing out of tendencies and trends.

Above all, these consist of the insights gained from my four years of work as a social worker for acknowledged Convention refugees, in particular Chechens, as well as various interviews and conversations held with those concerned. The objective is, as mentioned above, to point out the problems, but in particular also the chances of the Chechen juveniles in the Diaspora, and further to gain more acceptance and understanding for this target group from the social majority. However, it is to be pointed out that this involves tendencies that have been recognized exclusively within the context of practical work and, as such, can by no means be used as generalizing statements about the ethnic group of peoples. Three practical examples follow to serve as an illustration for the better understanding of Chechen juveniles' situation in the Diaspora. The interviews with Madina,

Zelim and Alina were held during the course of social working activities in an integration hostel.

Madina[1]

"We must find something that unites us and not look for that which separates us. That's how friendship works and that's how integration works." This sentence comes from a young Chechen girl, who attends a college for social work in Austria. The story of Madina reflects that which serves us as a perfectly positive example of successful integration[2]: A young woman flees from the war turmoil in Chechnya to Austria together with her family. The family establishes itself, after the first transit refugee station Traiskirchen, during the duration of the asylum proceedings in Vorarlberg, receives the acknowledgment as Convention refugees according to the Geneva Refugee Convention and thus the right to stay in the country, with unrestricted access to all support benefits. The daughters successfully learn perfect German, Madina passes the entrance examination to a college of higher education.

Zelim

"A 7 months suspended sentence for 3 years, 2 months of which must be served." This sentence was heard from the mouth of a judge at the regional court in Vienna in October 2007 concerning 18-year-old Zelim from Chechnya. The young man fled with his mother and his younger sister four years ago from Chechnya to Austria. The family, granted a positive asylum ruling, lives in Vienna. In contrast to Madina, Zelim's story is not considered an exemplary case of successful integration work. His offence – ABH – actual bodily harm during the course of a fight – reflects the story of exactly that failed and even "threatening" development, which various mass media as well as some politicians welcome as a deterring example. An example, which turns public discourse about migration, integration and asylum from a neutral discussion with factual reasoning to a biased, emotional and anxiety provoking debate.

---

1 All names have been changed by the author.

2 Integration *(Latin >>reconstructing of a whole<<)*, (...) 1) general term: construction of a unity, incorporation into a larger whole. (...) 4)sociology: designation 1) for a societal process that is marked by a high degree of harmonious, conflict-free correlation of the diverse elements (roles, groups, organisations) as well as 2) for processes of conscious or educational incorporation of individuals and groups into or their adaptation to generally binding moral and behavioural patterns. (cf. http://lexikon.meyers.de/meyers/integration, updated 13.03.2008)

Alina

"I do not know how I can prevent her. She is determined and her friends think in exactly the same way." This sentence comes from a desperate Chechen woman, whose 16-year-old sister just got married in a religious Muslim ceremony. Alina fled with her younger sister (the parents and the brothers died in the second Chechnya war) to Austria three years ago. The two sisters having been granted a positive asylum ruling live in Vienna. Just like Zelim, Alina represents a story that does not rank among those successful ones, but rather those of a less favourable development in Austria.

These three case examples should offer an insight into the conditions under which some young Chechens live in Austria. They clearly light up two major challenges that both the persons involved, but naturally, also the supporting persons are confronted with.

Therefore in the following, the topics "violence and crime" and "marriage of female minors" will be covered. The conclusion forms the analysis of possible causes for these behaviour patterns in young Chechens, as well as those factors that can steer against such behaviour and can lead to a successful biography of integration. For the evaluation of the degree of integration, the parameters "language acquisition", "gainful employment", "participation in social and cultural life" as well as "contact to the social majority" are referred to. A positive asylum ruling creates a valid entrance to the education and social system for all recognized Convention refugees in Austria, and opens up chances and possibilities of integration into the local society. Nevertheless, young Chechen people see themselves confronted repeatedly with insurmountable hurdles which prevent a successful development like the one example shown in the case of Madina.

Violence and Crime

"Common everyday brutality. After an excess bashing incident in the Munich underground juvenile delinquency, migrants as offenders and counter measures will be discussed in Austria" (Kurier, 14.01.2008, pages 9–10). According to this article in the daily newspaper "Kurier", the juvenile delinquency rate in Austria is also on the rise. The number of the suspects under investigation for acts of violence between the ages of 14 to 18 rose from 2,305 in the year 2001 to 3,873 in the year 2006 (Kurier, 14.01.2008, page 10). The official crime statistic sheds no light on the nationality, nor the ethnic background of those condemned, but only differentiates between Austrian citizens and foreigners. Therefore, information cannot be obtained about the number of Chechen juvenile delinquents.

A numerical classification is not absolutely necessary. Social work in hostels for asylum seekers and/or integration housing for recognized Convention refugees shows that violence is one topic, among others, in working with male Chechen youths. The report about Zelim serves as an illustration here, and by no means represents just one individual case, but a recognizable tendency in everyday life of some of the young Chechen men in Austria. The question which arises now, for social workers, politicians and society in general is what are the causes for this increased readiness for violence, noticed by social workers, and/or what measures could steer against this tendency? As already shown in the previous paragraph, juvenile delinquency is a widespread phenomenon on the rise, which *cannot* be reduced to a particular group of peoples. Merely the differences in the causes and motives for this inclination to violent behaviour can be recognized. With Chechen juveniles a multiple fabric of possible causes and explanation patterns was noticeable, the background of which is to be found in a combination of some aspects of Chechen culture, the historical development of the mountainous Caucasus region as well as the social and socio-political situation in Austria. Chechen society is developed strictly hierarchically and takes the form of a clan system[3], structured in *taips*[4] and *tukums*[5]. The legal basis of coexistence is anchored in the so-called "*adat*"[6]. Respect and obedience towards the elders, the concept of honour, a close solidarity, and support within the family – whereby the term family is substantially broader than in the understanding of Western and Central Europe – and a loyalty toward the entire Chechen people, are the foundations of the Chechen way of life. Family ties are even more noticeable in the Diaspora, and extended to some degree to the entire group of peoples. This collective consciousness resulting from the loss of the homeland, due in addition to an historically caused century-long defensive role against an overwhelming opponent, is particularly strongly pronounced amongst young people, which leads in disputes mostly to their appearance in large groups. The concept of honour having moved strongly into the

3 Clan: in ethnology, an ethnic group which deduces its origin from a common ancestor (e.g. a supernatural being). (cf. http://lexikon.meyers.de/meyers/Klan, updated 15.03.2008)

4 *taip* – Chechen term for a clan comprising several settlements and kinship groups which goes back to a common ancestor

5 *tukum* – Chechen designation for a Chechen's regional affiliation

6 *adat* – Caucasian moral law or customary law that is transmitted orally

foreground, serves again and again as an explanation for the beginning of a conflict, or for the use of violence as a defence for verbal attacks, as in, for example, "I had to defend my honour", "he insulted my family", "I must strike back, otherwise I lose my honour", etc. The absence of a reaction during a dispute, or a verbal solution to a conflict would equal a "surrender" and a "not facing responsibility", would therefore be linked to losing face within the Chechen society, and thus for those young people concerned constitute no acceptable alternative. Likewise the state of affairs for those people that, although not directly involved in the conflict, are called to help.

It is noticeable that the cultural identity of young people in the Diaspora is changing towards retaining and even strengthening archaic values such as honour, laws of the jungle, etc. whilst moderate elements such as modesty, rational and reasoning behaviour, in contrast to emotional, unreasonable behaviour is forced into the background.

These cultural aspects are closely connected to the historical development of the Chechen people[7]. For more than 400 years, the entire Caucasus region has been influenced by a permanent, more or less severely escalating confrontation with the Russian, respectively Soviet super power.

The fight against this overwhelming opponent thus plays, since the time of the first czars, a central role in the consciousness of every Chechen person and is passed on from generation to generation. The deportation of almost the entire Chechen population to Central Asia under Stalin in the year 1944 is a further milestone in history, which until today has left its marks burned deeply into Chechen consciousness. Beside these historical injuries, young Chechens have personally experienced both Chechnya wars in the late 90's last century. The long history of suppression passed down by fathers and grandfathers, as well as their own socialisation in a state of war, in combination with the experience of violence, has left its traces in the behaviour patterns of many young people. The violence experienced can release feelings such as frustration and despair or be expressed in anger and aggression towards others. A permanent confrontation with violence means that peaceful conflict solutions retreat into the background or disappear completely. In addition, the brutally led conflict on both sides has annihilated

7 Forced marriage designates a form of marriage in which one or both of the two partners are not willing to getting married. The choice of the partner is not made by the person concerned but by other persons, often family members. (cf. http://www.bmuk.gv.at/medienpool/13107/fl_zwangsheirat.pdf, updated 17.03.2008)

whole generations of men. The youngsters were thus robbed not only of their fathers and grandfathers but also of their male heroes. What remained were either the fighters in the forests, who were quickly stylized to heroes; or physically- and mentally-broken former inmates freed from Russian prisons, who fled abroad to find a new existence. The proud and modest Chechen male, who is characterised by a calm and considerate nature, is therefore only to be found in literature and in tales, therefore no longer perceived by young people as a real role-model. We also find, apart from the reasons just described, further possible causes for this readiness for violent behaviour in the situation in the host country. Unemployment for example, due to which few or no perspectives are left open, is experienced by young Chechens as a huge barrier in the process of integration. Legally compulsory schooling ends in Austria at the age of 15. This means that children and youngsters arriving in Austria before the age of 15 receive places at school accordingly. Those already exceeding this age limit can proceed to graduation participating in external programs and courses. Substantial difficulties exist for both groups. Mostly the first group is just not up to the expected standard required and due to the lack of German language knowledge fails the exams. When first entering school, the older someone is the more difficult this integration process becomes. Youngsters that first arrive in Austria at the ages of 12 or 13 have few chances to catch up on their deficits, which besides poor language abilities are also due to school absence in their homeland as a consequence of the war. Youngsters, no longer eligible for compulsory schooling, are often unable to deal with the requirements needed for external courses, which are built on self-discipline and responsibility, and accordingly the drop-out rate is high. This shows the tendency noticed by social workers that young Chechens between the ages of 15 and 20 are unable to present either a school graduation certificate or a college attendance paper let alone find an apprenticeship or a job and are therefore in many cases without employment. These male youths mentioned here kill this abundance of free time mainly with sports, in particular the Chechen national sport of wrestling, boxing and other kinds of martial arts. This physical and fighting superiority is often seen as the only possibility to show other youngsters that they are capable of "also doing something", are "no worse, than others" and are "cool". Therefore, conflicts are often looked for and provoked instead of being avoided. This behaviour, although it doesn't foster closer ties to the host society, does allow the youngsters to rid themselves of excess energy and also diminishes frustration and, for a moment, permits them to experience the feelings of success and superiority.

Marriage of Female Minors

During the course of social work a new phenomenon of marriages among Chechen female minors became noticeable which differ fundamentally to the much discussed forced[8] and arranged marriages[9] that we know of from other cultures. When it comes to the marriages of 14- to 16-year-old girls, one thinks about the biographies of someone like Necla Kelek, that she describes in her book "The Foreign Bride" (Cologne 2005). A forceful family in the background that chooses a husband for the daughter, a young girl without rights who is more or less forced into taking this step, a so-called marriage of convenience, the likes of which have existed for centuries. The marriages of young Chechen girls in the Diaspora differ essentially from this concept in that the decision is one of free will. Whereas a forced marriage, as the name already states, is connected to force, and shows a classic perpetrator – victim couple, we now meet young women, who take this step entirely of their own free will, without family pressure, and sometimes even against the will of their parents. Where does this strong desire for marriage among young Chechen girls in the Diaspora come from? The mothers of the girls concerned indicated during talks that they had married mostly between the ages of 20 to 25, after having completed formal education, as was the custom. Their daughter's will is not always understandable for them either, moreover in a country that provides for every prospect of educational and vocational development equally as in the case of their male contemporaries.

Let us return at this point to the example of Alina's sister. Why does a 16-year-old girl from Chechnya, who succeeded in escaping to Austria, marry an 18-year-old compatriot of her own free will without being forced? Why is this girl suddenly completely veiled, and no longer goes to school? Why does it come to a complete withdrawal of this young girl from public life and her submission to the command of her husband? The reasons for this tendency are naturally just like the phenomenon itself, very complex. Two important aspects, which refer on the one hand to the historical situation, on the other hand to life in the host country, can contribute to a better understanding. Just as with the young male Chechens described above,

8 An arranged marriage is characterized by the fact that the parents of the marriage candidates determine the conditions for the marriage (e.g. time, dowry, etc.). It is however assumed that the marriage is contracted of the concerned spouses' free will. It is not possible though to make a clear distinction compared to a forced marriage, because the pressure exerted on the spouses by their families often makes it difficult to discern a free will. (cf. http://www.profrau.at/de/zwangsheirat/definition.htm, updated 17.03.2008)

9 cf. (2004) Russia's colonial heritage in Caucasus. In: NZZ Fokus. Pulverfass Tschetschenien, 22.

young Chechen girls show a socialisation which was shaped almost entirely in a state of war. Influenced strongly by the historical tale of permanent suppression, and partly traumatised by the personal experience of violence, we hear the sentence again and again: "I must also do something for my country and my people."

Many girls struggle with these feelings of guilt having abandoned their homeland and their relatives "to enjoy a life without worries in the Diaspora". Marrying a compatriot, then bringing up as many children as possible, appears in this situation at least a possibility of contributing their part to the "protection of the Chechen people", whose numbers were substantially decimated due to the wars. Furthermore, the role of mother and housewife corresponds more to the newly awakened religious understanding in the Diaspora than that of the successful career woman.

In addition, life takes on a somewhat different shape to that which was expected in the new homeland. Of course, there are all those often mentioned numerous possibilities of educational and vocational development, however, their realization is associated with substantial complications. As I already described, the end of official compulsory schooling, coinciding with turning the age of 15, also represents a break in a girl's development. Many opportunities for further education, like high schools or colleges, remain out of reach due to poor German language knowledge. The acquisition of knowledge requires much more effort than with colleagues of the same age; compensating linguistic and school deficits demands an excessive commitment and great dedication from those concerned. Besides which school attendance is often made more difficult by frustrating experiences. On the one hand, the girls are exposed to the pressure of achievement at school. The teaching staff, that has little or no intercultural training to offer, is hardly able to reduce this burden. On the other hand, they are repeatedly confronted with rejection and hostilities from fellow pupils. Whereas young Chechen men enjoy great freedom in the choice of their leisure activities, girls are for the most part very strictly educated and compared to their brothers have very little freedom in choosing outside school activities. Therefore, young girls differ even more from their school colleagues of the same age. Feelings of "being excluded", "not belonging", are strengthened, the enjoyment and fun of attending school and learning lessens and the high performance required from the start cannot be fulfilled. Hence, the frequently mentioned opportunities for education are reduced. Often resulting from this disillusionment and apparent lack of perspectives there is a retreat into the familiar environment, friendly relations are reduced to interaction with compatriots, who are better able to understand the situation, possibly being a part of it themselves. In this position, the role of wife and mother seems easier to fill and offers a satisfactory alternative in gaining acceptance and recognition. In the last years this tendency has reached such proportions that one can almost speak of it becoming "modern" to marry. Now even girls who show quite good school results increasingly tend to follow this path. During talks with the parents concerned we heard in consultation a certain lack of understanding for the behaviour of their daughters, but in addition, a certain relief about no longer having the responsibility for them. The family's honour is protected by the marriage of their daughter, whereas an extramarital affair would spoil it. From this point of view, fathers of young Chechen girls explained, repeatedly, that it was far more difficult for them to protect their daughters in an environment like that in the Diaspora than in their own country. The behaviour of many young people in Austria does not correspond to the moral expectations of Chechen people, and can therefore only affect the behaviour of their daughters in a negative way. Instead, therefore, marriage to a compatriot, even if entered upon when very young, is seen as far more favourable than the risk of any dishonourable behaviour by the daughter, which would bring disgrace upon the entire family. Through marriage, the father rids himself of his responsibilities and transfers them onto the son-in-law. Therefore, in regard of these views little support can be expected in the battle against this tendency.

Upon first sight, as a result of these early marriages there are apparent advantages for all involved. Parents experience relief by honourably "getting rid of" the responsibility for their daughters and retaining the honour of the family within a "Europe of dangers" shaped by degenerated moral concepts. Those girls that are eager to marry can then withdraw after the disappointing encounter with their "new liberty and its manifold possibilities of further development" into a well-known satisfying role, making their "contribution" to their people, thereby receiving acknowledgment and respect. The young husbands – mostly influenced by a, as was described in the previous chapter, traditional, archaic cultural understanding – likewise receive confirmation of their position through their "very young, naïve, poorly educated wives" from whom little protest is to be expected. This strengthening of the role of the patriarch is particularly welcomed in those countries of the Diaspora in which the rights of the women are spelled out clearly, and the topics of domestic violence, divorce etc. are publicly discussed. A further important aspect in the analysis of this topic is the wide-spread religious wedding ceremony. This form of marriage ceremony is mostly preferred to that of the civil wedding. This results on the one hand from religious belief, on the other hand also from reasons of convenience. As a result of the bride's under-age status (sometimes the status of both bride and bridegroom), and/or missing documents like birth certificates, passport, positive asylum ruling, etc., the bureaucratic hurdles of a civil wedding are not taken into consideration. A religious marriage ceremony has the further advantage for those involved, apart from the non-bureaucratic handling, that it can also be settled rapidly and independently both time-wise and location-wise. From the point of view of the outsider, this fact often leads therefore to unconsidered and hurried decisions being made, some of which are made after just a few meetings between the parties involved. The subsequent problems, which result from this tendency, are complex. On the one hand, these marriages are already dissolved sometimes after just a few weeks or months. This is likewise done in religious form and therefore requires no bureaucratic involvement. The dissolution of the marriage is, seen from the patriarchal viewpoint, the affair of the husband and results mostly from being discontented with his newly betrothed wife. For the girls concerned this experience apart from being an emotional burden also means the loss of their honour and in further consequence difficulty in finding a new husband. On the other hand – after a longer marriage –, the young wife withdraws from public life into the household, to continue with the education of the children. Schooling is ended abruptly, all the strength and energy is concentrated on the household and the children's education. It is not unusual for 20-year-old women to already be faced with looking after three small children. This enormous burden on young and inexperienced parents can be too great a challenge and lead to frustration. In care situations, therefore, topics like domestic violence, child-care neglect and/or educational problems, apart from those concerning financial difficulties are on the agenda. The poor education level of the parents resulting from dropping out of school as well as a careless way of thinking, due to lack of experience, makes problem solving difficult. The effects that this tendency has on the development of the children are not yet assessable. The perspectives of this new generation of Chechens, growing up since their birth in the Diaspora, are conceivably unfavourable under these premises.

Success Story – Favourable Factors

The first practice report about Madina shows that life in the Diaspora for young Chechen people, besides the above-mentioned hurdles, also offers possibilities and chances for further development that are there to be taken advantage of. Therefore, the aim for politics and care facilities must be to filter out factors, which work against the described integration-hampering challenges, and to work in favour of a successful approach process towards the social majority. First of all, the strengthening of some aspects of the established social structure of the Chechens offers a possibility of influencing the development of young people. Above all, the dominating position of older family members as well as their influence on younger relatives can very positively affect the process of integration. Experience shows that the so-called "elders"[10] embody a calmness and composure, mostly taking a moderate and well-considered position in regard of culture, religion, behaviour patterns and in dealing with other attitudes, people and points of view. Priority is always given to the respectful dealings with one another, aiming at finding a compromise. Lately it has been observed that these family members' influence over young people has decreased following a shift in competence and knowledge within the Diaspora. Younger family members learn the language of the host country much faster and adjust more rapidly to the new forms of conduct and conditions. They take over any administrative business and other concerns for the family, communication with the authorities etc. which was traditionally done by the father, grandfather or uncle, etc. New forms of media communication such as mobile telephones and internet are well known and are used without any difficulty. The "superiority" of experience and knowledge on the part of older family members loses its importance more and more, the adaptability and flexibility of the youngsters gain in significance. The family's dependency shifts, particularly in public life when formal communication with outsiders is needed, in favour of the younger family members, and the influence of the elders is reduced further. Their moderate and well-considered attitude in many areas loses its meaning and influence for the next generations. The result is a shift in values towards archaic, radical elements of Chechen culture, as was described in the chapter on "violence and crime", respectively also on marriage of underage girls. A positive contribution toward a more successful integration of young Chechens is also to be expected from the well-educated urban middle class. The goal therefore should also be the strengthening of their position. Due to the high

10 Note: Elder Chechen men who can boast a rich wealth of experience and knowledge.

number of refugees belonging to the ethnic group of Chechen people, the host country has to deal with a cross-section of the population structure. This means that members of both sexes, of all ages and education levels as well as all socialisation milieus from urban and rural areas of Chechnya can be found among those people entitled to asylum. Accordingly, different opinions, viewpoints and ways of life will be exposed to the process of integration. This fact is only too often disregarded in a tendency to careless generalization and lets the chances of exerting any influence go unused. The care work shows that the well-educated middle class is characterised by great personal effort and willingness towards integration, which is reflected particularly in a strong desire for education, also for their daughters. In talks with those concerned it turned out that nearly all Chechen girls, who were studying successfully at Austrian universities and colleges (see: Madina), showed the family background that has just been described. The families come from the larger Chechen cities, mostly Grozny. The parents themselves have finished high school and place emphasis on a good education for their children. Their ethical and moral values are of a very secular nature. Parents show sufficient trust in their daughters to permit them to attend evening courses, live in student homes and associate with both male and female colleagues. Through the strengthening of their position, support for a moderate attitude can be created. Emphasising these positive examples of integration and successful biographies in public life, shows that there are real possibilities of how opportunities and benefits can be used in the Diaspora. A standard of achievement, which seems impossible, developmental steps, which seem too distant to reach, take on real forms which can be turned into role models.

Apart from this structural stabilization of some aspects of the Chechen social order, basic conditions for young people can be created, which makes it easier for them to master challenges in their host countries. The creation of realizable perspectives and possibilities must therefore be a basic requirement for an honest approach to the topic of integration. Particularly within the field of education, to compensate for the deficits in school performances brought about by the war in their homeland, and to further the standard of knowledge, possibilities are needed. A restrictive end of compulsory schooling at the age of 15, due to an insufficient school performance, without the possibility of any further stay in the regular educational system, can only function if enough external courses, which meet the needs of those youngsters, are available. In the case of young Chechens besides a tight structure, the courses should offer social and psychological support. The particular disadvantage of the described target group must be taken into account both in respect of the financial and personnel resource costs of social work. Young people are most of all "double losers" in the course of the war and flight. Older Chechens can fall back onto a socialisation in a peaceful environment and have mostly a completed compulsory schooling, and/or further education to show.

Children indeed are aware of destruction and war since their birth, but due to their youth, have the chance to attend school in the Diaspora for several years, become socialized in their new homeland, and rapidly learn the language of the host country and benefit from the advantages of the system. Youngsters bring with them from their homeland neither a solid footing nor do they have full admission to the support facilities in the Diaspora. The "normality/stability" necessary for a successful development is missing; integration efforts must be orientated towards answering their needs all the more.

Cultural Aspects of Chechen Integration in Poland

ZUZANNA OLSZEWSKA AND ANNA MACIEJKO

This article[1] examines the prospects for the integration of Chechens, who constitute the majority of asylum seekers arriving in Poland, in Polish society. It takes as its starting point and seeks to test the assumption that the majority of Chechens are not integrating well into Polish society and prefer to travel to Western European countries. While fundamentally the reasons for this may be economic, or due to flaws in the still-developing asylum system in Poland, this article explores how these factors impact, and are in turn affected by, the cultural norms and values of Chechen refugees and Polish hosts. Based on interviews with both Polish people working in various areas of the asylum system who worked closely with Chechens, and Chechen refugees and asylum seekers themselves, this analysis attempts to rise above the individual moral judgements and generalisations

1 Certain sections of this article first appeared in Polish as a report for the Society for Legal Intervention (Stowarzyszenie Interwencji Prawnej), which issued a paper series in 2007 (Maciejko/Olszewska 2007). This article is a result of an independent research project titled "Flight from Atrocity: The Social, Legal and Political Dimensions of the Influx of Chechen Refugees into Central Europe," entirely funded by the John D. and Catherine T. MacArthur Foundation. The analysis presented here is based on in-depth interviews carried out in Poland from April 2006 to February 2007 with social workers of District Family Assistance Centres, employees of Social Policy Departments of Voivodship Offices (provincial administration), UNHCR employees, employees of non-governmental organisations (NGOs) providing social assistance to asylum seekers and refugees and Chechens (55 respondents) who were, at the time of the interview, either still in the asylum procedure, had been recognized as refugees or had received tolerated stay in Poland. Interviews were conducted in Polish, Russian or Chechen (the latter through an interpreter). According to the wishes of most of our respondents, excerpts from these interviews are quoted anonymously in this article. All translations of interview excerpts and sources originally in Polish are by the authors.

we frequently heard from our respondents and to synthesise an objective, multi-faceted assessment of the situation.

Above all, it defines both "culture" and the process of "integration" as notions which are dynamic and dialogic, determined by historical conditions, and whose meanings must constantly be interrogated, particularly in situations of mass displacement and political upheaval.

This bifocal perspective on the situation, from the point of view of both hosts and refugees, produced some dissonant results. We found that – notwithstanding the goodwill expressed by both sides, the gratitude of many Chechens for their reception and the empathy of many Poles for the difficult situation of the refugees – there were often cases of frustration, incomprehension and mistrust on both sides. Similarly, due to the bitter divisions in Chechen society, the Chechen community itself was divided and refugees were perhaps most mistrustful of each other[2]. Finally, Polish social workers were often greatly chagrined when their clients, despite their great and often highly personal efforts to help them settle down in Poland, would suddenly disappear without warning, apparently having departed for a Western European country.

Similar conditions in other places have prompted Daniel and Knudsen (1995) to argue that mistrust is perhaps a paradigmatic characteristic of refugee situations, from the loss of trust in one's own society from which one was obliged to flee, to the lack of trust in host country officials. "Unlike life under 'ordinary' circumstances, or more correctly, under circumstances over which one exercises a certain measure of control, in the life of a refugee, trust is overwhelmed by mistrust, besieged by suspicion, and relentlessly undermined by caprice" (Daniel/Knudsen 1995: 1–2). Trust is built on familiarity, shared meanings and interpretations of actions, intentions and events, which may not be shared by hosts and refugees. In the following, we examine a number of different factors contributing to integration, and the differences in how they were perceived by Poles and by Chechens. We pay particular attention to incidents of cultural dissonance which could breed incomprehension and mistrust, and suggest how they might be overcome in order for successful integration to take place.

2 These divisions have largely resulted from the so-called "Chechenisation" phase of the conflict from 2003 onwards. According to the Russian human rights group Memorial, the process "has promoted bitterness [on] both sides of the conflict, as well as increase of fear and feeling of vulnerability among the peaceful population. The conflict has gained a new dimension – intra-Chechen – and it will be much harder to 'extinguish' than the Russia-Chechnya confrontation" (Human Rights Center "Memorial" 2005).

What is Integration?

Before beginning a discussion of integration, it is helpful to define the concept, since it is not uniformly understood. For the purposes of this article, we understand integration as a complex social process, during which: (1) new arrivals with a different culture gradually learn to function effectively in a given host society – that is, to take advantage of the opportunities, rights and liberties available in that society and to participate in public life, with the aim of securing a decent life; they should (2) simultaneously adapt to local legal norms and responsibilities and, to an extent, to the cultural and behavioural norms and customs of the host society. "Adaptation" does not, however, need to entail complete "assimilation," since in most open societies integration generally allows for the maintenance of a distinct identity, language and religion of ethnic minorities and immigrants. This process probably never occurs without periodic misunderstandings and conflicts, but it is worth underlining that the host society usually also adapts and changes under the influence of the immigrants' culture.

The majority of our interviewees, both Polish and Chechen, understood integration as such a two-way process, in which each side should give something of itself and learn from and about the other. Our definition is, however, a more complex one, comprising two elements which in our opinion are inseparable: (1) a pragmatic aspect (effective functioning in order to secure a decent life) and (2) a cultural aspect (adaptation to local norms and customs). Our research indicates that the two sides participating in this process (Polish helpers and Chechen refugees) perceived the relationship between these two categories in different ways, often leading to a mutual lack of understanding, which will be discussed in greater detail in this article.

It should be emphasized, however, that our respondents, regardless of their background, generally identified the same objective barriers to the integration of Chechens in Poland, although they described them in different ways:

- the limited number of jobs, a disadvantageous situation on the labour market, lack of job stability and poor working conditions – informal employment, non-payment of wages by dishonest employers;
- the lack of language training and suitable qualifications of the Chechens, which adds to their employment difficulties;
- difficulties in accessing affordable housing;

- too short duration (12 months) of Individual Integration Programmes (IIPs) for recognized refugees;
- and the lack of integration assistance for people with tolerated stay[3].

The Chechens also drew attention to two other problems, which in their opinion were at the root of their integration problems in Poland, since they had serious consequences for their effective functioning in all other areas of their lives:
- what they perceived as low refugee recognition rates[4];
- serious health problems – both mental and physical – as a result of warfare and trauma; the lack of effective medical treatment and rehabilitation.

On the other hand, Polish respondents who worked with Chechens located the key barriers elsewhere: they often expressed the opinion that their Chechen clients did not make enough effort to integrate, since Chechens treat Poland as a transit country and assume in advance that they will not settle there permanently. These differences indicate rather different interpretations of the situation, which will be discussed in greater detail below.

Methodology

55 in-depth interviews were carried out with citizens of the Russian Federation living in eight Polish towns, as well as 4 in Slovakia, and 1 in Austria. Of the 55 in Poland, 54 declared Chechen nationality, while one was Ingush. 26 of them were recognized refugees, 7 had "tolerated stay", 7 were in their first asylum procedure, and 15 were in subsequent asylum procedures, having previously received tolerated stay. All of those in the asylum procedure in Poland were staying in one of 7 different asylum residential centres – along with many of those with tolerated stay, unofficially or semi-officially, for lack of any other place to go.

3 "Tolerated stay" is a form of protection given to those who cannot be deported on the basis of art. 3 of the European Convention on Human Rights, but who do not meet the stringent requirements of the Refugee Convention. Note that an amendment to the Polish Law on the Protection of Aliens on the Territory of the Republic of Poland (May 2008) introduces a new form of subsidiary protection in line with EU directives, which will grant its holders access to 12-month integration assistance packages on the same terms as recognized refugees.

4 Above all, this was a hindrance because of the lack of integration assistance. The low recognition rates also breed mistrust, because to Chechens, they are a sign either of lack of understanding of their situation, which they see as a genocide against the Chechen nation, or of political unwillingness to risk the enmity of the powerful Russian Federation. Nonetheless, Poland's old anti-communist opposition is still a political force in the country, and often assists in Chechen pro-independence activism. Warsaw is probably the only city in the world with a roundabout named after Djokhar Dudayev.

Of our 60 respondents, 31 were men, 23 were women, and the remaining 6 interviews were carried out with married couples with the participation of both spouses, although the women sometimes removed themselves to take care of various household duties. Of the 23 female respondents, 11 were heading their households because they had been widowed, divorced, or otherwise separated from their husbands, and they had their own children, siblings' children, adopted children, grandchildren and/or daughters-in-law to take care of (male-headed households also often included several generations, siblings and extended kin). 5 women were alone. The remainder were with their husbands and children but spoke for their families, either because we had met them earlier, or because they were the ones whose situations had led them to flee. Of the 31 male respondents, only 3 were alone, either because they had not married yet, or (in one case) because his whole family had been murdered.

The earliest date of arrival into Poland among the sample was 1996, although this respondent did not enter the asylum procedure until 2000, when visas began to be required of Russian Federation citizens in Poland. Three respondents arrived in 2000, at the beginning of the second war; two others came before the end of 2003. Other than these 6, who had managed to stay on in Poland mainly thanks to their language skills, close contacts with Polish friends, and transferable qualifications, all of the remaining respondents arrived after May 2004 – the accession of Poland to the EU and at the same time to the Dublin II Regulation which to a great extent bound them to this country. Undoubtedly, our respondent recruitment methods influenced this outcome to some extent, since social workers were more likely to be in touch with people in the asylum procedure or in integration programmes. But it proved to be difficult to find others who had stayed in Poland for more than 3 years, and it may be assumed that very few Chechens from the early migration waves have remained in Poland.

Of the total sample, despite the fact that 36 respondents had the right to work legally in their host countries, only 8 were in relatively secure, formal employment – most of them with NGOs. Most of the others were working, or had worked in the past, largely in informal, short-term, unskilled and low-paying jobs, including construction and renovation, as au pairs or cleaners, in restaurants, or seasonally during fruit and vegetable harvests. A handful were conducting business on their own, importing used cars from Germany. Although they did not have the right to work legally, many of those in the asylum procedure were working or had worked illegally in the past, usually in similar short-term, low-paying jobs (9 of the 22 respondents in the asylum procedure in Poland openly declared that they had worked)[5].

Poles and Chechens on Chechen Integration Prospects

When speaking about the barriers to Chechen integration in Poland, our respondents from NGOs and social workers acknowledged the "extreme caution, bordering on fear" regarding Chechen refugees on the part of Polish society. We repeatedly heard the view among NGO workers that representations of Chechens as terrorists – for example in the Russian media – played a role in shaping such an attitude. On the other hand, they spoke at length about the limitations on the part of the Chechen community. Our respondents noted that Chechens have experienced a group migration, and have a well-developed system of internal control, restricting the ability to adapt easily to a different culture. To make integration assistance more effective, one respondent said, group control in the Chechen community would have to be relaxed, which would, for example, encourage men to exert less influence on decisions taken by refugee women. We also encountered the opinion that Chechens should change their "mentality" and "tear themselves away from the Chechen sense of victimhood", particularly in relation to gaining greater financial independence in exile. It is important for Chechens, as one social worker put it, to realise that "no kind of work is shameful, but they should realise the extent of their professional abilities and look for work appropriate to their skills." She added that "handouts do not mobilise them to work, but make people lazier." There was an unmistakeable hint of moral and cultural judgement to the

5 Given the importance of trust in the material discussed in this article, it is perhaps relevant to make a note here about the ethical considerations of the study. Our survey was recorded anonymously and all respondents were assured of the same. We did not push them if they seemed unwilling to give more than a general answer or when they or the interpreter verbally or non-verbally signalled discomfort with the question. Not believing this to be the main purpose of our study, we were reluctant to compromise the trust of our respondents by subjecting them to thorough questioning on often very painful matters, and we told them that their comfort was important to us. Moreover, we wished to establish a supportive and trusting rapport with our respondents and accepted their answers at face value, without probing for inconsistencies. That said, a large number of our respondents spoke openly and in great detail about terrible experiences at home and difficult conditions in exile. In a follow-up session with our Chechen interpreter, he expressed his approval of the depth of most people's responses.

statements of many (though not all) respondents, suggesting that the Poles believed that cultural adaptation and a change in "mentality" was the key to integration.

Our interviews with Chechens themselves had a rather different tenor. In their own opinion, Chechens are good and honest workers, who are capable of managing their lives and do not like to live on state handouts. They are also open to other cultures, used to living in proximity to non-Muslims like Russians or other Caucasian peoples, and are hospitable and friendly – which we had the opportunity to experience on several occasions. From interviews and from observations of life in residential centres and outside, it appears that Chechens are more active than it seemed to their helpers, but their activeness takes place within their own circles, invisible and incomprehensible to outsiders. Considering the fact that the large majority of them have fled conflict involving a direct threat to their life or health, it is not surprising that many Chechens seek above all a calm place where they can ensure their survival. Several people, when asked about the reasons for their departure from Chechnya, said that "We had to wait this out somewhere." At the same time, living in uncertainty of what tomorrow will bring, they are unable to make long-term plans. As a result, they are more focused on the "pragmatic" aspect of integration, according to our definition, than the cultural. This could explain why they seem to be most interested in actions bringing rapid, tangible effects.

A pragmatic approach to survival in exile explains the fact that Chechens seem to prefer not to remain in Poland, despite their frequent assertions that Polish culture is closer to them than that of Western Europe, that they can manage the language, and that it is "closer to home" in case of a sudden need to return. One might formulate the hypothesis that the desire to go further west is simply based on a rational calculation, according to which the risk of being caught and deported is still worthwhile. The main reasons cited by Chechens for wanting to go to Western Europe are a wish to reunite with family members (at least two-thirds of our respondents had relatives in Western Europe, of which nearly half were close kin – siblings, children, parents); easier and faster access to high-quality medical treatment (particularly surgical procedures) in the case of frequently serious health problems; and finally, better social benefits, making it easier to survive. At the time of our research in 2006–2007, for Chechens, especially those with large families, receiving tolerated stay in Poland was a tragedy because it did not come with an integration programme as in the case of Convention refugees.

Most of our respondents who were still in the asylum procedure were convinced that if integration was possible at all, it was only possible with an integration package from the state[6].

Despite Poland's accession to the Dublin Convention in 2004, many Chechens continued to attempt crossing over to Western Europe using smuggling networks for several more years. Some were apparently able to remain; others were detained in deportation centres and eventually returned to Poland. Until 2005 there were still incidents of mass disappearances of large groups of asylum seekers from residential centres. Although their numbers dwindled after that, the press continued to report isolated illegal attempts to smuggle Chechens across the southern border[7]. A 30-year-old mechanic from Grozny said that he knew about the Dublin Regulation, but his brother who lived in Denmark convinced him to go there at the end of 2005. When interviewed in late 2006, he had recently been returned to Poland and entered the asylum procedure. However, at the beginning of 2007, a 38-year-old teacher from Grozny, having admitted that his sister in France was ready to send him money to pay for smuggling his family to France, was more resigned: "But what's the point? They would deport us anyway." On the other hand, the trend of recognized refugees leaving after the end of or during their IIP continues, although proportions of successfully completed IIPs have risen slightly (Kosowicz/Maciejko 2007: 65). In the Mazovian Voivodship (Province) of Poland in 2006, one-third of integration programmes were terminated due to the disappearance of the client (Department of Social Policy of the Mazovian Voivodship Office 2007: 15). Following Poland's accession to the Schengen zone on 21 December 2007 and the lifting of border controls, it seems that the trend of mass departures of asylum seekers from residential centres has returned, with 900 people disappearing by mid-January (PAP 2008), despite probable knowledge of the Dublin II Regulation and its consequences.

Having considered the problem from both angles, we believe that the problem of the apparent lack of integration of the vast majority of Chechens in Poland does not stem from their passivity, but in many cases from its opposite – the activation of a dynamic network of mutual assistance and support, often stretching on a transnational plane from Western Europe all the way to Chechnya. This is a consequence not only of the insufficient social assistance in Poland, but also of

6 It will be interesting to monitor the effects on Chechen integration after May 2008, when integration assistance will be extended to those with subsidiary protection.

7 See for example Dziennik Polski Podhalański (2007: 1, 3) and Gazeta Wyborcza (2006: 3).

historical adaptation. When the state is unable to fulfil its obligation of providing citizens or refugees with a decent life (among others because of insufficient finances), ordinary human solidarity and enterprise step in. Unfortunately, the short-term pragmatism of such a solution can mean that many – if not most – Chechens exist in their own world, investing their meagre resources in maintaining their ties with their compatriots, but not placing much emphasis on learning the host country's language, contact with local people or broadening their knowledge of the local culture. In effect, they are most interested in heading further west because the larger social networks they have there make it easier to survive by relying on their own circles. Frequently, those who remain in the "new" European Union countries are the weakest, the poorest, or those who for various reasons cannot or do not wish to ask their kin for help.

Chechens are most likely to trust each other and depend on their relatives, friends or neighbours from home. Cousins and members of *taips* (clans)[8] find each other in residential centres scattered all over Poland, and try to visit each other as often as possible. However, in the politically divided Chechen milieu, many people told us that it is only possible to really trust people they have known well for a long time. Relatives in Western Europe send money and parcels; kin and friends who have lived in Poland for a longer time help those who have newly arrived. The mobile phone of our translator, a young man who had lived in Poland for 6 years and spoke excellent Polish, was constantly ringing with requests for help in explaining or translating something, assistance in taking care of administrative affairs, or accompaniment during hospital visits. When it was an older person calling, Chechen etiquette required that he responded immediately, regardless of the situation. We even heard indications that asylum seekers who received monthly cash allowances for school-aged children used them to financially assist families with tolerated stay, since it was the latter who were considered to be in more dire need.

A 34-year-old widow with three children from Grozny rented a 2-room apartment near the asylum residential centre in one small Polish town after receiving refugee status, and in this way she was able to maintain regular contact with her compatriots. Like many other people, when asked if she received assistance from friends and relatives, she replied, "Yes, they help me. Without it, I don't know how I'd survive." She did not have good contact with her Polish neighbours, who regularly called the police whenever her children were noisy. In one residential centre

8 For a detailed discussion of Chechen family and clan structures and the kinds of obligation incumbent on them, see (Adger-Adajew 2006: 177–85).

we met a 38-year-old man, a teacher by training (he was also a car dealer and claimed to have been well-off before the 1st Chechen War) who had tolerated stay, while his wife had re-entered the asylum procedure. He was a good example of Chechen self-sufficiency: "My wife has been waiting two years for a major operation; she'll have to wait one more year. I buy medicines myself from the Belarusians (informal traders) in the market, or they send them to me from home. My sister also sends some from France. The medicines which they give in the centre haven't helped anybody yet, not one child, not one adult. There's just one pill for everything. I was ill with the flu for four months, until finally I cured myself. When my one-year-old son got burned, I cured him myself with a traditional method, now he doesn't have a single scar. Folk medicine is the best."

A 30-year-old Chechen man with refugee status, a geophysicist by training, but unable to speak Polish well, found a good job as a driver for an international organisation working with refugees in Poland. Paradoxically, this was not thanks to an employment service, but thanks to his own efforts and by a very circuitous route: he learned of the job through internet contact with acquaintances in Ingushetia, where the organisation also operated.

The adaptive capacity and mobility described here are a result of a long history of adaptation to difficult conditions and existence on the margins of the state. For example, in the pre-war Checheno-Ingush Republic in Soviet times, unemployment and discrimination on the labour market meant that the majority of industrial jobs (particularly in the petrochemical and oil refining industries) were reserved for Russians, and every year over 100,000 Chechens and Ingush were obliged to travel to other republics of the USSR to work in seasonal jobs. In the 1970s and 80s, many were able to afford large houses and cars through such seemingly unstable work (see Tishkov 2004: 40–44). After the collapse of the USSR, Chechen men travelled to Turkey and Arab states for trade purposes, returning with goods that they could trade in informal marketplaces, such as clothing, footwear and kitchen appliances[9].

It is therefore not surprising that similarly enterprising Chechen women take certain food items which they are offered in residential centres but which don't

9 Tishkov, in his ethnographic account of life in Chechnya during and after the 1st Chechen War, writes that by the end of 1994, "there were hundreds and possibly thousands of young male Chechens who exchanged the long-time practice of seasonal 'moonlighting' for making shopping trips to Turkey and other countries, thus providing themselves with a reasonable means of subsistence. (...) A small-scale but energetic barter trade stimulated economic activity and gave the appearance of a market saturated with goods, chiefly at the level of street trade" (Tishkov 2004: 67).

appeal to them, and sell them in the market, in order to buy products more suited to their families' tastes. Indeed, informal trade in asylum centres is booming, albeit on a small scale, from yoghurt and fruit juices (and, as one Polish interviewee suspected, possibly also items from the packages of necessities provided for newborn babies) sold in bazaars, to attractive children's books from charity donations being sold back to Polish staff[10]. There is also an internal market within the centres, e.g. women bake and sell traditional cakes to other families, while families leaving the centres frequently sell their audio-visual equipment to other residents at discount prices. The problem lies in the fact that, as a result of the new conditions imposed by the "war economy" in Chechnya after 1994, and perhaps also because of the lack of formal education and qualifications on the part of young men due to the war, many Chechens appear to prefer informal economic activities in their own circles. Polish interviewees who worked with Chechens on a daily basis often acknowledged this attitude and ability to manage difficult conditions – but on the margins of the law and mainstream society. As one of them pointed out, with some insight, "It seems to me that there is a certain assumption of transience in all this mobility. These are people who have strong clan ties and are very well oriented as to what's happening where, they're active but also rather closed (within their own group). (...) Poland is not the place in which they'd like to invest their lives in the long term. For them, that ideal lies elsewhere. (...) They function a little bit as if they're just trying to deal with things as they come, to go here, to get some medical treatment there, now here, now there. There's rarely any long-term planning. (...) with the Chechens, there's no ideal that he'd (sic!) like to be like a Pole. With the Belarusians, it's different. They say, 'There, you'll be a minister!' Or 'You won't become a minister if you don't study.' (...) For Chechens, it's not so appealing to be and work the way Poles do. For them, it's important to have a family and some money, yes, but what counts are contacts, trade, cars, movement." This might account for the "secretiveness" of many clients of District Family Assistance Centres (DFAC) as to their future plans, or the "simulation" of legal activity on the surface to keep their terms of the IIP, which many social workers alleged. This should be viewed through the lens of an apparent Chechen preference for informal economic activity in their own circles.

10 Both of these activities invite the incomprehension and disgust of Polish staff, who think that their clients simply fail to appreciate what is given to them; and also the bitterness and resentment of their Polish neighbours, many of whom (in the areas in which residential centres are located) are poor and cannot afford to buy such "luxuries" for their own children, let alone receive them from the state.

Unfortunately, the situation on the Polish labour market merely heightens such tendencies. It should be emphasised that such informal activity is a problem of the Polish economy rather than one introduced by foreign immigrants. Even people with the right and will to legal employment find themselves being informally employed so that the employer can save money. Deprived of the rights guaranteed by a contract, they are in a vulnerable position in case of disputes with their employers, for example if they reduce the agreed wages without notice, withhold wages, or when it turns out that the employee is not covered by social security despite the employer's assurances. We often heard of such cases. For example, a 22-year-old man told us: "My wife works in (a café). Her employment agent (at one of the NGOs) helped her find the job. One day she went to the doctor with all her documents, and to our surprise we discovered that she did not have medical insurance and that this was not a valid employment contract! We had to pay. Her boss also told her that if she gets pregnant, she will lose her job immediately – there will be plenty of people to take her place, that's the situation on the labour market."

Other Chechens were frustrated by the fact that "where a Pole makes 14 Polish zlotys per hour, a Ukrainian makes eight, and a Chechen makes six. For employers, hiring people legally is not worth it, and Chechens don't know the language or their rights, so they are exploited." Others claimed that despite active job searches and completed vocational courses (e.g. floristry or fork-lift operation), they could not find work. Several respondents mentioned that they would like to know more about how to start a business in Poland, since they had ideas for their own small businesses such as restaurants or *halal* (Islamic) butcheries. Others asked about the possibility of working on the land and farming it as they once did at home. Interestingly, both groups were considering these possibilities without feeling the need to learn Polish, which would have been necessary at the very least when registering the business. Chechens with their pragmatic attitude often indicated their belief that "it's easiest to learn Polish on the job, from Poles." Frequently, these were the ones who had already worked in Poland (usually illegally), for example in seasonal jobs in fruit or vegetable harvests, in construction, at sawmills, or dealing in used cars.

It may be difficult to imagine that someone who does not seem to be in the least "integrated" (that is, he or she is not learning the language and is not interested in contact with the local population), can be getting by quite well and earning a living, albeit illegally. We encountered several such cases. However, such activity on the margins of law and society is not a good solution, because it creates a negative impression of refugees among Poles. Meanwhile, it would be misleading to state that refugees who speak the language well, have a wide network of Polish contacts, acquaintances and friends, know how to use Polish government offices and public services, and sometimes were even educated in Poland, were functioning effectively in society. Perhaps they more frequently relied on their Polish associates for help than on other Chechens, but very few of our respondents could be said to have no problems securing the basic necessities of life for themselves and their families. The majority lived in poverty or on the verge of it; many told us openly that they had only survived thanks to the goodwill of other people. It is therefore necessary to pay attention to both aspects of integration – the pragmatic and the cultural, since they are intertwined and are essential to improving the plight of refugees and pulling them away from the margins of society.

Poor Mental and Physical Health as Symbols of the Broken Nation

There is, in addition, a third category of people – those who genuinely descend into helplessness and apathy. In our opinion, in many cases this is probably caused or intensified by depression, physical illness or post-traumatic stress disorder (PTSD), frequently experienced by refugees from areas affected by armed conflict[11]. Narratives about poor physical and mental health seemed to have taken on cultural status among our respondents, obliquely reflecting the Chechens' sense of having been persecuted as a people, with each sick body metonymically symbolising their fragmented and ailing nation. Yet, judging by stories told to us not only by asylum seekers but also by social workers of the indifference of doctors in residential centres towards asylum seekers' requests for treatment, the extent of their suffering was not always believed. Among our respondents, almost half of them reported about having been held at gunpoint during a raid, arrested, detained at a "filtration point", imprisoned, held for ransom, or otherwise harassed by federal security officials or unknown, masked perpetrators; while a *further* 10%

11 The typical symptoms of PTSD include depression, insomnia, anxiety, hyperarousal, intrusive memories, nightmares and flashbacks; cf. Herman 1997. For a summary of the newest studies on the psychological consequences of armed conflict around the world, including Chechnya, see Murthy/Lakshminarayana 2006.

declared that they or their close family members had been physically tortured during such events. The actual percentages are likely to be somewhat higher, since we did not ask directly about their wartime experiences and most people probably preferred not to speak about such matters. Nonetheless, every such incident could lead to trauma, and 22% of our respondents admitted the existence of psychological disorders in their families (including anxiety, insomnia, aggressiveness, memory loss or withdrawal), although they most frequently referred to their children or spouses, and rarely spoke about their own problems, particularly men – it is thus possible that the proportion of those suffering from mental health problems may have been underreported and significantly higher[12]. In the opinion of a psychologist who conducted psychotherapy sessions in residential centres for asylum seekers under the auspices of Médecins Sans Frontières (MSF) for one-and-a-half years, all Chechens arriving in Poland ought to have at least psychological counselling, which seems a sensible proposition, while many could benefit from more intensive therapy. She believed that their experiences certainly caused difficulties in their everyday lives and in establishing contact with Polish society[13]. At present, the psychotherapeutic services offered are insufficient to cover all residents of residential centres, and there is no screening on arrival.

Chechens themselves also mentioned the need for greater attention to mental health. A 46-year-old man living in a residential centre and in the third year of his asylum procedure said, "Russian soldiers go and get their 'nerves' treated after three months in Chechnya, but what about us after 14 years of war? We don't get any medical or psychological assistance." We often heard from people who could not concentrate on their language studies, since they were overwhelmed by a constant "hum" of thoughts and problems in their minds; others said they suffered memory problems after their wartime experiences. "As soon as I learn a new word, the next day it flies out of my head," said a 46-year-old man with a wife and four children, who had worked in the border guard of Chechnya during its brief independence. He suffered from depression, physical ailments and memory loss. He had refugee status, but his Individual Integration Program (IIP) was due to end

12 See two reports on the psychological consequences of war and torture in Chechnya: de Jong/van der Kam/Ford et al. (2004); Medical Foundation for the Care of Victims of Torture.

13 Another psychologist whom we interviewed in Austria, involved for many years in psychotherapy for refugees, explained that men and women typically experience different symptoms of PTSD: women usually become depressed, whereas men are more likely to act aggressively or feel that they have lost control over themselves. Perhaps the latter is a factor in explaining the "demanding" nature of Chechens that many Polish respondents noticed, as well as conflicts in residential centres.

in two months' time, he did not have a job, and he assessed his situation as "very bad," with no prospects whatsoever.

Although we did not ask directly about the health status of our respondents' families, it was a commonly recurring theme in their narratives. As many as 49% complained of their own or their family members' serious health problems, frequently requiring specialist tests (such as Magnetic Resonance Imaging scans) or long hospital stays. These figures are not surprising given the war and the collapse of the health care system in Chechnya, which has lagged far behind other regions of the Russian Federation[14]. Meanwhile, the vast majority of interviewees repeatedly told us that the health care facilities in reception and residential centres were very poor, and complained about the unhelpful attitude of doctors and nurses towards the residents (with a few exceptions). The health care problem in Polish asylum centres was often raised as a reason for the onward migration of Chechens, for example to Austria[15].

A further example of a cultural dissonance between Chechens and Polish society was the question of diet. Chechens living in the asylum reception and residential centres regularly complained about the food prepared in the cafeterias or supplied by outside caterers. It either did not suit their tastes (particularly their children's), did not meet their cultural dietary requirements (although officially no pork is served in the cafeterias, not all residents believed that this was the case, particularly in the case of processed meats like sausages), or they refused to eat meat not butchered in the Islamic manner. We often heard from our interviewees that their children were going hungry, and they themselves had lost weight since their arrival – one man claimed to have lost 16kg. They frequently spent the cash allowance granted to families for every school-age child, ostensibly for school supplies, on food for their families or other necessities. The vast majority stated that they would prefer to receive cash allowances or foodstuffs in lieu of cafeteria food so that the Chechen women could prepare food for their own families.

Nonetheless, a 50-year-old man with refugee status, a former militant and a respected leader in the community, summarised the situation as follows: "The

14 According to a report of the World Health Organisation (WHO), "The general health status of the people in the North Caucasus republics still compares unfavourably to the Russian Federation average. Due to the collapse of the health system, access to health care is limited and the quality of health services is poor throughout the region" (WHO 2006: 1). WHO's activities in Chechnya focused on interventions in the following areas of particular concern: maternal and child health, HIV/AIDS, tuberculosis, mental health services and psychosocial rehabilitation (ibid).

15 See e.g. Rozumek 2003.

biggest problem is not the cafeteria food. It's the matter of health care. People are depressed, traumatised, and poor health care only worsens what they have already experienced. A sick person cannot function." It is remarkable that in their interviews, our Polish respondents rarely drew attention to the poor physical and mental health status of their clients, as if they did not notice or dismissed it. In fact, this is perhaps the key problem of this group of refugees, requiring well-planned intervention.

Women and Gender

The narrative of cultural dissonance, particularly when told by Polish respondents, was frequently highly gendered. We encountered a number of different opinions on the social status and role of Chechen women. It was commonly assumed by Polish respondents that Chechen women are of an inferior social status to men, their role is to stay at home and look after the children, and they are at risk of domestic violence. However, the reality is more complex, and appears to have been deeply affected both by years of Communist rule and more recently by the experiences of war and exile.

Issa Adger-Adajew, a Chechen refugee intellectual and ethnographer living in Poland, notes that although the Chechen social system can be described as patriarchal, there are what appear to be traces of a matriarchal past in some Chechen myths and customs, and in any case: "The position of women in the patriarchal Chechen society is exceptionally high, guaranteed by law, tradition and upbringing in the family. A man's relations with women are shaped in childhood through the cult of the mother. A son cannot go to war or on a dangerous expedition if he does not obtain his mother's blessing. (...) The two most precious beings in a man's life are his mother and his older sister. (...) The mother is the guardian of the family hearth (*c'en nana* – "mother of the fire"); the father – the head of the family. The grandfather is the patriarch, head and founder of the lineage" (Adger-Adajew 2006: 177–78).

Adger-Adajew also notes that among the differences between Chechen *adat* (customary law) and Islamic Shari'a law (although the two have co-existed to varying degrees in the region from as early as the 12th Century), is the superior position of women in the *adat* – including the requirement of a woman's explicit consent to marriage and her freedom in the choice of a marriage partner (Adger-

Adajew 2006: 199). Although as a native ethnographer writing after the war, his is perhaps an idealised portrayal of Chechen society; nonetheless, ideas about proper Chechen etiquette and social relations and their strict requirements featured prominently in our respondents' interviews, showing that they are very much current in society – and perhaps more self-consciously so following the years of attempted Chechen nation-building and self-definition. The rights and obligations of persons are determined not only by gender, but also by age and marital status. Women's status, like that of men, rises with age and marriage. Most Chechen respondents agreed that the requirements of proper comportment were difficult on the individual – regardless of gender – but that this was a burden they said they gladly shouldered, as integral to their identity as *nokh-chii,* Chechens.

Adger-Adajew does not mention cultural ideas about appropriate dress and modesty, but these were very much in evidence among Chechens in Poland. The Chechen dress code for women, however, differs slightly from the *hijab* observed by Muslim women in other parts of the world. A married Chechen woman should cover her head with a scarf, although the scarf is usually tied behind the head, leaving the neck free. Some women replace the scarf with a symbolic headband, because the most important part of the head to cover is the front, just above the forehead. A woman should dress modestly, but this does not necessarily mean covering up all her skin and disguising the shape of her body. The important thing is that she should wear a skirt or dress, but never trousers. Arms, necks, and lower legs are often left uncovered and there does not appear to be a taboo against this. Out of all the women in our sample, only one was dressed in trousers, and she said that she often suffered harassment from Chechen men for this reason. The women in our sample with higher education (but also a number of others, including former militants' wives) did not cover their heads, but did wear skirts. Many people, particularly more religious men, noted feeling very uncomfortable when seeing scantily clad women in warmer weather or in the media, but this discomfort was greatest when they were with their families. Modesty and shame were *relational* qualities that emphasised relative social standing and helped to ease social interaction within the Chechen community, but most Chechens did not believe that they would come in the way of their interactions with Poles.

However, as Tishkov notes, most Chechens had lived most of their lives under civil, socialist law, and education and work had been accessible to both men and women (Tishkov 2004: 162–63). All but one of our female respondents and all the women in the husband/wife pairs had completed at least the minimum level of secondary education required by the Soviet state; the remaining one woman, a determined 46-year-old grandmother who was heading her family and trying to join her husband in Austria, had been home-schooled by her mother. Many had vocational training in addition to their high school diplomas. An additional 5 of our 23 female respondents had higher education, with all but one of them arriving between 2000 and 2003 and representing most of the "long-stayers" in our study, who had been more successful at integrating in Poland. Two-thirds of our female respondents and women in husband/wife pairs had worked outside the home in Chechnya or elsewhere in the Russian Federation, in occupations including medicine (paediatric surgery, gynaecology, nursing), accounting, public administration, teaching, dancing, shopkeeping, baking/cooking, and tailoring.

Our study indicated that where no adult male was available to head a household, women (including widowed grandmothers, mothers or divorcees) tried to provide for their families with equal – sometimes greater – determination. This is not uncommon in other refugee situations around the world, where men feel the loss of social status more acutely than women and are less able to cope with this, while women, directly responsible for caring for the family, tend to be more able to practically adapt (see e.g. Al-Ali 2002). This was noted in a group interview with language teachers from an NGO offering Polish lessons to Chechens, who had had a chance to get to know their clients in a more sympathetic and familiar context. They sensed that there had been a depreciation of the role of the Chechen male. He, who had hitherto been the breadwinner of the family or even a militant, a freedom fighter, lost that social role, along with the pride and status that it conferred when he became a refugee. This could be one reason, they felt, why many Chechen men were unable to find a place for themselves in Poland. On the other hand, Polish respondents perceived an "emancipation" of Chechen women, as the ones who took over the initiative in the family and struggled to make ends meet. One language teacher declared that the most successful refugees were the single mothers. They thought the reasons for this were likely to be their observation of Polish women, and their wartime experiences, in which women whose husbands went to fight, were murdered or went missing, took responsibility for their families. One of them declared that "Chechen women are fighters", they are more involved, and they feel the need to "build a home wherever they are." Social workers and NGO employees shared this opinion that Chechen women were more open to integrative influences. Indeed, one NGO worker stated that the greatest "integration potential" lay with Chechen women who ran away from their husbands, since they break away from a culture in which men have the deciding voice and who dominate family life. It is worth taking advantage of this fact, she claimed, when planning integration activities for Chechen refugees.

A recent study of gender relations among Chechens in a Czech refugee camp, Zastavka near Brno, similarly suggested that these could be adjusted and renegotiated during conflict and in exile (Szczepanikova 2005). The author found that while ideals of masculinity and femininity may have remained unchanged, in practice the period of conflict had led to a greater public role for women already in Chechnya, while men played a greater role in childcare and household duties in the camp in the Czech Republic, for example. Nonetheless, she found that "the atmosphere of mistrust, powerlessness, and the feeling of being under constant oppressive control by the camp staff also intensified (if not to say stimulated) conflicts in the refugee families and made refugee women more vulnerable to violence" (Szczepanikova 2005: 295). Being far away from traditional protectors such as brothers and male kin also decreased their bargaining power vis-à-vis their husbands.

In Poland, too, we learned of a few incidents of domestic violence or violence against women living alone in the residential centres. However, the centre personnel tended to prefer to let the elected, exclusively male Chechen "elders" deal with such issues – indeed, it would often be the female residents who brought persistent cases of (often alcohol-related) domestic violence to the attention of an elder, through their own channel – his wife. The elders had little power except persuasion and perhaps religious authority to enforce a halt to the violence, however, and formal complaints could not be lodged without the cooperation of the victims, who usually declined out of fear or shame. So far, this issue has not been dealt with in any concerted manner by the Polish authorities, although it is clearly a sensitive matter in which trust and cultural understanding are crucial to achieving an effective solution, one in which the Chechen community itself must take centre stage.

There are other indications, however, that "emancipation" of women may not quite be proceeding in the way the Polish NGO workers imagined. Szczepanikova suggests that Chechen women in exile still idealise "the strong association of women with the domestic sphere and caring for the family remains crucial in their perceptions of ideal womanhood" (Szczepanikova 2005: 295). This could be a response to the chaos and uprooting that they have experienced, and a desire to return to an idealised past. Similarly, men's assertions of their dominance may be a way to recover their masculinity, threatened by the disempowering conditions of exile – and this need not necessarily have oppressive consequences if it is a cultural expectation. Conversely, in situations where women behaved in ways that might have led Poles to see them as "emancipated" – such as choosing to wear trousers, or running away from their husbands, paradoxically they were more vulnerable to abuse because they broke the rules of their community and alienated themselves from its support structures[16]. Indeed, in Poland there have been several such cases, the subject of discussion in refugee assistance NGOs in recent times. Seeing a woman – usually a single mother with children – taking steps to integrate in Polish society (for example by becoming friendly with Polish staff) can result in negative feelings, perhaps motivated by envy, among her compatriots. At best, she may be verbally abused (labelled a "prostitute" or symbolically expelled from the community as "not a Chechen") or at worst, as in one recent case, even raped. While it might appear that the "integrative potential" of such women is high, it may be simply that they are more visibly seeking assistance from their Polish helpers because they can no longer turn to other Chechens for help or protection. In other words, where gender relations may be facing a degree of flux, as is to be expected in a situation of conflict or displacement, it is necessary to avoid outsider assumptions and to understand the meaning of particular actions from *within* a refugee community. Particular delicacy is necessary to avoid increasing the vulnerability of certain people, like single women, through well-meaning gestures which may be misinterpreted.

Conclusion

This article has examined three areas important for successful integration of a refugee population: livelihoods and economic adaptation, physical and mental well-being, and adaptation to cultural norms in the host society (seen here through the prism of gender roles). All of these have been shaped by historical forces and been giving cultural meaning by both Polish and Chechen respondents, and thus should be seen, in a broad sense, as cultural factors. The dissonance in interpreta-

16 This situation occurs in other communities of immigrants from honour-bound societies and may be similarly misinterpreted. In her work among Pakistani immigrants in the United Kingom, Kaveri Harriss shows that a woman who breaks social norms to work long hours outside the home, for example, paradoxically becomes more isolated from potential allies who no longer wish to associate with her, weakening her position when she faces conflict with her husband (personal communication).

tion of these cultural meanings is a key factor in the frequent mistrust between refugees and hosts. Their Polish helpers were convinced that cultural aspects of integration (e.g. learning the language and customs) are a solid basis for long-term integration and life in Poland perhaps did not see the immediate practical difficulties of Chechens. They tried to encourage Chechens to greater motivation, a greater role for women, and language lessons, while the Chechens were increasingly desperate and disappointed, claiming that despite their greatest efforts they were unable to function in this country without their primary needs of housing and stable employment, with a baggage of physical and mental ailments, and feeling as if their claims to refugee status were not given sufficient attention. Many of them thus turned away from the Polish state and attempted to survive on their own terms – preferably, beyond the borders of the country. We believe that, in order to ensure a successful basis for Chechen refugees' integration in Poland, both pragmatic and cultural challenges must be met. For the latter especially, common ground and a common vocabulary of cultural meanings and values must be developed, so that refugees and hosts interpret each others' actions correctly and learn to trust one another.

Bibliography

Adger-Adajew, Issa (2006): Kamienie Mówią. Dzieje i Kultura Czeczenów [The Stones Speak. History and Culture of the Chechens]. Warsaw.

Al-Ali, Nadia (2002): Loss of Status or New Opportunities? Gender Relations and Transnational Ties among Bosnian Refugees. In: Bryceson, Deborah/Vuorella, Ulla (eds.): The Transnational Family. New European Frontiers and Global Networks. Oxford/New York.

Daniel, E. Valentine/Knudsen, John Chr. (1995): Introduction. In: Daniel, E. Valentine/ Knudsen, John Chr. (eds.): Mistrusting Refugees. Berkeley/Los Angeles/ London, 1–12.

Department of Social Policy of the Mazovian Voivodship Office (2007): Raport z realizacji w 2006 roku indywidualnych programów integracji (IPI) na terenie województwa mazowieckiego [Report on the Realisation in 2006 of Individual Integration Programmes (IIP) on the Territory of the Mazovian Voivodship]. Warsaw.

Dziennik Polski Podhalański (2007): Zdzierali z rodaków [They Ripped Off Their Compatriots]. 22 February 2007, 1/3.

Gazeta Wyborcza (2006): Warszawscy taksówkarze przemycali Czeczenów [Warsaw Taxi-drivers Smuggled Chechens]. 12 August 2006, 3.

Herman, Judith Lewis (1997): Trauma and Recovery. The Aftermath of Violence. From Domestic Abuse to Political Terror. New York.

Human Rights Center "Memorial" (2005): The Chechen Republic. Consequences of "Chechenization" of the Conflict. Moscow. Available at: http://www.memo.ru/eng/memhrc/texts/6chechen.shtml.
De Jong, Kaz/van der Kam, Saskia/Ford, Nathan/Hargreaves, Sally/ van Oosten, Richard/Cunningham, Debbie/Boots, Gerry/Andrault, Elodie/ Kleber, Rolf (2004): The Trauma of Ongoing Conflict and Displacement in Chechnya. Quantitative Assessment of Living Conditions, and Psychosocial and General Health Status Among War Displaced in Chechnya and Ingushetia. Amsterdam.
Kosowicz, Agnieszka/Maciejko, Anna (eds.) (2007): Integracja Uchodźców w Polsce w Liczbach [Integration of Refugees in Poland in Numbers]. Warsaw.
Maciejko, Anna/Olszewska, Zuzanna (2007): Preintegracja i Integracja Czeczenów w Polsce. Rzeczywistość i Rekomendacje [Preintegration and Integration of Chechens in Poland. Reality and Recommendations]. Warsaw.
Medical Foundation for the Care of Victims of Torture (2004): Rape and Other Torture in the Chechnya Conflict. Documented Evidence from Asylum Seekers Arriving in the United Kingdom. London.
Murthy, R. Srinivasa/Lakshminarayana, Rashmi (2006): Mental Health Consequences of War. A Brief Review of Research Findings. In: World Psychiatry, 5, 1, 25–30.
Polska Agencja Prasowa (PAP) (2008): Pogranicze w Ogniu [The Border in Flames]. 9 January 2008.
Rozumek, Martin (2003): Note for the File. Current Situation of Chechen Asylum Seekers in Czech Republic, Poland and Austria. Prague.
Szczepanikova, Alice (2005): Gender Relations in a Refugee Camp. A Case of Chechens Seeking Asylum in the Czech Republic. In: Journal of Refugee Studies, 18, 3, 281–98.
Tishkov, Valery (2004): Chechnya. Life in a War-Torn Society. Berkeley, Los Angeles, London.
World Health Organisation (2006): WHO Disaster and Preparedness Response Programme in the North Caucasus, Russian Federation. Annual Report 2006. Moscow.

Chechen Migrants on the Polish Labour Market: Challenges and Solutions

Emilia Małys

Introduction

The influx of Chechen asylum seekers to Poland and other EU member states is a relatively new phenomenon and experience for the receiving countries, both for its authorities and societies. It is also a big challenge in terms of national integration policies to work out a comprehensive and effective set of legal and practical solutions aiming at a successful integration of Chechens into their societies. There is an ongoing discussion at the EU-level concerning integration strategies, the nature of integration programmes, and the character of integration measures, whether they should be obligatory or not. Some member states considered their integration policies as not sufficiently effective and called for a revision. Poland, however, is just at the very beginning of creating the foundations of its integration policy, an endeavour which was actually motivated by a significant influx of forced migrants from Chechnya. There are many definitions of integration, although no legal definition exists in the Polish legislation. Generally speaking, integration is a bilateral and long-term process of mutual adaptation of both migrants and the receiving society from an economic, social, cultural and civil perspective. According to one definition, integration may be regarded as effective and successful if a migrant has a good command of the language of the receiving country, a job in line with his qualifications, decent housing conditions in a regular district, if he is financially independent and has a clean criminal record (Grzymała-Moszczynska 2000: 24). The economic and labour market inclusion is the starting point and crucial stage of the entire integration process. Forced migrants who are unemployed and not able to fulfill their own and their families' basic needs will not participate in any further stages of the integration process. Therefore, the primary aim of this article is to present the situation of Chechen migrants, so far the biggest group of forced migrants in Poland, on the labour market and to take a closer look at the major barriers and obstacles that impede their full and active participation in the labour market. The situation of Chechen women including single mothers has also been examined. Finally, I would like to suggest possible solutions and recommendations which, in my opinion, could improve, to some extent, the current and far from satisfactory situation of Chechen migrants on the Polish labour market. As regards methodology and information sources, I based my knowledge on the following information sources: The first source of information were my own observations and impressions collected within a five-year professional experience of cooperation with Chechen asylum seekers as well as on the basis of private acquaintances with Chechen families. The second type of information source were interviews (10) with Chechen migrants, both men and women, who have been living in Poland (Warsaw and surroundings) for a longer time (3–7 years) on the basis of either refugee status or tolerated stay permit. Another source of practical and useful information were representatives of NGOs acting on behalf of forced migrants, who are very involved and active in initiating and conducting actions aiming at improving the migrants' situation on the labour market. The last sources of information were studies, researches and handbooks published over recent years, mainly by practitioners and experts of migration research centres.

Characteristics of the Migration Flows of Chechens into Poland and Secondary Movements

A significant increase of the number of Chechens coming to Poland was observed in 2000, after the second Chechen-Russian war had outburst in autumn 1999. War activities made people leave their country of origin and look for protection, in the first place, in the neighbouring republics (Ingushetia, Dagestan) or geographically close countries (Georgia, Azerbaijan, Turkey). Many Chechen migrants had been living there for some time before they arrived in Poland or other EU countries. A significant increase of the number of Chechen asylum seekers in Poland can be observed when comparing the period of 1994–1999 with 434 asylum applications lodged by citizens of the Russian Federation with the period of 2000–2004 with almost 18 thousand applications lodged (only applications counted, one application covering all family members i.e. spouses and minor children). Since 2000, asylum seekers of Chechen nationality have remained the biggest nationality group seeking international protection in Poland. During the period 1992–2007, Russian Federation citizens lodged over 37 thousand asylum applications (out of a total of 65.6 thousand applications) and about 90% of those were of Chechen nationality[1]. The common travel route for the majority of Chechens leads through the territory of Russia and Belarus to the Polish border crossing point in Teraspol (Brest on the Belarusian side). People fleeing from the Chechen Republic are regarded as forced migrants looking for international protection, in contrast to economic migrants from other third countries (e.g. Ukraine, Vietnam). At the very beginning, geographic vicinity and the perception of Poland as a democratic country, with a similar historical experience, were the basic factors motivating Chechens to choose Poland. However, relatively low recognition rates and the lack of perspectives for settlement and a decent life were the reasons why Poland became increasingly considered as a transit country on the way to the western EU countries. After Poland and its southern neighbours, the Czech Republic and Slovakia, had joined the EU in May 2004, possibilities for secondary migration to richer countries were limited by the EU law which stipulated that a member state was responsible for examining an asylum application lodged by a third country national on its territory (so called Dublin II Regulation)[2]. In accordance with the basic principle laid down in the above Regulation, a member state responsible for examining an asylum application is actually the state in which an asylum seeker lodged his first asylum application. Since most Chechens arrive in the EU via Poland and file their first asylum applications there, Poland becomes the state responsible for examining their applications. In case they decide to continue their travel further west or south, the other member states are entitled to apply the Dublin procedure as a result of which Chechens may be sent back to Poland. At the beginning, there were many misunderstandings regarding the application of this procedure

1 Statistical data from the Office for Aliens.

2 Council Regulation (EC) No 343/2003 of 18 February 2003, OJ L50/10.

towards Chechen asylum seekers who felt trapped in Poland. They were accusing Polish authorities of denying them the possibility of leading a normal life in other EU countries. They were convinced that Polish authorities had been requesting other countries to send Chechens back to Poland, while the opposite was the case. Nevertheless, a part of Chechen migrants who had decided to take this risk was finally allowed to stay in other EU member states due to family or humanitarian reasons. Since the reception and living conditions as well as the integration assistance in other EU countries is at an incomparably higher level, more and more Chechens try to reach these countries. The additional pull factor is a well-established network of contacts and family ties e.g. in Austria, Belgium, France and Germany. This tendency was even strengthened after Poland had joined the Schengen zone at the end of 2007, the internal borders were removed, and physical movement facilitated. Due to some rumors about closing the external border for asylum seekers as well, the number of Chechens increased significantly prior to this event. Most of them went on to western EU countries, without waiting for the asylum decision in Poland to be taken, where in most cases they had repeatedly applied for asylum. A large number of them will be sent back to Poland on the basis of the Dublin proceedings. Some of them, knowing that the residence card issued on the basis of the tolerated stay permit entitles to free movement within the Schengen zone for up to 3 months[3], decided to wait for the final decision in Poland. The number of Chechen secondary migrations may decrease, at least temporarily, due to the upcoming amendment of the Act on granting Protection to Aliens which is to introduce a new form of protection. This form of subsidiary protection will entitle to integration assistance and, in most cases, should be granted to Chechen asylum seekers who at present are granted a tolerated stay permit and are not entitled to such assistance.

Legal Framework for Chechen Migrants to Stay and Work in Poland

Forms of Protection Granted to Chechen Asylum Seekers

Chechen asylum seekers are usually offered one of two forms of aliens' protection. The first form is international protection – refugee status – granted on the basis of the criteria set out in the Geneva Convention of 1951, and the second is

3 Art. 21 of the Implementation Convention to the Schengen Treaty of 14 June 1985 (OJ L.00. 239.19).

a domestic form of protection granted on the basis of the Polish Act on Protection for Aliens[4] and is called tolerated stay permit. The latter is a protection against expulsion to a country of origin where an alien could be deprived of life, exposed to torture, inhuman or degrading treatment or punishment, forced labour, unfair trial, or punished without a legal basis (art. 2–7 of the European Convention on Human Rights and Fundamental Freedoms). The majority of Chechen asylum seekers are no longer considered by the Polish authorities as refugees who have a well-founded fear of persecution because of their nationality or ethnicity, but qualified as victims of civil war, which affects all Chechens unless they can establish that due to their activity they are put at a particular risk of grave human rights violations and persecuted on an individual basis. In consequence, the civilian population of Chechen origin is usually granted a tolerated stay permit. During the period of 1992–2007, about 1.8 thousand refugee statuses (out of a total of 3.1 thousand) were granted to citizens of the Russian Federation (almost all of Chechen nationality). The tolerated stay permit has been granted from 2003, and during the period of 2003–2006 about 4.6 thousand of tolerated stay permits (out of a total of 8 thousand) were issued to Russian citizens, the vast majority of whom were of Chechen origin[5]. Persons granted refugee status are entitled to reside in Poland for an undetermined period of time, but the residence permit is valid for two years and is renewed at the refugee's request. The validity of the residence permit for foreigners granted a tolerated stay permit is one year and is renewed every year at their written request. Recognized refugees can apply for permanent residence after 5 years of interrupted stay in Poland, persons with a tolerated stay permit after 10 years. After 5 subsequent years of residing in Poland on the basis of a permanent residence, a refugee can apply for Polish citizenship. The situation of migrants with refugee status and migrants with tolerated stay permits seems comparable since both groups enjoy the right to reside in Poland, work or establish own business activities, the right to education, medical care and social assistance. However, there are some significant differences between these two forms of aliens' protection. Recognized refugees, unlike persons granted tolerated stay, are provided with the Geneva travel document enabling them to travel abroad. However, as mentioned before, the situation of forced migrants with tolerated stay permit has improved in this respect after Poland joined the

4 Act on granting Protection to Aliens within the territory of the Republic of Poland of June 13, 2003 (Journal of Laws 2003, No 128, item 1176, with further amendments).

5 Statistical data from the Office for Aliens

Schengen zone. The second difference resides in the fact that persons with tolerated stay permits do not have the right to integration assistance, which means that they are not covered by the annual Individual Integration Programme (IIP) and do not receive monthly financial assistance. They are only entitled to apply for social allowances on the same basis as Polish citizens. Once the asylum procedure is completed they have to leave the refugee centres and are left on their own. They are not provided with accommodation and if they do not have a job they are not able to rent a flat and stay in Poland. As a result, Chechen migrants renounce the tolerated stay permits and re-apply for refugee status in order to stay in the refugee centers where at least accommodation and food are provided. Lack of financial support for Chechen migrants with tolerated stay is regarded as a push factor to leave Poland and is criticized by NGOs which act on behalf of refugees. Fortunately, as it was mentioned, the situation will improve due to the amendment of the Act on granting Protection to Aliens. One of the crucial changes consists in the introduction of a new form of protection to the Polish system of aliens' protection, that is, subsidiary protection. It will be applied as a protection complementary to refugee status. In practice, it should be granted to Chechen asylum seekers who at present are granted tolerated stay permits. Asylum applicants for both granted refugee status and subsidiary protection will be entitled to one year IIP and financial assistance. This will improve the material situation of many Chechens and maybe encourage some of them to stay in Poland. Apart from the new form of protection, the legislator decided to keep the tolerated stay permit as an additional institution of national law which could be applied in relation to foreigners who do not meet the criteria of the two described forms of protection but could not be sent back to their countries of origin.

Individual Integration Programmes

The right to integration assistance is a special entitlement granted to recognized refugees which aims at supporting their integration process into the Polish society. Persons with tolerated stay permits are not provided with integration assistance, and this is a serious deficiency of the present aliens' protection system. This shortcoming will be corrected under the new legislation, and foreigners granted subsidiary protection will also be included. The legal basis for granting integration assistance to refugees in Poland is provided in two acts: the Act on Social Assistance[6] and the Regulation of the Ministry of Labour and Social Policy

6 Act of 12 March 2004 on social assistance (JO, No. 64, item 593, with further amendments).

on granting assistance to refugees[7]. The integration assistance is carried out in the form of IIP, conducted by District Family Support Centres (DFSC) and coordinated by the provincial governors. There is no legal definition of "integration" but we can learn from the above regulation that the level and effectiveness of the integration process is assessed on the basis of language education and of a functioning professional and social integration. Integration may be regarded as effective if refugees speak Polish, work and are economically independent, have established contacts with the local community and participate in the social, cultural, and public life. The duration of the IIP is up to 12 months. The integration assistance includes, first of all, financial assistance granted in the form of a cash subsistence allowance intended to cover expenses connected with housing charges, the purchase of food, clothing, footwear and personal hygiene products as well as learning the Polish language. The allowance is paid monthly and its amount depends on objective criteria such as the number of family members and the period of the programme as well as on subjective criteria i.e. the refugee's individual situation. The assistance also includes health insurance contribution payments to the National Health Fund and specialized vocational guidance services. Specialized guidance means mainly legal, psychological and family counseling services. The IIP is established between a refugee and a relevant DFSC and has the form of a contract signed by the two above-mentioned parties. The contract specifies the level, scope and form of assistance adequate to a refugee's family situation and the obligations both of the respective DFSC and the refugee. Among the main obligations of a refugee are: registration at the place of residence, registration at the relevant labour office at the date determined in the contract, active search for a job, participation in Polish language courses, cooperation and contact with the programme coordinator at agreed dates. If a refugee fails to fulfill the obligations agreed upon in the IIP, assistance may be suspended for a determined period of time and reinstated in case of cessation of the prerequisites based on which the assistance has been suspended (Ministry of Labour and Social Policy 2005: 8–11). The major disadvantage of IIP is its short period of duration which is not enough to guarantee an effective integration. After completion of the IIP, a vast majority of refugees are still not independent and face basic problems such as lack of accommodation or job and poor command of the Polish language. Another disadvantage is the exclusion of persons granted tolerated stay permits from the scope

7 Regulation of Ministry of Labour and Social Policy of 29 September 2005 on granting assistance to refugees (JO No. 201, item 1669).

of integration assistance. Anther significant shortcoming of the integration system in Poland is the insufficient number of social workers responsible for carrying out the IIP. Furthermore, it should be added that upon completion of the IIP, recognized refugees are entitled to welfare benefits on the same terms and conditions as Polish citizens. This assistance is also available to migrants granted tolerated stay permits. According to research data from 2006, in three voivodships it is difficult to unambiguously assess the efficiency of IIP in relation to Chechen refugees because in most cases they decided to leave Poland just after completion of the IIP or even prior to its completion, unlike refugees of other nationalities e.g. from Belarus or African countries (Samoraj/Bieniecki 2007: 99–100).

Right to Work and other Related Rights

Pursuant to article 87 of the Act on the Promotion of Employment and the Institutions of the Labour Market[8], foreigners both granted refugee status and tolerated stay permits are exempted from the obligation to have work permits and allowed to take up employment on the same basis as Polish citizens. The above two categories of migrants can work on the basis of employment or civil contracts and have the same rights as Polish citizens. They can work without any restrictions unless specific provisions require the possession of Polish citizenship (e.g. the post of a judge, prosecutor, official, or employee of a security company). The situation of asylum seekers is different. In general, they are not allowed to work during the procedure – with one exception: Asylum seekers can have earlier access to the labour market in case they have not been issued a decision (in the first instance) within one year after the asylum application was submitted and if they did not cause this delay. The second condition is that they need to have a work permit. In practice, this provision is not favourable for asylum seekers and remains a dead letter of the law. I have not heard of one single case of an employer having initiated the procedure on a work permit for a Chechen asylum seeker. However, Chechen asylum seekers, despite the prohibition, usually work illegally and take up casual jobs in the agriculture or construction sectors. Also, some employers do not pay attention to this prohibition and recruit Chechens even in the vicinity of refugee centres. The situation will definitely improve in this respect because according to the draft of the amended act, asylum seekers will be allowed to work without necessarily having a work permit if the first decision was not issued with-

8 Act on Promotion of Employment and Institutions of Labour Market (JO No 99, item 1001, with further amendments).

in a 6-month period counting from the date the asylum application was lodged. The delay must not have been caused by the asylum seeker. This is a clear improvement, opening up the possibility to accept a legal employment while remaining within the procedure for more than 6 months. Forced migrants granted refugee status or tolerated stay permits and their family members enjoy the same rights as Polish citizens, based on the constitution, the labour code, and labour legislation in general. This applies, among others, to all mechanisms of labour protection, the principles of labour law, the right to minimum salary, safe and hygienic working conditions, paid leaves etc. One of the labour principles laid down in the labour code is the prohibition of discrimination in work relations with regard to, among others, race, nationality, ethnic origin, or religion. It means that migrants with refugee status or tolerated stay permits should be treated equally as other employees, in particular in the sphere of recruitment process, work and wage conditions, promotion and access to vocational trainings. Taking into account what has been mentioned above, the foreigner is entitled to question the decision on refusal to offer him/her a job if the grounds for the employer's decision were not related to the migrant's qualifications but based exclusively on the migrant's origin or his/her legal status. In such a case, the alien concerned can file a complaint with the labour court and require for a remedy which must not be less then the minimum wage. It is worth adding that non-discrimination provisions apply only to employment contracts and exclude civil ones (Gracz 2006: 31–36). In accordance with the mentioned Act on the Promotion of Employment and Institutions of the Labour Market, recognized refugees and persons with tolerated stay permits, after being registered with the labour office, are entitled to: unemployment benefits, information on vacancies by the labour office, free-of- charge trainings, professional assistance in finding an adequate employment offer; furthermore, they may be appointed to perform intervention or public work, professional vocational advising, or participate in classes of the Labour Club. Finally, they are entitled to a free-of-charge medical insurance premium, which means free medical care, and to single financial assistance to set up a business activity. Asylum seekers who were granted the right to work are entitled only to services of professional advisors and offers from labour offices but are excluded from the right to apply for unemployment or other types of benefits. Apart from the above-mentioned rights, registered unemployed persons are obliged to appear once a month at the local labour office to confirm their readiness and ability to take up a job, if available and in line with their qualifications. Pursuant to the 2004 Act on the Freedom of Business Activity[9], foreigners granted both refugee status and tolerated stay are entitled to set up and perform a business activity on the same terms as Polish citizens. There are no restrictions in regard to the choice of the form of business activity.

Obstacles to Effective Participation of Chechens in the Labour Market

When analysing the situation on the labour market in the context of potential chances and possibilities of Chechen workers we should first look at their educational and professional background and consider how the professional skills and qualifications they already possess could be best used on the labour market. The most popular education backgrounds of Chechen men are related to the oil industry or the economy. Among the most popular professions performed by Chechens in their country of origin are: construction worker, mechanic, and driver. Chechens are famous for constructing and renovating houses. One of my Chechen respondents was praising the traditional Chechen techniques of building houses. This is why many of them take up casual jobs in the construction sector. Unfortunately, they are not offered employment contracts but are rather treated as seasonal and cheap workers and offered minimal wages. Besides, a lot of Chechen men used to practice sport professionally and work as bodyguards or security guards protecting governmental offices or other institutions. As regards Chechen women, because of the cultural approach, they usually do not work professionally, but take care of children and the household. All kinds of house work, cooking as well as taking care of children and elder people are natural for Chechen women and can be useful on the labour market, especially for those women who have never worked professionally or do not have education. If they used to work in Chechnya, they were usually teachers, nurses, saleswomen, dressmakers, seamstresses. In Poland, women with a teacher's experience could try to find a job as a Russian language teacher in public or private language schools since the Russian language seems to be more and more popular. Taking into account the abovementioned qualifications of Chechen migrants and the current situation on the labour market, with staff shortages in many sectors, especially construction, agriculture, textile industry, trade, gastronomy and catering, we may conclude at a

9 Act on Freedom of Business Activity (JO 2007, No 155, item 1095).

first glance that it should not be a problem to find adequate jobs for both Chechen men and women. In fact, the situation is more complex. There are many factors affecting the situation, from the approach of society, employers, and authorities towards forced migrants and their needs, to objective and independent factors restricting the possibilities for migrants to take up an employment (like invalidity, diseases, psychological problems, lack of education or qualifications, single mothers/widows with numerous children) as well as the cultural conditions and the migrants' approach itself. A mixture of the above-mentioned factors may sometimes create a barrier hard to overcome, and the only solution is to look for a dignified life somewhere else.

Prejudices and Stereotypes

Unlike many other EU countries, Poland is not a multicultural society, and the number of foreigners living and working in Poland is still very low. Polish employers are not used to recruit foreign workers unless special qualifications or foreign languages are needed. Due to staff shortages the situation has been changing dynamically and more and more foreign workers are being employed. Naturally, foreigners from western countries are perceived differently than those coming from eastern countries, which are regarded as poorer and less democratic. Migrants from eastern countries are often treated as cheap labour force and are subject to discrimination and exploitation practices. Chechen migrants are usually included in this category. Chechens complain that Polish employers are reluctant to employ them because of some existing prejudices and stereotypes. When they are looking for a job on their own without assistance of a Polish citizen and they are speaking on the phone with eastern accent, in most cases, they are perceived rather negatively and with suspicion. My Chechen respondents complain that such phone conversations are usually very short and they are answered that the offer is not valid any more. On the other hand, sometimes it may be true that Chechens have the irresistible impression that employers are afraid to employ them and do not want to have anything to do with them. In fact, it is a clever excuse which protects employers from being accused of discrimination on grounds of nationality. In most cases, Chechens are judged just by their eastern accent and regarded as Russian citizens or citizens of other post-Soviet countries. When employers are aware that they are Russian citizens but of Chechen nationality, they might be confronted with a mixture of prejudices, partly related to the country of origin (Russia) and partly to their Chechen nationality. Some employers are afraid of potential problems with the mafia in case of any misunderstandings, while others have a more ambivalent image of Chechens. They are perceived as victims of Russian domination fighting for independence on the one hand, and in view of well-known terrorist attacks in Russia, as potential criminals and terrorists on the other.

Lack of Knowledge

Lack of sufficient knowledge creates a space for prejudices, stereotypes, and false convictions and may be at the root of discrimination practices and as a result constitute a serious obstacle to equal and full participation of migrants in the labour market. The problem with the lack of satisfactory knowledge concerns both Polish employers and Chechen workers. Many employers are reluctant to employ Chechens because they do not have sufficient knowledge on their legal status and the rights linked to this status. Very often, employers do not even know that refugees and persons with tolerated stay permits have free access to the labour market and do not need to have work permits to perform work on the territory of Poland. On the other hand, Chechens are also not well informed on elementary issues such as where and how to look for a job, about the current situation on the labour market. Most of my Chechen respondents were looking for a job through the network of their relatives or Polish friends. The main reason was that their direct efforts to find a job e.g. by searching in newspapers and calling employers had been unsuccessful. Some of them did not know any other methods or found them ineffective. One of my Chechen interlocutors, who had been living in Poland for eight years, was very well informed on the job opportunities and on how to look for a job, which was partially the result of his long residence in Poland, but also his resourcefulness and determination played a considerable role. During the first time of his stay, after having obtained a tolerated stay permit, he was looking for a job through the internet and responding to the selected job offers posted on different job websites. All his application letters remained unanswered and he was not invited to any interview. He did not give up and finally found a job through a temporary job agency. Afterwards, he changed workplaces many times, once he worked illegally, another time legally. At present, he has a well-paid and legal job in the construction sector. The obligation to spread information on available vacancies and vocational courses rests with the local labour offices. However, according to my Chechen respondents and NGO representatives, they do not seem to be prepared for this role since most of the clerks working in these offices do not speak foreign languages and are not provided with adequate training on cultural differences. Besides, Chechens complain that labour office employees are simply not committed and interested in effectively helping them. In addition, Chechens are not aware of their rights and obligations at work. They do not know about the basic rules of the labour law, disadvantages of unregistered work, and how to defend themselves against dishonest employers. They are also not aware that discrimination on grounds of nationality or ethnicity is prohibited, and therefore are not making use of their rights. It is rather natural that the level of knowledge and experience should increase simultaneously with the length of residence in Poland, but of course this is not the only indicator. One of my Chechen respondents is a positive exception, and his level of awareness is related not only to his long residence in Poland but also to solid education obtained in his country of origin, and personal features. He knows his worker's rights and how to make use of them. He defended his and other workers' rights twice by lodging complaints with the State Labour Inspection.

Unregistered Work and Exploitation

If they succeed to find a job, most Chechens living in Poland usually work in unregistered employments, below their qualifications, and low-paid. This phenomenon is rather not related to the legal status of a migrant. There is not a significant difference between asylum seekers taking up illegal work, migrants with tolerated stay permits, or recognized refugees. The phenomenon of unauthorized employment is a broader problem of the Polish economy, concerning not only forced migrants and foreigners in general but Polish citizens as well, and is strictly connected with high tax burdens and high costs of employment in Poland (so-called extra remuneration costs, i.e. security and medical insurance contributions, contributions to different funds). In order to avoid these additional costs, employers, usually owners of small, often family companies, prefer not to sign any contracts or rather civil contracts instead of employment ones. The sectors most affected with the problem of irregular work are construction, agriculture, and gastronomy. The phenomenon of unregistered work should be treated as pathological and unfavourable, especially for migrants, who are often unaware of the disadvantages of unauthorized work. They are not covered by medical insurance and in case of any accidents at work they are not protected. Furthermore, they are not covered by security insurance schemes and, in the future, will not be entitled to pension rights. The phenomenon of unregistered work is a conspiracy of silence, and both sides of this unwritten contract benefit, although they are not equal partners. Employers are not interested in employing migrants on a legal basis, especially for casual and seasonal work, and migrants decide to take up irregular jobs because employers who are not burdened with extra costs can pay them more than in the case of a legal employment. This was confirmed by my Chechen respondents who were working illegally in the construction sector. One of them was working illegally for a couple of months as the bricklayer's assistant. There were a few more Chechens working with him. When he asked about signing a written contract he was answered that he would be paid 15 zl per one metre, and without a contract 30 zl. According to him, the majority of people working there, including Polish citizens, were working without contracts. For forced migrants, who do not have many perspectives for other types of jobs and need money for maintaining their families, the choice is rather obvious. As mentioned, migrants are not always aware of the fact that illegal employment means lack of legal, social and medical protection and entails certain risks and threats. My interlocutors, employees of NGOs working in the interest of forced migrants, are often informed about cases of dishonest employers and exploitation of migrant workers. The most typical situation is when an employer promises to pay an agreed amount of money and on the payday pays less or sometimes puts the payment off, or does not want to pay at all. My Chechen respondents noticed that, in the construction sector, some subcontractors search for people to take up a job, pay them for the first two to three months and afterwards stop paying regularly and put the payment off for some reasons. The other common practice in this sector is that employers, instead of regular monthly wages, pay their workers so-called "advances" amounting to 100–200 zl. One of my Chechen interlocutors, whom I mentioned in the previous subchapter, was performing different types of work and has a profound professional experience in general and as a construction worker in particular. Once he was working as a site manager on a legal basis. He headed a group of 70 Chechen migrants with tolerated stay permits living in Warsaw and its surroundings. They were supposed to work legally mainly as bricklayers and bricklayers' assistants. He helped them to fill out the personal questionnaires and submitted them to the company's human resource unit. The Chechens were paid only for the first two months but still without the written contracts. Finally, when the employer owed them quite a big sum (wages of all Chechen workers), they felt deceived and wanted to solve this problem by their own methods. My respondent, who felt responsible for this group and wanted to prevent a conflict situation, decided to settle all unpaid wages for his compatriots from his own savings. Subsequently, he lodged a complaint with the State Labour Inspection against his employer. After the first control was conducted by the Inspection and the irregularities were revealed, he recovered his money. This story came to a happy ending only thanks to my respondent's knowledge, intelligence, and courage to defend his and other workers' rights. One of the employees of the NGO mentioned that some Chechen women, in order to avoid a dishonest treatment, had asked for being paid after a day or week, which is rarely accepted by Polish employers (the construction sector might be an exception). According to the experience of NGO employees, not all employers are dishonest by definition and sometimes there might be some misunderstandings regarding payment or other working conditions due to an insufficient command of the Polish language. Another disadvantage of unregistered work is the lack of medical insurance, which is especially risky when performing work in the construction sector. Therefore, Chechen migrants with tolerated stay permits or refugee status working illegally usually get registered with the local labour office in order to receive the status of unemployed and be entitled to medical insurance and free medical care. For recognized refugees entering the integration programme, registration with the labour office is one of their obligations. It is common practice for Polish citizens as well. This is why the official rate of unemployment is higher than it is in reality.

Low Wages and Casual Jobs

Although the situation on the labour market recently changed for the better and, due to staff shortages, employers had to raise wages to attract new or keep present workers, these changes have not been noticeable by Chechen migrants yet. My Chechen interlocutors working in the construction sector admitted that it was not difficult to find a job but the problem is that jobs available are usually physically demanding, low-paid, and casual. One of them was earning 1200 zl (about 350 €) per month working from 7 am to 7 pm. Since forced migrants are not provided with social flats and have to rent a flat at the free market, he was paying 1200 zl per month for a two-room flat. His wage just covered the costs of renting a flat. Without the assistance from family members residing in other EU countries he would not be able to maintain himself and his family. Another Chechen man who has been living in Poland for many years is at present working legally in a car repair shop on a daily basis earning 800 zl per month. Thus, he is forced to earn extra money taking up additional casual work. In another case, a

Chechen refugee worked illegally 12 hours a day (shift work from 7 am to 7 pm and from 7 pm to 7 am) as a guard with a security company and was paid 7 zl per hour. He earned approximately 1200 zl per month and had to cover flat expenses and maintain his family. Moreover, it was a casual job for a short period of time (4 months). This is another concern of Chechen migrants. They are usually offered casual, short-time jobs (up to six months) which is typical for unregistered and low-paid jobs. This lack of economic stability makes migrants' life difficult and unbearable, since every few months they have to look for a job once again and go through the same difficulties and problems. Apart from the economic consequences, this has many negative psychological effects. It gives rise to frustration or depressions, lowers a person's self-esteem and creates a state of perpetual threat and anxiety. One of my Chechen respondents is an exception to the rule. At present, he works in the construction sector on a legal basis and has a very good wage (several thousand zl). At the same time, he is very resourceful and hardworking. As regards Chechen women, who perform mainly cleaning and housework services or take care of children or elderly people, they usually earn around one thousand zl per month. They rather work illegally, at private houses. One of my respondents, who was cleaning in the office and had a legal job, was earning 1100 zl monthly. Some Chechen women also work in Turkish bars and help in the kitchen; they also earn around one thousand zl. There are also a few exceptions of Chechen women who earn more but this is directly related to their education and previous professional experience and of course personal features. Another survival strategy consists in temporary labour migration of Chechen men to other EU countries (e.g. Germany or Belgium) and taking up an illegal employment there while their families are staying in Poland. Since wages in these countries are better and the living costs in Poland are lower, they are able to maintain their families for a longer period of time. It is not surprising that Chechen migrants share the opinion that it is not worth working if wages do not cover their basic needs. My Chechen respondents repeatedly stressed that they would like to have a regular and decent income that would allow them to maintain their families and live with dignity. They are not dreaming about high salaries and luxurious lives. Some of them underlined that Chechen people are diligent and would like to feel useful and needed. Taking into account that it is not easy to find a decently paid and regular job, rents are high, and the average Chechen family is rather numerous and (at best) usually only one person works, we may conclude that it is a serious challenge and struggle for Chechen migrants to survive in

Poland. As a result, many of those who feel disappointed and discouraged by the lack of opportunities to lead a normal life decide to leave Poland and move to other EU countries.

Lack of Documents and Work below Qualifications

The next obstacle making it difficult for Chechens to integrate into the Polish labour market is the lack of documents confirming their education, vocational qualifications and skills gained in their country of origin. In many cases, their documents were lost during the war or, in some cases, left behind in the rush before departure. In the case of one of my respondents, all her personal documents including school certificates and labour book ("trudovaja knizhka") confirming her four-year professional experience as a dressmaker were burnt because the house was set on fire as a result of bombing. In other cases, migrants decided not to take any documents on purpose because their life was exposed to particular danger and they were hence hiding their identity while leaving the Chechen Republic, sometimes using forged passports. Knowledge about education and qualifications of Chechen migrants arriving in Poland is still insufficient. Some information has been collected and analysed in relation to recognized refugees qualifying for integration programmes and also for social assistance. According to the report on individual integration programmes conducted in 2006 and based on the examination of the personal files of migrants, the majority of migrants do not have their education background documented in Poland. Only 13.7% of those questioned were in possession of certificates confirming their education, and half of them had higher education. Almost two thirds of the questioned migrants declared they had secondary education, more than 20% primary education, and two persons did not have any education. The situation is similar concerning the documents confirming the migrants' vocational qualifications. More than two thirds did not possess such documents in Poland. Therefore, the authors of this survey decided not to publish the data on professions since the picture would be incomplete and not credible. Half of the interrogated persons declared not to have any profession. The second part of the above-mentioned research containing statistical data of migrants who were beneficiaries of social allowances will not yield credible information due to the lack of respective documents. Over 30% of the adults declared to have primary education, over a half of the adults had secondary education, 14% of the adults had higher education, and there was one person without any level of education. The above information is based only on the migrants' declarations and is not supported by any documents. It is difficult to say whether migrants did not present their documents or did not bring them to Poland. The information on vocational qualifications is also very sparse. In 30% of all cases no information on a profession exists, 41% of those questioned declared to have a profession which, however, was not documented, and there was one single case of a documented profession. The most popular professions declared by men were construction worker and driver, among women dressmaker, teacher, and nurse (Klaus/Chrzanowska 2007: 141, 173–174). Undocumented education or professional experience is one of the basic obstacles for migrants to perform work in line with their qualifications. It usually takes a lot of time, perseverance, and effort to achieve a similar professional position as the one they had in their country of origin, and sometimes it turns out to be impossible. In order to maintain themselves and their families, they have to take up any work which is, in the vast majority of cases, below their formal qualifications. However, the absence of documents is not the only problem. The other one is the lack or poor command of the Polish language or the mismatch of the migrant's education and experience on the one hand and the needs of the local labour market on the other. All of my interlocutors were working below their qualifications in the first years of their residence in Poland and many of them are still working in a job which is not in line with their formal qualifications. Although they possess higher education and some professional experience they perform casual jobs in the construction or security sectors. Finally, the character of a migrant plays an important role; if he or she is persistent, resourceful and enterprising enough to overcome all the difficulties. I know few Chechens who are satisfied with their jobs, salaries, and other working conditions, and a few more who are determined, and I believe that sooner or later they will succeed. One of my Chechen respondents with a higher linguistic education who speaks several foreign languages works as a construction worker. Although he earns good money, he would like to have a more challenging position in line with his possibilities. He would be determined and resourceful enough to achieve it. He plans to set up his own business and establish a temporary employment agency which would be employing workers from Eastern Europe and "lending" them to Polish or foreign employers. As regards the education and qualification level there is a significant difference between the first wave of Chechens, who arrived after the breakout of the second war, and the recent flows. During the first years of the second conflict Chechen migrants coming to Poland included representatives of the independent Chechen authorities, judges, prosecutors, commanding officers, representatives of the academic and cultural spheres, and other well-educated and qualified people. They left Chechnya because they were more aware of the threats in the first place, but also thanks to their higher social status they could more easily afford the costs for travel and documents. A major part of them left for other EU countries and just few decided to stay in Poland. Chechen asylum seekers having arrived in Poland during the last two or three years were primarily poorly educated and low-qualified young people who had grown up during the time of war and did not have a chance to obtain regular education and gain professional experience. Among them, we find a certain percentage of illiterates.

Lack or Poor Command of the Polish Language

At first glance, it seems that because of some similarities between the Russian language, spoken by the majority of Chechen adults, and Polish, Chechen migrants should not have major difficulties learning Polish at a satisfactory level. However, this presumption may turn out to be too simplistic. First of all, it must be realized that Russian is not the Chechens' mother tongue. Some of them do not speak Russian at all or at a poor level. This mainly applies to old people who used to live in the mountain area, or young people who did not learn Russian at school due to the turmoil of war. For them, the first opportunity to attend a Polish language course is offered in the refugee centres, where asylum seekers wait for the decision on their asylum applications to be taken. Taking into account that asylum seekers are not allowed to work during this procedure and have a lot of spare time, it seems to be the best moment for them to take this opportunity and learn Polish in order to increase their future chances on the labour market. The reason for a different approach may be linked to the chosen strategy or have a cultural background. The first situation occurs when Chechen asylum seekers assume that the command of Polish will not be useful for them because they do not intend to stay in Poland for a longer time. At present, this is what the majority of Chechens assume, being more or less aware that living conditions for refugees in Poland are problematic in comparison with other EU countries. There are also some cultural conditions that should be taken into account when organising classes for asylum applicants of different culture and religion. Chechen women usually do not attend Polish language courses due to several reasons, among them domestic responsibilities, lack of a babysitter, or reluctance of their husbands since groups are coeducational, or sometimes all these cumulated factors are involved.

Consequently, groups are composed usually of men. Finally, it must be admitted that the quality of Polish language classes organised in refugee centres leaves much to be desired. Chechen asylum applicants complain most of all about the small number of classes per week (one hour once or twice a week), about the fact that classes are not held by adequately prepared professionals but by non-experienced teachers from primary schools or even volunteers and that there are no advanced groups because of frequent rotation. The situation seems to be better in the case of Polish language classes for persons granted with refugee status who enter the integration programmes. They are obliged to attend Polish courses. There are two Polish courses worth mentioning: one of them is offered by the Lingua Mundi Foundation and governor Mazoviecki from the European Social Fund. As one of my Chechen respondents underlined, the course is very intensive, four hours three times a week, with usually 10 people in one group. They are not time-limited and refugees can attend them as long as they need. The language skills are confirmed by an exam and a certificate. The second course is conducted in the context of the project of The Intercultural Center of Professional Adaptation, from PIW EQUAL funds. Both courses provide teachers well prepared to teach the Polish language as a foreign language, a reasonable number of hours and child-care facilities while parents attend classes (Pawlak/Ryabinska 2007: 120). According to my Chechen respondent with higher linguistic education, who speaks Polish fluently, a good command of Polish is a key condition for socio-economic integration and a must if somebody wants to live in Poland. In his opinion, Polish classes should be mandatory and if Chechens do not want to learn Polish on a voluntary basis, they should be motivated to do so. He suggested that refugees partially cover the costs for Polish language classes. He confirmed that the basic reason why Chechens do not invest in learning Polish is their intention to leave Poland, and that the level of language competence can be a yardstick of their readiness to integrate.

Lack of Sufficient and Professional Assistance in Finding Employment

Chechens with refugee status are entitled to participate in a one-year IIP which specifies not only the refugees' rights but also his/her obligations. The supervision whether obligations have been met within the IIP rests with the DCFS. One of the six responsibilities of a refugee is registration with the district labour office and active job search. The basic factor affecting quality and efficiency of the IIP, according to employees of DCFS, is whether they intend to stay in Poland or leave.

Chechens usually comply with the obligation of registration with the district labour office but not because they are aware of the role of this institution which should assist them with finding a job but rather because they intend to obtain medical insurance entitling them too free medical care. The obligation to register and personally sign a list every month is not clear for them and not linked with seeking employment. According to employees both of DCFS and the labour offices, most Chechen refugees do not look for a job during the IIP or start to do so only towards the end of the programme. One of the possible reasons could be some unfounded rumors that they would lose part of the financial assistance if they took up a job, which has been denied by DCFS employees. From a Chechen's perspective, the labour offices are not very supportive since they do not offer any vocational training or retraining courses. Even if there are courses available, they are usually addressed to Polish unemployed because a fluent command of Polish is mandatory, and information on these courses and trainings is not provided by clerks but spread by other refugees. Unlike the staff of DCFS, employees of the labour offices are not prepared to work with foreigners including forced migrants. They do not speak foreign languages and sometimes are not fully aware of the legal situation of recognized refugees and persons with tolerated stay permits. This is due to the fact that the majority of the labour offices' suppliants are unemployed Polish citizens. It appears that the district labour offices are not able to fulfill their basic task, which is training, vocational stimulation, and vocational counseling for unemployed migrants (Samoraj/Bieniecki 2007: 84–91). Other institutions which are, to some extent, involved in assisting forced migrants in finding a job and in vocational counseling are welfares centres which mainly deal with persons granted tolerated stay permits but also with recognized refugees after completion of the IIP. Migrants benefiting from social assistance usually apply for different kinds of social allowances, mainly to cover their expenses for food, clothes, and accommodation, and very rarely apply for non-financial assistance like support in obtaining a social flat or finding a job. The Act on Social Assistance[10] envisages the possibility to conclude a so-called social contract between a migrant and a welfare centre regulating the rights and obligations of both parties. The welfare centre is to provide a requested type of social assistance and the migrant commits himself to undertake certain required activities. If not fulfilled as agreed, social assistance may be suspended or withdrawn. The objective of signing such contracts

10 Act on Social Assistance of 12 March 2004 (Journal of Laws No 64, item 593, with later amendments).

is to stimulate refugees to be active and intensively look for a job. Therefore, activities connected with seeking employment are among the typical migrants' responsibilities within the social contracts. According to the previously quoted report on forced migrants benefiting from welfare, 80% applicants were unemployed, over 18% declared they worked but in most cases rather had casual and unregistered jobs. As far as social contracts are concerned, in over 32% of the cases there was a direct commitment to intensively search for a job, one person was obliged to see employers and ask for vacancies, more than 16% of the migrants were obliged to actively participate in the Job Club, and almost 14% to register with the labour office. One of the main weaknesses of this system is the fact that the same rules apply both to Polish citizens and forced migrants although the latter require much more attention due to cultural and language differences and often traumatic experiences. To conclude, welfare centres do not offer forced migrants any practical assistance in finding employment, but their activities are rather aimed at motivating and encouraging people to do it on their own (Klaus/Chrzanowska 2007: 162–163; 177–190). Comparing the activity of the abovementioned institutions with the activity of NGOs as regards professional stimulation of forced migrants and their inclusion into the labour market, the latter match the migrants' needs better and their assistance is more practical and effective. At the same time, it must be said that, for the time being, there is not a single NGO acting on behalf of forced migrants which would exclusively specialize on matching employers and migrant workers on the basis of similar rules as professional job agencies. However, there are a few organisations where Chechen migrants can request practical assistance in finding a job or vocational trainings. These organisations provide assistance to refugees and other migrants in general. They do not have special sections with professional advisors or agents but there is usually at least one employee who helps migrants in a practical way. One of these organisations is Polish Humanitarian Action which runs a Job Club for migrants. There is one person acting as a labour agent and vocational advisor. Another one is the Association of Legal Intervention with really involved staff who provide migrants with legal and practical assistance in most of their everyday difficulties, including job search. The Intercultural Vocational Adaptation Centre deserves special attention, a project managed by the Institute for Social Prevention and Resocialization within the EU EQUAL Project. The overall objective of this project is to combat social exclusion and discrimination of different groups of migrants. The Centre offers three basic types of activities: conducting classes and training sessions, running the Immigrant and Refugee Counseling Centre, and intervening in selected crisis situations. Classes and training sessions are offered to immigrants and forced migrants (e.g. classes of Polish language and culture, how to set up a small business) and to professionals dealing with introducing immigrants, repatriates and forced migrants into the Polish labour market (e.g. intercultural trainings for vocational counselors, social workers, rehabilitation specialists, educational managers, employers, negotiators, and police officers). Besides, the Centre promotes multicultural workforce and provides assistance in validating foreign diplomas and updating vocational skills of its customers. Since May 2006, the Centre offers assistance in finding employment, among others helps to contact selected employers and arrange an appointment. Migrants can ask for an appointment with a legal adviser, cultural counselor, counselor, or career consultant. The range of vocational courses and trainings offered by the Centre both for men and women comprises computer courses (beginners and advanced), driving license courses (cat. B and D), tour guide courses, massage courses, hairdresser, dressmaking and nail care courses. The most popular were computer and driving license courses. In 2006–2007, 41 Chechen migrants participated in the above courses. New offers to be introduced will include a tiling and terracotta laying course, an accounting course, and a culinary course. Other NGOs offered, among others, the following courses: cutting and sewing courses, maintenance of fiscal check-out, or a warehouse attendant course (Kosowicz/Maciejko 2007: 50–51). One of my Chechen female interlocutors was attending a one-month nail care course organised by The Intercultural Vocational Adaptation Centre in cooperation with The Education and Personnel Development Centre. It was a quite intensive course, three hours three times a week, in the afternoon (there was also a morning option). The course was conducted in Polish and the participants who completed the course were provided with a Certificate of Achievement both in Polish and English. My Chechen respondents were satisfied with having the opportunity to attend vocational courses because they were learning something new and they were provided with certificates. What they regretted, however, was the lack of further assistance aiming at developing already gained skills and knowledge which should finally lead to employment. Forced migrants cannot always count on professional and thorough assistance. Vocational trainings organised by private educational or vocational training centres are not always well-informed on the legislation regarding foreigners and their legal status. For example, a certain centre organised a vocational course preparing participants to work as security staff members. This course was especially popular among Chechen men who had some military experience. However, according to the Polish legislation, only Polish citizens are allowed to work in so-called "uniform services", i.e. army, police, border guard, customs services, or security companies. Foreigners can only work as supervisors of possession but not as security staff members (Samoraj/Bieniecki 2007). Looking at the scope of the activities and practice of the main institutions assisting forced migrants in finding employment and on the basis of interviews with Chechen migrants, I must conclude that this assistance is neither sufficient nor comprehensive, taking into account all the obstacles to finding an employment on the Polish labour market. In most cases, my Chechen respondents found or switched their job through relatives or friends who were already working on the workplace now vacant because they were changing for a better job, or through Polish acquaintances.

Cultural Differences

Sometimes cultural differences, mainly of religious or traditional character, can affect effective participation in the labour market. There are some types of jobs which are not performed or reluctantly performed by Chechen migrants. As a rule, Chechen men will not take up a job which is traditionally performed by women, e.g. cleaning, sweeping, washing the dishes and other housework jobs. This would not be acceptable in the Chechen culture, where a strict division of roles persists and such responsibilities have always been attributed to women. What limits Chechen men on the labour market may be the exclusive asset of Chechen women who are excellent housekeepers. Another job that neither a Chechen man nor a Chechen women would take is waitress /waiter. For Chechen men it is not a typical job. As regards Chechen women, their reasoning is connected with their traditional upbringing. Chechen women are supposed to be modest, innocent and bring no shame or disgrace to the family. Therefore, they have to pay much attention to their reputation. The profession of a waitress cannot be accepted by them and their families because this kind of job may expose them to undignified treatment and lack of respect (e.g. in frequent situations when male customers are drunk). A lack of awareness of cultural and religious differences may sometimes lead to misunderstandings between Chechen employees and employers. It must be highlighted that family life and family relations are a priority issue for Chechens and sometimes may affect the fulfillment of other commitments, including professional ones. For instance, an unexpected visit of relatives may be a reason for a Chechen to stay at home from work. There are many other cultural differences including those of religious nature, and it would be useful if employers were aware of them and tried to respect them, e.g. Muslims do not eat pork, which should be taken into account if meals are provided, or they are less efficient at work during the Ramadan period, and they need a three-day leave at the end of Ramadan due to the most important Muslim holiday (Chrzanowska 2007: 119–123). My Chechen respondents working in the construction sector did not complain about their relations with Polish co-workers, but there was one "phenomenon" that affected their cooperation. As a rule, Chechens, as Muslims, do not drink alcohol, whereas some of the Polish construction workers are used to drink alcohol at work. One of my Chechen interlocutors, together with four other Chechens working illegally as bricklayers, were perceived as a threat and competitors for the Polish workers because they were not drinking and doing frequent breaks but worked faster and harder. They were not paid per day but for each metre. This even led to some misunderstandings and to a conflict with their superior who disliked this difference in work speed because he was paid per day and wanted to extend the work as long as possible in order to earn more. Besides, non-drinking Chechens were perceived as odd and unwilling to integrate, and they preferred to keep aside. All these social, cultural and religious differences should be brought to the attention of Polish employers and workers, who have little experience with Muslims and are not aware of these fundamental differences.

Health and Psychological Problems

Health and psychological problems are the objective obstacles to taking up and keeping an employment not only for Chechen migrants but for everybody. However, Chechen migrants, as well as other forced migrants being victims of war, are more often handicapped or suffer from different serious diseases and need a special medical treatment and rehabilitation. Additionally, most Chechens who were victims or witnesses of tortures or other brutal, inhuman or disgraceful treatments, suffer from post-traumatic stress disorder and need special psychological assistance. According to the quoted report on refugees and persons with tolerated stay permits benefiting from public welfare, half of the migrants had health problems, and every third was sick for a long time, including invalids. Mental disorders were not covered. It can be observed that 95% of persons with long-lasting sicknesses, 70% with temporary health problems, and all handicapped persons were Chechens

(Klaus/Chrzanowska 2007: 142). Forced migrants have access to free medical care and enjoy the same rights as Polish citizens, but it is common knowledge that the Polish health service is underfinanced and therefore the quality of services leaves much to be desired. This is especially problematic in the case of Chechens who often require specialist treatment and expensive operations. The lack of financial sources to conduct such treatment and the poor quality of medical services is another reason why Chechens move to western EU countries.

Lack of Social Accommodation and Difficulties Renting a Flat

The difficult housing situation is a further fundamental obstacle to effective integration of Chechen migrants and the key factor that pushes them out of Poland. Just as in the case of the phenomenon of unregistered work or medical care, the housing problem does not only concern forced migrants but Polish citizens as well who, if they cannot afford to buy a flat on the free market, queue for the allotment of a municipal flat. Due to the lack of municipal flats the Polish state is not able to provide all forced migrants with accommodation. To demonstrate this miserable situation, it can be mentioned that every year there are five municipal flats to be offered to all recognized refugees in Warsaw. In practice, these flats are not given to newly recognized refugees but to those who have been residing in Poland for some time and who have been waiting in the queue. In 2006, only one Chechen family consisting of 5 members was granted a municipal flat (Kosowicz/Maciejko 2007: 57). This possibility is not offered to persons with tolerated stay permits. The remaining recognized refugees and forced migrants have to rent flats on the free market, which means that a large part of the financial assistance will be spent for covering flat costs. The situation of Chechens with tolerated stay permits is most dramatic since, for the time being, they are not included in the integration programmes and do not receive financial assistance (they can only apply for social allowances which are very low). However, even renting a flat is a big challenge for a foreigner with an eastern accent or not speaking Polish at all. On the basis of the experience quoted by my Chechen respondents, Polish citizens are usually reluctant to rent out a flat to eastern migrants, especially to families with numerous children, due to the existing prejudices and fear that flat costs might not be paid on a regular basis. From an objective perspective, these fears are partially justified since it is almost impossible to pay the flat costs and maintain a family when performing unregistered and low-paid work. Therefore, only determined and resourceful people stay, who usually work and are supported by relatives residing in western EU countries. Another difficulty when renting out a flat is to get registered. The majority of Polish citizens, even if they decide to rent out a flat to a Chechen family, are rather reluctant to register them, and this is for two reasons: first, the conviction that it would be more difficult to get rid of the tenants when they are registered and second, the fact that owners usually do not want to sign a contract in order to avoid paying taxes. Whereas registration is needed in order to obtain PESEL (numbers in joint electronic system of population's record) which are essential e.g. in taking up employment or registering with a health center. It seems to be a vicious circle, because obtaining PESEL is a must within the integration programme. Fortunately, there are two other possibilities. A non-registered foreigner may obtain PESEL when he is in possession of medical or social insurance. If he does not meet any of these criteria and would like e.g. to take up employment, he should apply for PESEL directly at the Ministry of Interior and Administration (Cegiełka/Gracz/Jasiakiewicz et al. 2006: 91–92). My Chechen respondents indicated that the housing situation in other EU countries is far better than in Poland. Their relatives and friends are provided with municipal flats and they have to pay only bills for consumption of water, gas and electricity, or when they are within integration programmes which usually last 3 years, the state covers all the costs, and afterwards the costs are equally divided between the state and the refugee.

Barriers for Chechen Women on the Labour Market

Participation and the position of Chechen women on the labour market depend on a number of factors linked to their marital status, age, educational background, vocational qualifications, and individual features. Culture and tradition also have considerable influence. Unlike forced migrants of other nationalities (e.g. from African countries, India, Pakistan), Chechen migrants usually arrive with families, often with many children, sometimes with old parents or other relatives. There are also single mothers like widows with children, who lost their husbands during the war, or whose husbands were kidnapped and their whereabouts remain unknown. Sometimes these women come only with children, sometimes with other closer or distant relatives. There are also cases of divorced single mothers with children.

Cultural and Traditional Factors

The cultural model of a Chechen family and the different roles of women and men doubtlessly have much to do with the participation of Chechen women in the labour market, be it in their country of origin, in Poland or elsewhere. As a rule, Chechen women who are married and have children do not work professionally but are responsible for raising the children and running the household. The responsibility for ensuring decent living conditions for the whole family rests with Chechen men, who are family providers and the head of the family taking the most important decisions. Their social position is measured by their ability to guarantee the well-being of their families. Considering this division of social roles, Chechen girls are brought up to be good wives, mothers and housekeepers, and the emphasis in their education is rather not on preparing them for professional life. This does not mean that there are no well-educated or professionally working Chechen women. Three of my female respondents were well-educated but not all of them had professional experience. It often happens that Chechen women with higher education and even profession do not work because they are occupied with upbringing children and running the house and additionally, it may be their husbands' decision. The described cultural patterns and social roles have undergone some modifications and changes due to the war and the subsequent phenomenon of migration. The situation caused by the war, the lack of possibilities to perform a regular and legal job and the necessity to survive and maintain the family has created a new socio-economic reality for Chechen men and women. When Chechen men were involved in war activities and spent most of the time outside or later, when they were subject to detention and kidnapping and it was risky for them to go out, Chechen women had to be more active and assume the role of the family provider, for instance by trading on the market places. Further changes and challenges came along with the life in emigration. It is observed that those who have the biggest problems with adapting to the new reality are Chechen men whose traditional role has been diminished. Their helplessness arising from the lack of possibilities to ensure decent living conditions to their families has a considerable psychological effect on Chechen men and causes frustration, a loss of dignity and of the image of family provider. In some cases, it can lead to aggression towards the family or susceptibility to different addictions like alcohol or drugs. Of course, there are also resourceful and enterprising Chechen men, who are able to overcome problems and find their place on the labour market. This is an individual thing depending on the character and personality and also on objective factors like education and qualifications. At first glance, it appears that complete families have better chances to confront the difficulties than single mothers with children. However, taking into account what was said on the depreciation of the social role of Chechen men and the experiences by NGOs or family support centres, it can be noticed that often, in the case of full families, neither husbands nor wives work professionally. Wives do not work because they have children to take care of, and husband cannot find a job or cannot work due to health problems or invalidity. It should be added that situations when social roles have been switched in case a man does not work or is unable to work are not observed. If a woman decides to go to work, in most cases she will have to reconcile her work with running the household (Chrzanowska 2007: 117). This observation was confirmed by my respondent who was working professionally and maintaining the whole family including her husband who was neither working nor assisting at home.

Are Chechen Women more Susceptible to Integration than Men?

Education, qualifications, professional experience, and individual features are the key factors determining the position and possibilities on the labour market. There are a few Chechen migrants who, thanks to the above-mentioned qualities but mostly to their individual features, after passing through a long path, managed to find a job in line with their qualifications. On the basis of my professional experience and own observations, interviews with representatives of different NGOs and Chechen women, I would venture the opinion that Chechen women are more diligent, resourceful, persistent and determined to adapt to a new reality than men. Of course, the adaptation strategies may differ and depend on many factors like the education level or previous professional record, but the bottom-line is that women are more self-motivated, open, willing to learn something new, and active in looking for new possibilities to improve their situation. One of my respondents is a good example of the above observations. She has been living in Poland together with her family since 2000, on the basis of refugee status. She has higher medical education and had been working for a few years in the hospital before the first war. When her asylum procedure was completed she quickly started to look for job opportunities. First, she accepted casual jobs in order to improve her family's living conditions. At the same time, she set herself a goal to find a more satisfying job in line with her education and qualifications and to have her diploma recognized. The first step was a very intensive course of the Polish language including specialized medical vocabulary. Subsequently, she passed the Polish language exam in the Supreme Medical Council. The next step was to submit all the required translated documents to the relevant department of the Ministry of Health. Fortunately, she was in possession of her diploma and other documents confirming her professional experience. Otherwise, it would have been more difficult and time-consuming to achieve this goal. Finally, her diploma was recognized and she was provided with the equivalent of the Polish diploma. The last condition she had to meet in order to work as a doctor in Poland was to complete a one-year internship at the hospital. She was paid one thousand zl per month. During the internship, she was working as a nurse in a private gymnasium. She highlighted that she was able to reconcile the internship with her work at the school thanks to the understanding of her superiors in both places. After completing the internship she was offered a job in the hospital but due to the low salary decided to continue her job in the gymnasium as a pediatrician. For her, it is important that she has formal possibilities to work as a doctor and take up a job in a hospital or other medical institution any time. She is very much involved in her work at school and satisfied with both salary and working conditions, with her relations with the superiors, and the general atmosphere. Since she is a very active woman she is involved in other activities, on behalf of Chechen refugees. Naturally, it is easier to adapt to a new reality for women who are well-educated and have a profession, especially one that is needed, whereas many Chechen women are not so well-educated and have little or no professional experience. Some of them perform unregistered work, usually below their qualifications and for a minimum salary. They do cleaning services, look after children, or work in supermarkets. Nevertheless, it is my impression that they are gradually striving for changing their situation and improving their living conditions. They are better motivated to raise their vocational qualifications or learn a new profession. Women with elementary and secondary education are eager to attend vocational trainings and courses to obtain additional skills and knowledge, for example by taking hairdresser, dressmaking, nail care or floriculture courses. According to the employee of one NGO, Chechen single mothers are very resourceful and enterprising and are most susceptible to integration influences, more than married women or men.

Situation of Single Mothers

Paradoxically, the level of participation in the labour market is higher in the case of single mothers with children than in the case of full families. Chechen women are more determined and persistent when it comes to feeding children and ensuring them normal life conditions. It is their priority, and therefore they are readier to make compromises than men. However, determination to take up a job is not enough, and they have to face various obstacles resulting from the position of being a single parent. It is easier for them to find a job if they have professional experience, although the important question remains what to do with the children when they are little. The situation is definitely worse if a single mother has never worked professionally and has no relatives or friends nearby to support her. The NGO representative, for example, described the situation of a Chechen woman who was granted tolerated stay, had a poor command of the Polish language, and several kids. She was forced to leave her husband who was addicted to alcohol and spending all the money on alcohol. Her decision was not approved by her husband's family and she did not have any relatives to support her. She was determined to find a job to pay for the rented flat and maintain herself and her children. Finally, she found a legal job for a minimum salary as a cashier at the supermarket, at first for a 3-month trial period. At the times when she was working, her elder kids were taking care of the younger ones. In the first month, she had to take leave when her younger child got ill. This situation reoccurred when her other children were also infected. As a result, after the three-month period, the employer decided not to extend her contract (Chrzanowska 2008: 78–79). One possible solution to help single mothers get access to the labour market, as suggested by the NGO representative, is to establish unpaid integration kindergartens that both refugee and Polish children could attend and where both refugee and Polish mothers could work as kindergarten teachers. Such kindergartens could be financed by the state or local governments and benefit from EU co-funding. An additional supportive solution would consist in self-assistance by Chechen women. Those who want to work professionally could pay other Chechen women to take care of their children. As I found out from the employee of the NGO, such arrangements have already been carried out in some refugee centres. Chechen women, who want to work or have to leave to make certain arrangements, and do not have relatives to leave their children with, can ask other women to take care of their children for 10 zl a day. One of my Chechen respondents, divorced, and living in Poland for a couple of years on the basis of a tolerated stay permit, would like to establish a foundation to support single mothers. First of all, she would like to make it easier for them to access the labour market, by organising a day room or kindergarten where children could stay, play and learn something useful. The foundation would also provide women with information on their rights and obligations related to their legal status. The respondent underlined that she would like to point out to Chechen women the perspectives and possibilities of residing in Poland by explaining procedures of granting permanent residence permits and Polish citizenship. The foundation could also assist women by preparing application documents, finding employment, or setting up a business activity. One idea for a small business could be catering services. Since Chechen women are good at cooking they could prepare traditional Caucasus cuisine to be served at parties, banquets, conferences or on other occasions. Another idea suggested by the respondent could be cleaning services. Another initiative she would like to include in her foundation's agenda is to set up a multicultural women's group which could be a platform for meetings and discussions among women of different religions and cultures in order to enhance solidarity between women.

Possible Solutions and Recommendations

This package of recommendations is addressed to all relevant actors involved in and responsible for working out a wise and effective integration strategy for Chechen migrants, especially in the socio-economic context. While authorities at the central, regional and local level should take the lead, collaboration regarding the conception, development, organisation, and evaluation of integration policy should involve a wide range of stakeholders including employers, social partners (e.g. employer's organisations, trade unions), NGOs, and the research community, but also civil society and migrants themselves. Since integration policy is designed at the national level and implemented at local levels, a good co-operation and information flow between all actors involved must be ensured. There should also be good collaboration between the authorities and NGOs which play a central role in advocating on behalf of migrants. Employers and social partners could contribute by facilitating everyday integration in the workplace through highlighting the significance of cultural differences and enhancing social responsibility. We must take into account that integration policy needs to be planned on a long-term basis and that it has to be coherent within the overall legislative framework but at the same time responsive to the specific needs of the particular groups. The following solutions and recommendations attempt to respond to the observed obstacles for the integration of Chechens into the labour market and include remarks and ideas proposed by NGOs or Chechen migrants themselves as well as my own considerations, in particular as regards complex and practical assistance in finding employment, vocational stimulation and awareness-raising activities.

Reform of Integration Programmes

IIP are so far the only form of institutionalized integration assistance for refugees in Poland. Although they have been functioning for seven years now, they are neither effective nor adapted to the individual needs of refugees. This conclusion is confirmed by a large number of persons who decided to leave Poland during or after completing the programmes. Therefore, the IIP are in urgent need of prompt reform. First of all, they should cover all forced migrants who were granted any form of international or national protection and are allowed to reside in Poland. The first step towards this approach will be extending the IIP to migrants who will be granted subsidiary protection. Taking into account the requirements it is assumed that this form of protection will be granted mostly to Chechen migrants. However, forced migrants granted tolerated stay permits will remain outside the scope of the programmes. Secondly, the duration of the IIP should be extended to a 3-year-period depending on the individual situation of a refugee and his family. Annual programmes are not sufficient since a vast majority of refugees is not ready to start independent lives after completing the programme. Forced migrants, including Chechens, were often victims of torture or other kinds of inhuman treatment; they are people with traumatic experiences and need much more time and attention to get familiarized with a new reality. Due to the situation in their country of origin, Chechens have lost the habit of existing within an institutional framework and performing work on a regular and legal basis. Therefore, they should be given more time to learn Polish, acquire new skills, have their education and qualifications recognized, and finally find a legal and regular job. Last but not least, integration programmes should be adapted to the individual needs and possibilities of forced migrants. With regard to the exceptionally difficult position of Chechen single mothers, the authorities, in cooperation with NGOs, should work out a special integration programme for single mothers in order to increase their chances on the labour market and make their integration process more successful. One of the initiatives to improve the difficult material situation of single mothers could consist in establishing a special centre where they could stay after completing the asylum procedure and leaving the refugee centre. Such a centre should be established and run by the relevant authorities but also supported by NGOs. The centre should also provide a kindergarten for children of those women who would like to take up employment.

Polish Language Courses – Practical, Job-oriented Workshops

A good command of the Polish language is undoubtedly the basic precondition for successful economic integration of all migrants, including Chechens in Poland. An unsatisfactory command of the Polish language will always be a barrier and limit their job opportunities to physical and low-paid jobs. Considering all the mentioned obstacles for Chechens to effectively learn Polish, especially in the context of their economic integration, I would recommend the following solutions:

a) better quality and organisation of language courses.
Polish language classes should be organised by the central and local authorities, supported by NGOs, and conducted by professionals adequately prepared to teach Polish as a foreign language. The courses should be more intensive, with a differentiation of groups on the grounds of age, sex, and level of advancement. For those who would like to reconcile learning and working there should be a possibility to attend evening courses.

b) Separate groups for women and men.
This recommendation takes into account the cultural aspect and is especially important in the case of Chechen women, since it could increase the number of Chechen women participating in the courses and allow them to be more active during the classes. Consistently, classes for men should be conducted by a man, and those for women by a woman. Such a division would respect the needs and interests of both men and women.

c) Assistance for mothers.
Without practical assistance single mothers or women with small children who do not have anybody to leave their children with would not be able to take part in the courses. Refugee centres should be equipped with a kindergarten or a day room where children can be left and receive proper care when mother or parents are absent. It could be run by other Chechen women for money. To ensure the participation of women who left the refugee centers to attend classes within the integration programmes, there should be a day room in the same building where the classes are conducted.

d) Make classes more practical and useful.
Apart from grammar, vocabulary and the most common topics, Polish language courses should acquaint migrants with the cultural and social conditions of living in Poland, with the functioning of a big city, the rules and procedures of the basic institutions refugees may have contact with, or the situation and possibilities on the labour market. Language classes should be coupled with practical workshops, where migrants could learn useful things e.g. how to look for a flat or job, how to write a CV or a cover letter and prepare for an interview.

e) Increase motivation.
Polish language classes should be mandatory from the very beginning. One of my Chechen respondents underlined that refugees should not only have rights but also some obligations. Repeated and unfounded absence should be punished by decreasing the amount of pocket money or financial assistance (IIP), whereas particular involvement and progress should be awarded by increasing the amount of pocket money or financial assistance. The aim is to make refugees aware that learning yields measurable benefits.

Vocational Stimulation and Assistance with Recognition of Qualifications

Vocational stimulation of Chechen asylum seekers should start at the earliest stage possible. The capacity of the labour offices should be enhanced in order to ensure the migrants' access to professional counseling, to possibilities of raising their qualifications and retraining. The offer of vocational and retraining courses should be wider, and a certain number of places should be reserved for refugees. Besides, some employees should be appointed and trained not only to inform but also to advice forced migrants on the choice of vocational courses on the basis of their education and qualification background or on retraining possibilities taking into account trends and shortages on the labour market. The next issue raised by my Chechen respondents was that a thorough command of Polish is mandatory to attend the vocational courses offered by the labour offices. Migrants have to speak Polish since they would be using Polish at work. However, the communication level should be sufficient to be admitted to the courses. There should be more governmental and non-governmental initiatives focusing on the stimulation of migrants by provision of vocational courses and counseling. NGOs should be supported financially on a regular basis by the authorities in order to increase their activities related to vocational stimulation of forced migrants. What is missing is further assistance aiming at developing already gained skills and knowledge, which should finally lead to employment. It would be of significant help if people completing vocational courses were offered remunerated practices or internships and if the staff of labour offices or NGOs could act as agents assisting with organising such practices and internships. Finally, authorities should think about facilitating the procedure of recognition of education and qualifications as well as a decrease of/exemption from fees, especially in the case of high and needed qualifications.

Complex and Practical Assistance in Finding Employment

According to Chechen migrants, the labour offices are not very supportive in finding a job and none of my Chechen respondents found a job through the office. Furthermore, there is not a single governmental or non-governmental institution which would offer forced migrants complex, practical and effective assistance in finding a legal employment. There is a strong and urgent need to establish a specialized employment agency to assist forced migrants which could operate on a similar basis as a private employment agency. This agency could be run by an NGO and co-financed by the state. It could cooperate with the regional labour offices, which would share the vacancy notices submitted by employers. Following are some elementary ideas for the scope of activities offered by such an agency:

- creating and updating the database containing information on migrant employees and job offers gathered from different sources;
- assistance with the preparation of application documents (CVs of migrants looking for a job could be posted on the database);
- providing migrants with knowledge on the labour law, the situation on the labour market, and deficit professions;
- vocational counseling and assistance during the procedure of recognition of qualifications;
- selecting job offers from the database which match a migrant's qualifications with an employer's demands;
- contacting employers and arranging appointments with employers which could take place in the agency;
- participation of the agent and assistance during interviews with employers;
- negotiating working and payment conditions, and analyzing contracts prepared by employers, at the migrant's request;
- organising trainings for employers on the legal situation of forced migrants as well as the cultural and religious differences;

- arranging (non-)remunerated traineeships/internships with selected companies.

The agency should be equipped with a suitable number of rooms, including one for migrants where they could read newspapers with job offers, use computers with access to the internet, or print documents for free. The staff of the agency should include employment agents, agent assistants, vocational counselor(s), and administrative staff. The agency should also cooperate with interpreters and lawyers. It could be a good idea to employ forced migrants e.g. as agent assistants, including Chechens who have resided in Poland for a longer period of time and who speak Polish. The agents should have regular and professional trainings, especially in the areas of acquiring and updating knowledge on most wanted professions and vacancies (apart from newspaper and internet search, information from the labour offices, and own market analysis), recognizing an employer's expectations and employment conditions in the professions that are most popular with migrants, as well as requirements concerning documents and certificates.

Additional Instruments Supporting Forced Migrants on the Labour Market

One of the additional and relatively new instruments for improving economic integration of forced migrants into the Polish labour market could be society cooperatives, regulated by the Act of 20 April 2006 on Society Cooperatives[11]. Society cooperatives are socio-economical institutions aimed at realizing the needs of persons vulnerable to social exclusion, who hardly have any chances of finding a regular employment (for example physically handicapped people or the unemployed). The institution of the cooperative has to meet two objectives: By running this kind of business, its members make their own profit in order to maintain themselves and their families. Secondly, performing work within the cooperative positively affects social and professional reintegration of its members, which counteracts their social exclusion (Wilga 2007: 2–5). Both recognized refugees and persons granted with tolerated stay permits can become founders of the cooperative. NGOs can become members of the cooperative and support its functioning since forced migrants, at the beginning, are not acquainted with legislation regarding business and the socio-economic reality in Poland. While the idea itself is very interesting and could be a solution for the unemployment of migrants, there are some provisions that require improvement. One of the major difficulties for migrants when founding a cooperative is the lack of personal financial re-

11 Journal of Laws, No 94, item 651

sources and their inability to apply for such resources at the Labour Fund, which demands a return guarantee, as well as the lack of knowledge and managerial skills to run a company. Therefore, it is recommended to amend the act by introducing a possibility for social organisations to set up cooperatives and then attract forced migrants to join them. This conclusion was drawn by the Legal Intervention Association, the NGO that started the discussion on applying this form of social economy to the needs of forced migrants, especially Chechen ones. Prior to setting up a cooperative, the needs, interests and skills of forced migrants should be identified, and the same should be done for market niches for the activity of society cooperatives. According to one of the employees of the above-mentioned NGO, Chechen men would be interested in launching a business activity within the cooperative in the construction and renovation services sector, whereas some Chechen women declared interest in providing catering services. In fact, it would be a pioneering activity since not a single cooperative has been established by forced migrants in Poland yet. Another idea to be considered by the Polish authorities could be to introduce incentives for employers to encourage them to employ forced migrants on a legal and regular basis. This would be a kind of positive discrimination towards forced migrants who by definition face bigger problems with their integration into the labour market. It could be a similar idea as proposed in relation to repatriates of Polish origin from Kazakhstan and other countries of the former Soviet Union. Every employer who decides to employ a repatriate for at least 24 months is entitled to a partial return of the costs incurred for remunerations and social security contributions. Costs connected with creating a new workplace for a repatriate, or costs related to conducting training for a repatriate for the purpose of his/her vocational stimulation can also be partially returned.

Assistance with Provision of Accommodation

The difficult housing situation of forced migrants requires urgent solutions. As pointed out before, the number of municipal flats offered annually to recognized refugees is negligible, which is linked to the lack of municipal flats in general. In this case, other possibilities should be analysed, especially good practices of other EU member states. One possible solution worth considering could be partial coverage of the flat expenses by the state or local governments. This kind of support is very much in need after completion of the annual IIP. One possible option could be that state or local authorities would cover the expenses related to renting a flat, and migrants would cover the rest, i.e. costs incurred for consumption of water, gas and electricity, or all costs could be divided equally between the state and refugees. This assistance could be granted for 2–3 years, taking into account the individual situation of the migrant's family, and could be prolonged in particular cases. There should also be a possibility to apply for additional financial assistance within the IIP in case the integration benefits are not sufficient to cover all flat expenses. Finally, due to difficulties signalized before, forced migrants should be assisted in finding and renting a flat by staff of the regional family support centres and NGOs.

Awareness-raising Activities

Since the number of Chechen migrants who decided to stay in Poland is very small, it is not surprising that many Polish employers have never met them, and their knowledge is superficial and based upon existing stereotypes. In fact, interests of forced migrants who need to work and employers who lack workers are convergent, and therefore they should get to know each other better. In order to achieve this, all the interested stakeholders (central and local authorities, NGOs, media, employers' organisations) should undertake activities aiming at raising awareness and knowledge addressed to Polish employers. A basic initiative could be a wide-ranging information and education campaign in the mass media encouraging employers to offer employment to forced migrants (in TV and newspapers). It could be part of a wider social campaign addressed to the Polish society. The campaign should include the most essential information on the migrants' legal status (e.g. that they are allowed to work without work permits) as well as cultural aspects of the major migrants' groups in Poland and promote the migrants' national skills. Another source of information for employers could be trainings on the legal status of forced migrants and the cultural differences, organised by local labour offices, specialized employment agencies, and NGOs. All the above actors, jointly and separately, could organise labour fairs, where employers would present their job opportunities and working conditions to unemployed migrants. Finally, employers should be invited to attend seminars, conferences or social events dedicated to forced migrants in order to deepen their knowledge and learn more about the culture and customs of the migrants they employ or intend to employ (e.g. on the occasion of International Refugee's Day or International Migrant's Day).

Enhancing Contacts between Migrants and the Polish Society

The social aspect of integration means personal social relations between migrants and their host community, and membership in formal and informal social groups. The success of integration depends both on the goodwill and the involvement of migrants adapting to a new reality as well as the readiness of the receiving society to accept newcomers. It is difficult to achieve this goal without some basic knowledge that members of the receiving society should have on the phenomenon of forced migration, on the migrants' countries of origin and cultural differences. Since the level of knowledge and awareness among the Polish society is rather low, the number of educational campaigns should be increased. It is of particular importance to conduct such actions in local communities in the close vicinity of refugee centres, which are usually located in small towns or villages, where the general level of education is lower than in big cities. Apart from the aspect of preventing or reducing the phenomenon of intolerance and xenophobia, the awareness-raising activities should also make people aware that forced migrants are in need of practical support to be able to adapt to the new background. Assistance by Polish friends and acquaintances in communicating with different offices, when renting a flat or searching a job can be very useful and precious for migrants. All my Chechen respondents who have been residing in Poland for a longer time underlined that they would not have managed to find their flats or jobs or arrange other important issues without the assistance of their Polish friends. Some of them even claimed that they would have left Poland a while ago if they had not been supported by their Polish friends. One of the concepts for successful integration outlines two crucial conditions: a satisfactory job and supportive friends among members of the host society (Gracz 2007: 203–205). It is highly recommended to create more platforms for meetings and cooperation between migrants and members of the local community. This task should rest, in particular, with municipal or local authorities as well as social organisations.

Conclusion

Instead of my own final comments, I would like to quote the fragment of a text written by a Chechen migrant, who has been living in Poland since 2005, which portrays most of the problems and difficulties mentioned that impede an effective participation of Chechens in the Polish labour market and reflects the current state of socio-economic integration of forced migrants in Poland. At the end, he points at a set of basic indicators necessary for a successful integration of migrants into a new society.

"It's not that we, refugees, are sitting in the centre and waiting for manna from Heaven. For honest work there should be a decent payment. Naturally, there are also people among us who will not lift a finger to earn a loaf of bread if they have it in the centre. But there are also such people among Poles, who prefer to lie in bed if they are to work for 600 zl. When I was staying in the refugee centre, different people were coming and making promises. So, first we went near Bialystok to pick strawberries. We managed to stay there only for a week; I was getting 20 zl per day. There was no accommodation provided, so I was sleeping outside covered by a jacket. Subsequently, I was working for a man who was building a hotel. He promised big money. When he came to look how we work he did not make any remarks. When it came to paying us he was not satisfied with the results and paid us only half of the agreed amount of money. My brother called him names and finally, we got the whole sum of money. Several months ago, my friend asked me if I would like to work in a certain company. I needed money, so I agreed. I have been working there for a couple of months now. I am the only one left from the entire group of Chechens working there. My boss is very honest, he never deceived me. I wish everybody had such a good employer. When we go somewhere together, he introduces me and says that I am from Chechnya and I am one of his best workers. My dreams? I would like to have a good job, buy a flat, get married and speak Polish fluently. I would also like to complete a massage course and then become one of the best masseurs in Poland. Have a long queue of customers. Earn enough to survive till the next payment. And I wish a good handbook for every refugee coming to Poland was published, where in the introduction it should be written that it will be hard but it is possible to live here" (Refugee 2007: Pl. Refugees' newspaper).

Bibliography

Chrzanowska, Aleksandra (2007): Cultural conditions of the functioning of forced migrants on the Polish labour market using the example of Chechen society. In: Migrants on the Polish labour market. Reality, problems, challenges. Warsaw, 117–123.

Chrzanowska, Aleksandra (2008): The situation of forced migrants on the Polish labour market. In: Equal chances? Equal rights? Analyses. Reports, Expertise. The Association of Legal Intervention, Warsaw.

Cegiełka, Dawid/Gracz, Katarzyna/Jasiakiewicz, Agnieszka et al. (2006): Legal framework for integration of refugees in Poland. Commentary for practitioners. Warsaw, 91–92.
Gracz, Katarzyna (2006): Work, unemployment and business activity. In: Legal framework of the integration of refugees in Poland. Commentary for practitioners. Warsaw.
Gracz, Katarzyna (2007): Forced migrations and perspectives for multiculturalism in Poland. In: Chrzanowska, Aleksandra/Gracz, Katarzyna (eds.): Refugees in Poland. Cultural and legal barriers in the adaptation process. Warsaw, 203–205.
Grzymała-Moszczynska, Halina (2000): Refugees. Handbook for persons working with refugees. Krakow.
Klaus, Witold/Chrzanowska, Aleksandra (2007): Integration and social assistance for recognized refugees in Poland. The results of file studies. In: Stop Poland. Analysis of integration programmes for refugees. Warsaw, 141–174.
Kosowicz, Agnieszka/Maciejko, Anna (2007): Integration of refugees in Poland in numbers. Warsaw.
Pawlak, Mikołaj/Ryabinska, Natalya (2007): Why refugees do not want to integrate in Poland. Assessment of the integration programmes from the refugees' perspective. In: Stop Poland. Analysis of integration programmes for refugees. Warsaw.
Ministry of Labour and Social Policy (2005): Guide for Refugees. Warsaw.
Refugee. Pl. Refugees' newspaper 4 (2007). Warsaw.
Samoraj, Beata/Bieniecki,Mirosław (2007): Evaluation of the Efficiency of Individual Integration Programmes. In: Stop. Poland. Analysis of integration programmes for refugees. Warsaw, 92–100.
Wilga, Grzegorz (2007): Society cooperatives as a new form of integration of forced migrants on the Polish labour market. In: Analyses. Reports. Expertise, no 1(5). Legal Intervention Association. Warsaw, 2–5.

The Chechen Diaspora in Europe and its Security Implications

ALEXANDER SCHAHBASI

Particularly after the terrorist attacks in the Russian Federation, such as the Moscow theatre siege (2002) and the hostage crises in Beslan (2004), Chechens were viewed with more suspicion by the European public with regard to terrorism, meaning attacks that are conducted outside the battleground in the Caucasus. So far, attacks that targeted the general public have been limited to the Russian Federation and have not taken place in countries of the European Union. With regard to the implications for European Countries and the Chechen Diaspora in Europe the issue of security has to be looked at from mainly three perspectives:

- Support for the resistance in Chechnya
- Radicalisation of Chechen youth in Europe
- Challenges and threats to European countries

Support for the Resistance in Chechnya

First and foremost there is the issue of support for the resistance movement in Chechnya through the expatriate communities in Europe. It is of course not possible to assess the scope of support that emanates from the European Diaspora, but it is clear that the interaction between Chechnya and Chechens in Europe is an intensive one. The role of a Diaspora has been well observed in Jordan, where it is suggested that the Chechen community has close interactions with Chechnya (Al-Shishani/Moore 2005).

Financial support for Chechnya, be it for humanitarian causes or resistance, appears to be vivid. Although not comparable in scope, money transfers to Chechnya seem to resemble those to the Middle East in means – they are effected in circumvention of official channels such as banks. Whereas in the Middle East the havala-system[1] is more established, in the case of Chechnya funds raised for the "Chechen cause" are presumably transferred via Chechens travelling to the region and handed over to confidants there. Financial support may serve various purposes, ranging from personal to humanitarian, but it cannot be ruled out that there are contributions in any form for the fight against Russia or terrorism-related activities. It has been generally observed – which is not a particular trait of the conflict in Chechnya – that funds that were purportedly for humanitarian purposes were in fact used to finance terrorism (Levitt 2003). The real destination of such money flows is hard to assess. In terms of organisational support through Islamic Charities, the Saudi Al-Haramain Foundation[2] has been accused by Russia's Federal Security Service (FSB) of financial support for Chechen rebels. The accusation has been denied by representatives of Al-Haramain claiming that their activities in Chechnya were limited to humanitarian purposes (LaFraniere 2003). However, the importance of financial support for the Jihad in Chechnya, which is to be seen within the ideological concept of "Al-Jihad bi-al-Mal"[3], has been voiced by senior clerics[4].

In terms of support for the struggle through "human resources", no information on active recruitment of Chechens for the resistance has yet surfaced. Evidently, radicalized European Muslims have fought alongside rebels in Chechnya, such as the German citizens that were killed in Chechnya by Russian forces

1 The havala systems requires a network of brokers in both countries. The sender deposits a certain amount of money with the broker in one country and the same amount of money is handed out to the recipient by a broker (a confidant) in the country of destination. Communication is usually via phone or e-mail and the recipient uses a password provided by the sender to identify himself.

2 "La fondation Al Haramein est présente dans 55 pays et a son siège à Riyad. Ses buts sont religieux et humanitaires, certes, mais son principal objectif reste le prosélytisme actif" (Sfeir, Antoine (ed.) (2002): Dictionnaire Mondial de L'Islamisme. Paris). In 2004, the Al Haramain Foundation was closed by Saudi authorities.

3 Al-Jihad bi-al-Mal or Financial Jihad includes fundraising for needy Muslims and support for Jihad warriors (mujahedeen).

4 As pointed out in a statement by the late Saudi scholar Hamoud al-Oqala al-Shuaibi: http://saaid.net/Warathah/hmood/h48.htm.

(Schirra 2002). The transfer of fighters is usually handled through established smuggling networks, where in the case of Chechnya Turkey seems to play a pivotal role (Thamm 2003).

Generally – compared to Iraq and Afghanistan – there is quite a low number of foreign fighters in Chechnya.

Radicalisation of Chechen Youth in Europe

The issue of radicalisation within the Chechen Diaspora prevails with regard to the disaffected youth. Those growing up in Europe are probably less prone to this phenomenon than those having lost crucial years of education and childhood due to warfare and flight. Particular youngsters who arrived in Europe in their teens find it difficult to integrate as they often lack language skills and education in general.

To be clear, radicalisation, within the framework of this article, refers to the process of adoption of radical thoughts – be they nationalistic or jihadist – that lead to the active support of warfare, terrorism, or acts of violence. The term radicalisation is not to be used in the context of any kind of legitimate religious practise or other genuinely cultural norms that are an integral part of Chechen tradition. These cultural norms, values and traditions as well as religious practises are to be valued and not to be diminished through misperceptions and false interpretations. For the purposes of this report terrorism – despite the ongoing academic debate – is defined as "premeditated, politically motivated violence perpetrated against noncombatant targets by sub-national groups or clandestine agents, usually intended to influence an audience"[5].

Until the first Chechen-Russian war in 1994, religion played an important but not crucial role for Chechens in terms of identity. Cultural norms and the adat, the traditional code of conduct, prevailed over the Islamic Law, the Sharia. This stance was of course reinforced by the Communist ideology of the Soviet Union. The role of radical Islam has not been an issue in Chechnya, but during the period of the two Chechen-Russian wars the role of religion changed and Islam, particularly its more radical traits, gained ground. Through the influx of foreign fighters and funding Chechens were confronted with the Jihadist ideol-

5 United States Department of State (2001): Patterns of Global Terrorism, p. xvi. Retrieved from: http://www.state.gov/documents/organization/10286.pdf.

ogy (Vidino 2005)[6]. This trend towards religion and at times radical Islam has also spread in the Diaspora and has even been reinforced through the Diaspora situation. The emergence of religion as a source of identity is clearly not an isolated development as this kind of trend has been observed in various Diaspora communities. In the case of Chechens there are thus two prime sources of identity, the national and the religious identity as a Chechen and Muslim. While the first is still largely dominant, the availability of a transnational identity seems highly attractive in a Diaspora situation – particularly when the host societies are perceived as alien and even hostile. Tendencies towards radical Islamic networks and thoughts are mainly observed on an individual basis. This feeling of alienation and lack of identity is particularly an issue for youngsters in their late teens, as they were quite young when they left their native land – too young to build an identity or to fight, but at the same time too old to adapt to their new surroundings in Europe, with crucial years of education lost on the way. Such disaffected young men and women might be prone to fundamentalist Islam in their quest for identity and respect. Radicalisation is a process that is fuelled by various sources, but the internet evidently plays a major role in this process and also increases the risk of identifying with the causes of global jihad which might lead to terrorism not for the nationalistic cause but rather to acts within the framework of global jihad. It has to be clearly stated that only a small number of Chechens adheres to radical Islamic believes and that involvement in international jihadi networks is mainly through individuals. Seen in the context of current trends and developments in terrorism, it is exactly this kind of individuals who are often self-radicalized through the internet, seeking a sense and a purpose in their lives (Sageman 2008). Of course the mere feeling of alienation is not a gateway to violence, but mobilization through networks is usually a transformative agent.

To prevent radicalisation and potential recruitment for terrorist causes is at the same time a challenge for security services as for those working in the field of migrant integration. Providing young people with a perspective in terms of education and labour market integration as well as social acceptance and respect for their culture and religion is crucial.

6 On the role of Al Qaeda in the Caucasus see also Gunaratna, Rohan (2003): Inside Al Qaeda. New York. p. 134–135.

Challenges and Threats to European Countries

To answer the question whether attacks perpetrated by Chechens could ever take place on the soil of the European Union, it has to be considered that there are ideologically two directions within the Chechen resistance movement: nationalism, and radical Islamic fundamentalism or jihadism. While the first does not likely pose a threat to European countries, the latter might lead to potential threats due to the global nature of its ideology.

Generally, European countries are perceived as safe havens, where Chechens found refuge in large numbers. Thus, actions that might interfere with that status do not seem likely, particularly because the Chechen community in Europe consists largely of refugees of the two Russian-Chechen wars. There have, however, been plans by a group called "the Chechen Network" consisting of Algerian and/or French nationals to target Russian institutions, the Eiffel Tower, and/or a shopping mall in Paris (Bakker 2006: 20).

Organised crime by Chechens is another issue that surfaced time and again – particularly in the field of ransom, smuggling, robbery and theft. To a large extent these activities are to be seen as what they are – criminal activities for monetary reasons. However, the development of organised crime structures becomes particularly worrying when it is regarded within the context of terrorism. "Officials in the Balkans are equally concerned about developing links between terrorism and mafia activity in Chechnya and other parts of the Caucasus spreading to Albania, Bosnia and beyond to Southern Europe" (Levitt 2003).

These considerations regarding the implications for security are to be taken into consideration when looking at the long-term perspective of a Chechen Diaspora in Europe. Clearly, the described developments and trends do not implicate any generalization, but try to point out areas of concern.

Bibliography

Al-Shishani, Murad Batal/Moore, Cerwyn (2005): Jordan and Chechnya. An Unquestioned Relationship. Retrieved from: http://www.watchdog.cz/index.php?show=000000-000004-000003-000117&lang=1; (28.12.2005).

Bakker, Edwin (2006): Jihadi terrorists in Europe. December 2006.

LaFraniere, Sharon (2003): How Jihad Made Its Way to Chechnya. In: Washington Post Foreign Service, Retrieved from: www.washingtonpost.com; April 26, 2003.

Levitt, Matthew (2003): Fighting Illegal Transfers through Alternative Means of Money Transfer. Retrieved from: http://thewashingtoninstitute.com/templateC07.php?CID=11.
Sageman, Marc (2008): The Next Generation of Terror. In: Foreign Policy. March/April 2008.
Schirra, Brun (2002): Erlösender Tod am Kaukasus. Deutsche Muslime kämpfen an der Seite der Rebellen in Tschetschenien. In: Die Zeit, 2002, 46, p. 5.
Thamm, Berndt Georg (2003): Selbstmordattentäter. Die Bestellung kam per Handy. Retrieved from: http://www.sicherheit-heute.de; (30. 12. 2003).
Vidino, Lorenzo (2005): How Chechnya Became a Breeding Ground for Terror. In: Middle East Quarterly, Summer 2005, 8, 3. Retrieved from: http://www.meforum.org/article/744.

The Potentials of Radicalisation within the Chechen Diaspora in Europe

Cerwyn Moore

Introduction

Both the 9/11 attacks and the Madrid bombings galvanised the European member states into action, so as to engage in the war against terrorism. In October 2004, the European Commission published a report entitled, "Fight Against Terrorism: Prevention, Preparedness, and Response" (European Commission 2004). Two of the major findings of the Commission report were the importance of the disruption of terrorist recruitment, and the opposition to radicalisation. Evidently, both the failed attacks and the bombings in London in July 2005 highlighted the ineffectiveness of measures designed to control borders, when terrorists are home-grown, or in the case of the London attacks, UK citizens.

Elsewhere, the issue of radicalisation has, in recent years, been the subject of debate by those involved in academia and, of course, those involved in a variety of institutions linked to policy circles at the national and supra-national level (Coolsaet 2008). In particular, the threat of radical Islam has been identified by some as a long-term threat to stability in the Middle East, and perhaps also to those ascension states currently seeking membership of the European Union (EU). Of course, this is not to say that Islam and radicalism are intimately intertwined. Nonetheless, research to date does indicate that the issue of radicalisation has been politicised following a series of events after 9/11.

Indeed, many years before the Commission report a series of "failed attacks" in Europe, loosely attributed to pro-Chechen groups, highlighted links between terror networks, radicalisation in Diaspora communities, and connections between regional terror networks, and affiliates in the global Salafi-Jihadi movement. Significantly though, it should be noted that Chechens have played little or no role in Al Qaeda operations, nor should the Diaspora community in Europe be viewed as a threat. Instead, it is important to note that the perception of Chechen asylum seekers results from regional terrorism tied into the ongoing conflicts in the North Caucasus, the media perception of Chechnya, the Russian narrative of Islamic threat, rather than from pro-Chechen terrorism. Even though the issue of integration of peoples, particularly from post-Soviet regions, is beyond the remit of analysis in this report, this does highlight two important introductory points: pro-Chechen terrorism may, in many cases, not be conducted by Chechens, and secondly, radicalisation is a multi-level phenomenon which may be both violent and non-violent.

This report seeks to analyse the potential for radicalisation in the Chechen Diaspora community in Europe. In order to do so, the report begins with an overview of the Chechen Diaspora community in different parts of the world. In each case a series of estimated figures for the Diaspora community, in a selection of countries is offered. These figures have been garnered from a close reading of existing literatures. However they are approximate figures, largely due to the difficulty in attaining up-to-date statistics, the unavailability of census data, the different waves of Diaspora, and finally the different status and labelling of the Chechen community within Turkey, Russia and EU member states. The report will then move on to examine the issues of radicalisation and Diaspora communities, and the role of Salafi-Jihadism.

The Chechen Diaspora Community and its Historical Antecedents

In order to contextualise the potential for radicalisation within the Diaspora community in Europe, it is important to consider the waves of migration from Chechnya to different parts of the world. This is important because the Diaspora community has, in different ways, played a role in the two conflicts of the 1990s (Moore/Tumelty 2008). Nonetheless, it is difficult to gain up-to-date and detailed figures for the Diaspora community due to the different status and labels used to signify migratory trends (for instance, including/excluding Circassians or including/excluding different sub-ethnic groups from the North Caucasus). Similarly, the different generations of migrants from Chechnya have been assimilated into the socio-political systems of particular countries such as Jordan, Azerbaijan and Kazakhstan. As such, the four sections which follow seek to offer a brief description of the historical antecedents of the Diaspora population in different regions, including some examples of areas where the Diaspora community may be located, whilst also offering some rough estimates for the Diaspora population. To begin, I will trace the lineage of the Middle Eastern Chechen Diaspora.

The Middle Eastern Diaspora: Syria, Jordan, Turkey and Iraq

The North Caucasus region is located in a hotly contested geographical area, having been the site of numerous confrontations between Tsarist Russia and Ottoman forces in the age of empire (Gammer 1995/2006; Zelkina 2000; Gall/De Waal 1997; Yemelianova 2002). Throughout the seventeenth, eighteenth, and nineteenth centuries conflicts erupted culminating in the Russian conquest of the region in 1859. At around this time a wave of Chechens fled to nearby regions such as Anatolia, Armenia and Azerbaijan, then still under the control of Ottoman forces. As a result, a small number of Chechen communities, in part hosted by the Ottoman administration, became settled in these regions, with other groups moving deeper into Ottoman territory into Jordan, Syria and present-day Iraq. The Chechen communities were also often used to protect the borders of the Ottoman Empire, becoming incorporated into some Middle Eastern communities. While many retained a sense of Chechen identity, their ability to express their own cultural identity was largely halted.

However, it was not until the Second World War, that a second wave of Chechens became located outside of the North Caucasus. The conflict between Nazi Germany and Soviet Russia in the early 1940s led to further instability in the North Caucasus. By 1944, under the command of Stalin, the Soviet authorities undertook a campaign of ethnic cleansing directed against ethnic groups in the Caucasus, leaving hundreds of thousands of people forcibly relocated to Central Asia (Gammer 2006).

In more recent years, it is the Jordanian Chechen Diaspora community which has played a significant role in domestic affairs within Chechnya proper, even though they have been integrated into socio-political life in Jordan (Jaimoukha

2001; Moore/Al-Shishani 2005). One reason for this may derive from the more relaxed approach to governance and the Hashemite system of rule in Jordan. In this way, the Jordanian government did not force or coerce the Chechen community to conform to traditional forms of socio-political identity, instead encouraging the Chechen migrants to assimilate, in part, into pre-existing communities and culture. The Chechen sense of identity – the traditional customs – were thus retained by this group, whilst some Chechens became important figures in Jordanian history and politics. As the table indicates, at present a rough estimate of the number of Chechen migrants in Jordan is around eight thousand.

In contrast to Jordan, it has been argued that this has not been the case for other Chechen communities in Syria, Egypt and Iraq. The small Chechen Diaspora community in Syria, numbered at approximately four thousand, in Egypt, numbered at around five thousand, and in Iraq, numbered at around two and a half thousand, have largely been assimilated into the societies and official political systems of these respective countries. The Chechen Diaspora communities in each of these countries have retained a sense of Chechen identity, although this is often subservient to the dominant modes of politics, often shaped by national political Islam.

The Turkish Chechen Diaspora of approximately one hundred thousand is the largest outside Russia. The vast majority of the Diaspora community resulted from emigration in the nineteenth century. The Chechen Diaspora in Turkey has a long tradition of involvement in the North Caucasus. Indeed, the Turkish community has maintained a sense of North Caucasian identity, with many notable contemporary Chechen writers and poets being based in Turkey. For instance, Tarik Cemal Kutlu penned two novels in the 1980s, whilst he translated the novel *Zelimkhan* into Turkish.

At present, there are Chechen communities in many of the larger cities of Turkey. Furthermore, Chechen communities can be found in a strip down central-eastern Turkey, including the provinces of Adana, Maras, Mus, and Sivas in Eastern Anatolia. The status of Chechen communities in Turkey has been shaped by the politics of empire, with these groups not officially being considered as a distinct ethnic minority (Cornell 2001). In part this resulted from the Treaty of Lausanne, signed after the First World War, which recognized only Greeks, Armenians and Jews as ethnic minorities. According to the constitutions, Turkish is the only language used in schools and the media, with resulting implications for the marginalisation of the Chechen language. As a result, there has been large-scale assimilation of the Chechen Diaspora. Nevertheless, a large number of support groups including the Caucasian-Chechen cultural association, the Caucasian-Chechen Solidarity Committee, the Caucasian Cultural Society, the Sivas Chechen Committee and other groups have offices in Turkey, channelling support to the North Caucasus.

Region	Diaspora Population
Turkey	100,000
Jordan	8,000
Egypt	5,000
Syria	4,000
Iraq	2,500

At least four points can be identified here, which are worthy of note. Firstly, the experience of the Chechen community in Jordan was very different from that of the ethnic groups in other Middle Eastern countries. The Chechen population in Jordan retained a sense of groupness and community, preserving their cultural identity, unlike the Diaspora communities in other Middle Eastern states who were forcibly integrated into the social, cultural and political life of other states due to national policies. For this reason, it appears that the Jordanian Chechens played an important role in the two Russo-Chechen campaigns in the 1990s.

Secondly, a number of Jordanians participated in the two Russo-Chechen wars of the 1990s. A small number of these volunteers were radical Jordanians and Gulf State Arabs who became concentrated around the Chechen Jordanian Sheikh Fathi, and latterly, Ibn Khattab (Moore/Tumelty 2008). Although linked, another group of volunteer combatants travelled to Chechnya and took part in hostilities driven, in part, by nationalist motivations. As a result, this illustrates how radical Salafist ideas became increasingly influential, particularly after 1995, as external groups loosely linked to the Diaspora community played a role in polarizing the war-ravaged community of Chechnya (Moore/Al-Shishani 2005).

Thirdly, in a political sense the Chechen community in Turkey has been supportive of the Chechen nationalist cause. Implicitly, this stance has been encouraged by support from Turkish politicians and the Turkish population, particularly in the first war. The political situation in Chechnya has re-engaged some previously assimilated Caucasians, who have not given up hope for liberation of their ancestral homeland, yet whilst support for the nationalist cause has been set up in Turkey, very few Turkish Chechens have actively become involved in the conflict. Moreover, due to Turkey's economic and political relations with Russia, the Turkish government has been cautious in this regard, bowing to Russian pressure to ban the May 2002 meeting of the International Chechen Congress in Istanbul, but resisting pressure to restrict the activities of Chechen organisations more broadly.

Fourthly, the historical antecedents of the different Chechen communities across the Middle East are part of a wave of migration, shaped in part by the Ottoman and Russian Empires in the nineteenth century (Cornell 2001). To some extent, this wave of migrants from the North Caucasus has been largely integrated into the various social, political and cultural communities across the Greater Middle East.

Post-Soviet Chechen Diaspora: The South Caucasus, Georgia, Azerbaijan and Russia

The largest concentration of Diaspora Chechens can be found in three centres. Firstly, many Chechens, amounting to approximately one hundred thousand, have relocated from the North Caucasus to Russia, particularly to Moscow and its environs. According to some reports, a small Chechen Diaspora can also be traced in Russia's Far East, with additional communities dotted throughout the rest of Russia. Many of these communities had been established in the Soviet era, but have grown markedly as a result of the two wars of the 1990s. Secondly, a significant Chechen Diaspora community exists in the South Caucasus, with many Chechen families having relocated or migrated to neighbouring countries, building on long-established affiliations in parts of Georgia and Azerbaijan. The exact figure for the Chechen community in these countries is difficult to gauge, but much like the Chechen Diaspora in Russia, the numbers rose sharply as a result of the two wars of the 1990s. This community retains strong links to Chechnya proper, given both its close proximity to the North Caucasus and the extensive trade links between countries in the South Caucasus and Southern Russia. Finally, a third Diaspora group remains in parts of post-Soviet Central Asia. These communities were established as a result of the policy of deportation, enacted by the Stalin regime in 1944 (Smith 2001). Accordingly, a small and yet important Chechen Diaspora community is centred in parts of Kazakhstan.

Region	Diaspora Population
South Caucasus (Georgia, Azerbaijan)	Unknown
Russia, including Moscow	150–160,000
Post-Soviet Central Asia	Unknown

The Global Diaspora

The global Chechen Diaspora is relatively small, shaped by the end of the Cold War and the two conflicts of the 1990s. Only a small number of Chechens appear to have migrated across the Atlantic, with a community of approximately one hundred located across Canada, and a slightly larger figure of around one thousand being located in the United States. The global Diaspora maintains an awareness of events in the North Caucasus, often through the extensive use of internet sites.

Region	Diaspora Population
Canada	~ 100
US	1,000

The Chechen Diaspora in Europe

Census data, or indeed the lack of it, reveals that a significant proportion of the Chechen population remains unaccounted for, with a further portion of the population cited as "wanting to leave the region". The key reason for this does not result from a lack of attachment to the North Caucasus, but results from the instability in the region throughout the 1990s (Tishkov 2002).

At present, approximately one hundred thousand Chechen asylum-seekers have settled in Europe. Interestingly, the Chechen Diaspora in Europe is, in generational terms, very young. In a sense then, the immigrants or asylum-seekers who have relocated to Europe in the 1990s appear to be a young generation of Chechens, who retain both a desire to return to the North Caucasus and who posses first-hand knowledge of the situation on the ground in the region. Evidently, the reason for the move to Europe is primarily driven by the political conditions in the North Caucasus. More often than not, these political refugees travel to France, or join communities in Austria, Belgium and Northern Europe, although the first place of migration is usually within the Russian Federation. Indeed, as a result of the ascension status of countries on the borders of the EU, and as a result of the continued instability in the North Caucasus, the Chechen Diaspora community will remain a highly politicised policy issue.

Chechen communities can be found in Austria, France, Germany and Belgium. In addition to these communities, sizeable Chechen groups can also be found across Scandinavia, in Poland and the UK. These Chechen communities may experience difficulties integrating into European countries, due to a lack of knowledge of existing norms and laws. Furthermore, in recent years a number of illegal immigrants from the Caucasus as a whole have been arrested. Due to the stringent policies designed to curb emigration to Europe, it is extremely difficult for Chechens to obtain legal entry into Europe, and this has brought immigrants into contact with people smuggling operations and other criminal elements (for example document forgers).

Finally, it should be noted that a considerable number of asylum-seekers have travelled into Europe, following the change in status of some countries due to the enlargement of the EU and the concomitant expansion of the Schengen zone. Accordingly, a significant upsurge in the amounts of Chechen migrants was noted recently, as Chechen families move from Central European states such as Poland, to many Western European countries. The mixed status of many of these migrants (from those seeking political asylum to economic migrants), many who had been denied access to Europe in 2002 and 2003, coupled with the aforementioned criminal networks which exploit migrants, mean it is incredibly difficult to track the exact number of people who have relocated in parts of Western Europe. At the same time, the differing policies of integration mean it is difficult to regulate the integration of migrants groups into EU member states.

Assessing Radicalisation and Diasporas

Radicalisation is understood here as a preparedness to pursue or support far-reaching changes in society. These changes may be incompatible with existing social and political norms, and to some extent, may be accompanied by a threat to established forms of governance. Amongst other things, the form of radical Islam known as Salafi-Jihadism, it is argued, is puritanical, intolerant and anti-Western. In the case of the European Union then, radicalisation would be viewed as a threat to national democratic norms, and also the protocol of governance tied into the range of actors involved in the European Union. Significantly though, radicalisation does not necessarily have to be violent; it can also be associated with the polarisation of beliefs in a particular community. In this way, radicalisation may be related to the stirring-up of ethnic differences and the demonising of other groups, extreme social isolationism, and a sense of taking the law into one's own hands.

For the most part, accounts of the second Chechen War have tended to assume that Islamist groups in the North Caucasus are merged with Chechen guerrillas and that this has effectively made the conflict in Chechnya into a religious one, depicted as Russia's "war on terror" (Russell 2007). In many ways, the broad and misplaced reading of radicalisation conflates types of militancy – from the political radical through to the religious radical. Whilst these two ideal types may exist within the same organisation (or even the same individual), they do not necessarily entail one another, and the processes and mechanisms of radicalisation may be significantly different. This representation, coupled with the isolation of Chechnya as a political issue, has done much to undermine the separatist core of the anti-Russian resistance in the North Caucasus, and its background in the Sufi tradition in the region (Zelkina 2000). At the same time, more nuanced academic accounts of the second conflict (Gammer 2007), along with grounded and insightful reportage (Nivat 2001; Procházková 2002) have illustrated the complexity of the situation across the North Caucasus. Evidently, therefore, the radicalisation of the insurgency in Chechnya occurred over a number of years, partly shaped by external groups tied into the Diaspora (Moore/Tumelty 2008). Nonetheless, radicalisation only occurred in one wing of the Chechen resistance, with many indigenous groups rejecting assistance from external support networks.

Furthermore, the level of analysis when considering radicalisation is also important here. A whole host of different paths for the radicalisation of an individual and of a group are often conflated, even though the motivations may be markedly different. There will likely also be interaction between individuals, whose behaviour within particular organisations may be profoundly distinct from their behaviour prior to joining an organisation. Other work in this area has noted how economic deprivation plays a role as a potential causal factor for radicalism, although this again has been contested.

There are a number of potential problems when identifying causal factors for radicalisation. These include the potential existence of a wide range of "paths to radicalism" for different individuals. Secondly, there will not be a mono-causal explanation, and elements may be missing from the trajectories of particular individuals that are present in others (Sageman 2004). Thus, rejecting a potential cause (for example, a Soviet-era technical education in a country with few opportunities) because some individuals who fit that category do not become terrorists ignores the interplay between causal factors and a multi-causal context.

Meanwhile, in recent years a series of articles and books on ethnic conflict have challenged the way that identity is deployed in the academic literature to explain specific conflicts. According to this body of work, a more refined account of loosely affiliated groupings highlighting the role of commonality, connectedness and groupness, could be used to move research beyond the account of political violence and "identity" (Brubaker 2004). Together, commonality and connectedness, along with an emotionally laden sense of belonging, creates a distinctive bounded group, which links a "felt solidarity or oneness with fellow group members and a felt difference from or even antipathy to specified outsiders" (Brubaker 2004: 46). Interestingly however, this body of work did not focus on the role of Diaspora communities, the issue of radicalisation, or the conflicts in Chechnya. Nevertheless, this reading of connectedness points towards the "multiple forms and degrees of commonality (...) and the widely varying ways in which actors (and the cultural idioms, public narratives, and prevailing discourses on which they draw) attribute meaning and significance to them" (Brubaker 2004: 48).

My argument here is that this multi-layered reading of connectedness and commonality can be employed to understand the Chechen Diaspora in Europe. More specifically, this reading of identity can be used to shed light on strong groupness in the Chechen community in Europe, and to reject the idea that this community has been influenced by radical Salafi-Jihadism. Instead, this nuanced, in places narrative or storied reading of Chechen Diaspora connectedness draws attention to the distinctive and powerful emotional ties to one's kin group, whilst also shedding light on the continued antipathy towards Russian policies towards the North Caucasus. In so doing, this helps to untie the Chechen community from small groups of radicals associated with one element of the Salafi-Jihadi movement in Europe, and at least in part, debunks many of the myths associated with commentaries and opportunistic readings of radical Islam in Chechnya proper. However, in the case of this report, this leads to a set of questions about pro-Chechen terrorism in Europe, and the emergence of a Salafi-Jihadi narrative which together, frame the potential for radicalisation.

The Potentials for Radicalisation

The European Experience: Pro-Chechen Terrorism in Europe

Although not conducted by Chechen groups themselves, a serious pro-Chechen terror plot was uncovered by the French authorities in the late 1990s. Members of a pro-Chechen network had been living as expatriates in France in the 1990s. In the late 1990s, a number of these Salafi-Jihadi volunteers travelled to Afghanistan and the Caucasus, in order take part in fighting. It appears that this channel to the Caucasus and Central Asia, and the movement of a small number of volunteers, also facilitated a further phase of radicalisation within one group of expatriates in France. On their return to France, a handful of these volunteers began to hatch a plot to attack sites in France. Prior to the attack though, some members of the network were exposed by French anti-terrorism police during raids. Chemicals, bomb-making instructions, and materials that could be used for making poisons and manufacturing lethal toxins were seized. Although some of these figures may have been volunteer combatants they are at best loosely "affiliated" to the radical wing of the anti-Russian resistance in Chechnya. Moreover, those arrested were not of Chechen origin and these acts should be read as "pro-Chechen" terrorism, located within a broader global Salafi-Jihadi movement.

Salafi-Jihadism and Global Terrorism

The influence of Salafi-Jihadism was brought into sharp focus in Europe as a result of the terror attacks in Madrid in March 2004, the killing of Theo van Gogh in the Netherlands in November 2004 and a spate of attacks in the UK in 2005 and 2007. However, these well-known events were accompanied by a host of other failed or foiled attacks including the Strasbourg plot in 2000, the 2001 September plot to attack embassies in France, Belgium and the Netherlands, the foiled attacks on transatlantic flights in December 2001, arrests in Bosnia in connection with radical groups plotting terror attacks in October 2005, and, more recently, the foiled attacks by a little-known group called the Islamic Jihad Union in Germany. For the most part, all of these attacks and plots centred on Europe; indeed, many have been associated with radical Islam. However, it would be misplaced to claim that all of these events have a shared history in radical Islam, or indeed, that the form of terrorism adopted by some of these networks is in fact new. Instead, they provide evidence that a range of conflicts have been co-opted by radical groups, and provide justification for attacks against Western interests, both within Europe, by also globally. It is essential then, to unpack the ways in which indigenous, nationalist and secessionist conflicts have been presented within a single radical Salafi-Jihadi narrative, how internal radicalisation within the Chechen separatist movement laid the ground for the adoption of particular methods, and importantly, how external groups including Diaspora communities, impact upon local conflicts.

Reports indicate that terror networks based in Europe manufactured poisons and extended links to groups in the Pankisi region of Georgia. Many militants had already been trained in covert operations, drawing on the modus operandi of Al Qaeda, drawn-up in a series of training manuals. For example, a number of groups who were tracked by national security agencies followed a set of similar security precautions such as having multiple identities, false travel documents, coding their communications and renting flats at ground level to facilitate easy escape. Prior to 9/11, European cells did engage in promoting conflicts that have since been connected to the global Salafi-Jihadi movement, although this was largely due to small-scale operations by individuals or groups. Nevertheless, another wave of jihadis did travel to Chechnya after 1999. My argument here is that, rather than those involved in the conflict itself in Chechnya such as Ibn Khattab or Abu Walid, the role of these individuals has done much to blur the representation of Chechnya as an indigenous nationalist conflict, and as a hotspot in Salafi and Wahhabi movements (Wilhelmsen 2005).

For example, as I have argued elsewhere (Moore 2006), two volunteer fighters from North Africa, known as the Benyaich brothers, had been members of Islamic Jihad in Dagestan, establishing connections between groups in North Africa and the North Caucasus in the late 1990s, and playing a small role in the conflict itself. Even though they had little real experience shaping or radicalising the indigenous Chechen movement, they evoked a Salafi-Jihadist agenda and became involved in the logistics for the Casablanca attacks in 2003, and perhaps also in the Madrid attacks in 2004. Other notable affiliates include a small number of former combatants linked to cells in France, who were connected to Al-Qaida-inspired plots, and members of the Hofsted group in Holland. Furthermore, according to some reports, one of the suicide bombers involved in the 2003 attacks on British Embassy in Turkey, Feridun Ugurlu, had fought in both Afghanistan and Chechnya. Such figures are better understood as "affiliates", whose experience of fighting in Chechnya fostered links with other radical groups. In this way, a whole group of other fighters who may have travelled to Chechnya played a role in shaping the image of Chechnya as a jihadi hotspot. However, these figures are not from Chechen origins, nor are they explicitly linked to the separatist wing of the anti-Russian resistance in the North Caucasus.

Elsewhere, some radical groups have been set up in order to radicalise the European Muslim youth, and encompass them to engage in armed jihad. Again though, it should be noted that this general comment masks a diversity within Islam, and sets up a series of questions about the nature of jihad, inter-generational change in social movements, radicalisation in particular communities, the role of ideologues, all of which are beyond the scope of this report.

Concluding Remarks

Undoubtedly, the radical Salafi-Jihadi network has legitimised some terror attacks as part of a global movement. Other groups which include the Algerian GSPC, a splinter group of which has been renamed and realigned as Al Qaeda in the Maghreb, have been raising funds, procuring weaponry, and recruiting fighters for jihad throughout the world for many years. Indeed, nearly ten years before the 9/11 attacks, radical elements in Algeria planned to hijack a plane, and crash it into Paris. Although "foiled", this plan demonstrates how indigenous movements seek to employ forms of political violence as a strategy and method, and how this process produces new waves of regional terrorism linked to indigenous movements. In turn, this also sheds light on the need to unpack the relationship between indigenous, separatist, secessionist and nationalist conflicts, in order to focus on how elements of global movements co-opt members from local theatres, gain support from and leverage in insurgencies, and how the flows between a series of local conflicts have shaped a radical wing of the Salafi-Jihadi movement. More generally, this also helps to indicate how a single anti-Western narrative may have emerged.

Even though the global Salafi-Jihadi movement has led to the radicalisation of individuals in Europe, the Chechen Diaspora community has remained divorced from this movement. In contrast, the young generation of Chechen migrants in Europe have maintained a highly politicized sense of identity, often maintaining a separatist ideology. Due to the traumatic experiences of a decade of political and military instability, the Chechen Diaspora in Europe may take time to integrate fully into widely differing European communities, although this should not be mistaken for isolationism or radicalisation.

Bibliography

Broxup, Marie Bennigsen (ed.) (1996): The North Caucasus Barrier. The Russian Advance Towards the Muslim World. London.
Brubaker, Rogers (ed.) (2004): Ethnicity Without Groups. London.
Coolsaet, Rik (ed.) (2008): Jihadi Terrorism and the Radicalisation Challenge in Europe. Aldershot.
Cornell, Svante (2001): Small Nations and Great Powers. A Study of Ethnopolitical Conflict in the Caucasus. Surrey.
European Commission (2004): Fight Against Terrorism. Prevention, Preparedness and Response. Available at: http://register.consilium.eu.int/pdf/en/04/st14/st14330-re01.en04.pdf
Gall, Carlotta/De Waal, Thomas (1997): Chechnya. A Small Victorious War. London.
Gammer, Moshe (1995): Muslim Resistance to the Tsar: Shamil and the Conquest of Chechnia. London.
Gammer, Moshe (2006): The Lone Wolf and the Bear. Three Centuries of Chechen Resistance to Russian Rule. London.
Gammer, Moshe (ed.) (2007): Ethno-Nationalism, Islam and the State in the Caucasus. Post-Soviet Disorder. Abingdon.
Jaimoukha, Amjad (2001): The Circassians. A Handbook. London.
Moore, Cerwyn/Al-Shishani, Murad Batal (2005): Jordan and Chechnya. An Unquestioned Relationship. In: Prague Watchdog. Available at: http://www.watchdog.cz/index.php?show=000000-000004-000003-000117&lang=1&bold=cerwyn

Moore, Cerwyn (2006): The Radicalisation of the Chechen Separatist Movement. Myth or Reality? In: Prague Watchdog. Available at: http://www.watchdog.cz/index.php?show=000000-000004-000001-000203&lang=1&bold=cerwyn
Moore, Cerwyn (2007): Inter-Generational Change and the Integration of Regional Groups in the Chechen Resistance. In: Central Asia. Caucasus Analyst, 9, 9.
Moore, Cerwyn/Tumelty, Paul (2008): Foreign Fighters and the Case of Chechnya. A Critical Assessment. In: Studies in Conflict and Terrorism, 31, 5 (in press).
Nivat, Anne (2001): Chienne De Guerre. A Woman Reporter Behind the Lines of the War in Chechnya. New York.
Procházková, Petra (2002): The Aluminium Queen. The Russian-Chechen War Through the Eyes of Women. Prague.
Ro'i, Yaacov (2000): Islam in the Soviet Union. From World War II to Perestroika. London.
Russell, John (2007): Chechnya. Russian's 'War on Terror'. Abingdon.
Sageman, Marc (2004): Understanding Terror Networks. Philadelphia.
Smith, Sebastain (2001): Allah's Mountains. The Battle for Chechnya. London.
Tishkov, Valery (2002): Chechnya. Life in a War-Torn Society. London.
United Nations (2004): Chechnya and Neighbouring Republics. Hear Our Voices. Geneva.
Wilhelmsen, Julie (2005): Between a Rock and a Hard Place. The Islamisation of the Chechen Separatist Movement. In: Europe-Asia Studies, 57, 35–59.
Yemelianova, Galina (2002): Russia and Islam. A Historical Survey. Basingstoke.
Zelkina, Anna (2000): In Quest for God and Freedom. Sufi Responses to the Russian Advance in the North Caucasus. London.

Chechen Transnational Networks on the Internet

KAROLINA ŁUKASIEWICZ

Introduction

"...there are voice rooms where you can meet Chechens from all over the world. You have people of all different ages and the topics are from current events to religion, and then you have your younger crew who listens to Noxchi music, etc. It's a nice way of learning and touching up your Noxchi mott and even Russian. It helped me!" [1] (http://www.facebook.com/group.php?gid=2246058387, 2007)

The above quotation comes from a Chechen discussion forum on the social networking site Facebook.com. When reading the forum, one can easily discover its relevance to people; due to the rapid technological development, Chechens living in Chechnya and abroad, particularly in Europe, are able to build transnational networks, share common interests and concerns, all without even seeing each other in reality.

The influence of technology on the emergence of social networks is significant for many groups of immigrants, and this phenomenon is particularly visible among refugees as they seek contact with family members and their home countries even more intensively than labour migrants. This is the case for Chechen refugees who have developed various kinds of transnational communities connected through social networks. The networks are based on the possibility to read about current events in Chechnya, the opportunity to call family members both in Chechnya

1 Nick names in quotations will be omitted due to privacy reasons. Each post quoted is described with a date when it was posted. In the bibliography are additional dates when it was retrieved. All the posts in the paper have been accurately quoted, mistakes included.

and abroad, and finally the opportunity to talk with other Chechens on online forums. In this paper, the latter topic will be of particular interest.

This new phenomenon raises various questions: How do Chechens in Europe build their transnational networks when visiting online forums? What topics do they discuss? What kind of interests do they share? What does it mean for them to be able to contact each other in virtual space? Answers to above questions are crucial, as they influence not only people's identity and actions, but the processes of adaptation to the host societies as well.

On the basis of grounded theory and computer content analysis, it is possible to identify and explain the mechanism of an emergence of Chechen transnational social networks through qualitative data content analysis of data collected from online forums and websites. In this paper, I will present research results on Chechen transnational networks. First, I will describe the theoretical framework of the analysis; next, the methods applied in the research will be introduced; then I will discuss the mechanisms of developing the networks; and finally, the topics covered by Chechens on online forums and websites will be analysed. Particular attention was paid to Chechens residing in Europe. On the basis of their popularity, the following internet portals will be analysed[2]: www.amina.com, www.facebook.com, www.chechnyafree.ru, www.kavkazcenter.com.

Chechen Social Networks

A number of features become apparent when reading Chechen online forums, i.e. the importance placed on Chechen identity, the recollection of crucial Chechen historical events (particularly related to the war and its victims), contact with other Chechens from the same *taips*[3] around the world, the opportunity to stay informed on the current situation in Chechnya; and finally the exchange of practical information (e.g. learning the language of the country of residence). Though the theoretical framework capturing the issues may derive from different paradigms in social science, I decided to analyse the phenomenon in terms of social networks, applying the grounded theory paradigm for collecting and analysing data (Corbin/Strauss 2008) rather than sociometric analysis. I named discussions

2 Other Chechen internet forums are e.g. on http://groups.yahoo.com/, http://groups.google.com/.

3 *taip* or *teip* is a Chechen tribal structure based on descent from a common ancestor and geographical location.

on Chechen online forums "social networks" to stress the structural relations among particular actors of the network rather than concentrating on the attributes of individual actors themselves. The notion of "social networks" was introduced by J.A. Barnes of the Manchester School of Social Anthropology. Barnes distinguished traditional analysis, focusing on communities and shared values in the paradigm of "Tonies's Gemeinschaft", from "networks", i.e. social structures based on personal contacts cutting across organisational boundaries (Barnes 1954). Another recognized forerunner of the paradigm was Elizabeth Bott, who made a considerable contribution to analysis through the application of the social networks perspective to conjugal role behaviour (Bott 1957). Such a perspective was related to Clyde Mitchell's systematic studies on social organisations' structures (Mitchell 1969). The author stressed the analysis of network content reflecting the meanings given by particular actors to the relationship. Furthermore, the content of the interaction determines the meaning given by authors to the cues, signs and symbols of the interaction. This issue will be an object of analysis in regard to Chechen online forums.

Further development of the social network theory led to the development of mathematical and spatial modelling applied by the Harvard and Chicago Schools to uncover small group structures and community networks.

Social networks, understood in terms of structures connecting people, are distinctly visible in the case of immigrants. The phenomenon has been described by a number of scholars, such as Vertovec (2001: 10), who observed:

"For migrants, social networks are crucial for finding jobs and accommodation, circulating goods and services, as well as psychological support and continuous social and economic information. Social networks often channel migrants into or through specific places and occupations."

A crucial issue related to social networks is that these networks often determine the exchange of social capital. In the case of immigrants, they can share not only culture, but also practical information as enumerated above.

Another concept evident in Chechen social networks is related to modern communication technologies. Chechens develop social relations beyond national borders and without making personal contacts – via the Internet. The process is accurately described as transnationalism, the novel element at present defined by Portes, Escobar, Radford (2007: 13) as "a frequent and durable participation of immigrants in the economic, political, and cultural life of their countries, which requires regular and frequent contact across national borders. Such contacts are made possible by innovations in transportation and communications technology unavailable to earlier generations of migrants."

Castels (2003: 20), in defining transnationalism, stresses an aspect of community building: "The rapid improvements in transport and communications make it possible for migrants to maintain their links with co-ethnics in the place of origin and elsewhere, while also building communities in the place of residence." Modern technology undoubtedly enables the development of Chechen social networks.

To sum up the theoretical discussion, I will define Chechen transnational networks on the Internet in accordance with Smith's definition, i.e. "a dispersed group of individuals from the same nation who maintain a sense of togetherness across geographical borders" (Smith 1998: 215). The stress will be put on the transnational relations of the group beyond national borders.

Since none of the existing theories is able to explain all the complexities of process observed on Chechens' online forums and websites, I applied a grounded theory approach.

Methodology

Qualitative data collection and analyses were introduced to explain mechanisms of the emergence of Chechen transnational social networks and the description of topics they cover on online forums.

In the process of collecting and analysing data, I have applied a grounded theory approach, forming the basis for computer-assisted content analysis. Grounded theory determines stages of collecting and analysing data to form a theory explaining the process being analysed. In accordance with this approach, I have collected data from five online forums in addition to four websites. These websites were selected due to their popularity among Chechens, as determined by empirical evidence. The popularity of these internet portals has been assessed through the interviewing of Chechens living in Poland, the examination of online advertising, and the analysis of data collected on www.alexa.com[4].

4 Alexa.com, a subsidiary company of Amazon.com, provides information on web traffic to many websites. It provides brief information on the content of particular websites, company details, traffic details, and links related to those being analysed.

During the process of collecting empirical data, memos[5] were made. Next, a QDA Miner[6] database was created containing descriptions of the online forums analysed, posts placed in the forums, and goals set by the authors of the particular internet portals. Finally, from the empirical data, a number of categories and particular codes emerged[7]. Categories and codes were analysed in correlation to variables such as the place of residence of Chechens and the number of persons logged into a particular internet forum or using the website. The following analyses are the result of the qualitative methodology applied.

Chechen Online Forums

From the multitude of Chechen online forums and websites, the following have been selected on the basis of their popularity:

I. www.amina.com
II. www.facebook.com
III. www.chechnyafree.ru
IV. www.kavkazcenter.com

After analysing the forums certain groups of topics appeared. These groups of topics will be discussed in detail in the below sections dedicated to particular portals. In this chapter, I will present some general topics present on most of the portals. The topics are grouped in categories, in accordance with the grounded theory approach. These categories include Chechen culture, religion, history, the Caucasus region in general, politics and economy, language, country of residence, and leisure.

The first category is that of *Chechen culture.* In this section, frequent topics of discussion include cultural traditions (including the posting of photographs and videos of Chechen music and dance), activities relating to theatre (e.g. arranging the showings of Chechen plays), Chechen radio and television programs, famous Chechens, and places crucial to Chechen national identity. In this category, posters frequently voice concern about the destruction of Chechen national heritage at the hands of Russia. Posters blessed their homeland; expressed their pride of

5 Memos are written records of analyses.

6 QDA Miner is a computer program assisting qualitative data analyses, offered by Provails Research.

7 Codes were organised into a code book in QDA Miner.

being Chechen; declared their desire to return to Chechnya (either for visiting or repatriation).

Religion was another essential issue found in the content of online Chechen social networks. Spiritual aspects of Islam, as well as related gender issues, were broadly discussed, as were traditions related to religious celebrations.

Furthermore, discussions on *Chechen history* often appeared. These discussions were often in regard to particular events related to the Russian invasion and Chechen history, both early and contemporary (e.g. the school siege in Beslan).

This category also includes deliberation on various Chechen *taips*.

These discussions expressed aspirations for Chechen independence and the need to fight for their homeland. Also stressed was the suffering and bloodshed incurred in the name of Chechnya.

Chechen social networks are often combined with discussion on *Caucasus in general*. In this category, appeals to fight for pan-Caucasian unity appear.

Next are *political and economic* discussions. These issues were related to Chechnya, their countries of residence, and other important political events as well. Also discussed in this section were issues related to the global and national economy.

Numerous discussion forums are dedicated to *language*. In these forums, Chechens discussed the Chechen language. It is important to note that the forums analysed in this paper were primarily in Russian or English, as well as other languages Chechens wanted to practice. The latter usually related to the language spoken in the posters' countries of residence, a conclusion drawn from the content of the discussions.

This leads us to the next group, that of *place of residence*. A significant group of topics was related to current countries of residence of Chechen Diaspora communities, with discussions often focusing on recent events having occurred in the countries of residence.

Finally, there is a group of topics related to *leisure* activities, particularly in regard to hobbies, sports, and holidays.

Mechanism of Developing Transnational Social Networks on the Internet

There are numerous ways in which people develop transnational networks through the use of online forums. Empirical analyses of Chechen online forums demonstrate several possibilities.

First of all, one often comes across online forums while browsing for current information or news regarding Chechnya. Chechens often recommend websites to one another as well. When entering an online forum, one often simply chooses a discussion group covering topics of personal interest. However, it is very common to enter online forums dedicated to particular *taips*. This is an opportunity to localise members of the same *taip* living in different parts of the world. It should be noted that, even in the case of entering a forum not directly dedicated to a particular *taip*, visitors are asked about their *taip*. Finally, it happens that Chechens visit a discussion group dedicated to learning a language. Usually, in the case of Amina.com it means that they want to practice the language of their country of residence. For example, when entering discussion groups dedicated to the German language on Amina.com, newcomers are usually asked where they are. The same applies to other European languages.

No matter how a visitor comes to join a forum, it often happens that the structure of one forum significantly overlaps others in terms of membership and the topics covered. After joining one forum, people tend to visit others, or leave messages about some interesting topics discussed on different pages, thereby inviting others to visit different pages. Some of these structures, once developed, are maintained for years while others vanish. Many discussion topics on the online forums are frequented by a core group of members, though the majority of the structures' members fluctuate – come and go – with some returning after a year or so of inactivity. It should be noted that some Chechens living in Poland, after their IP addresses had been discovered, were tracked by Russian security services and declared to stop using Amina.com out of concern for their family members residing in Chechnya. Those users who freely post on online forums (e.g. expressing critical opinions of the political situation in Russia and Chechnya) have often lived in the US or Europe for a long time and have few relatives remaining in Chechnya.

The transnational character of the networks is expressed in the fact that members of the forums are spread all over the world while at the same time may talk to each other on a daily basis. Furthermore, they also support their family members in Chechnya financially.

www.amina.com

Amina.com, a platform of communication and exchanging information for the international Chechen Diaspora, was established by Albert Digaev (a Chechen refugee residing in the USA) in 1997, making it the oldest Chechen online forum. It owes its name to a female name common among Chechens. Amina.com was established as an online portal for providing up-to-date information on Chechnya. Today, Amina.com features numerous online discussion boards, chat rooms, photo galleries, articles on Chechnya, and a private internet email service (Pohl 2005; http://www.selard.com/, 2007).

As of March 28, 2008, Amina.com had a record of users' simultaneous online visits amounting to 11,239 (http://www.selard.com/, 2008). According to data collected by Alexa.com, Amina.com has a traffic rank of 60,784 hits in a three-month period (January to March 2008)[8]. Amina.com had the highest number of users (reach) at the end of 2002. This was a rapid increase in the number of users, from less than 20 users per million (users of the Internet) up to 90. During 2003, the number of users fluctuated around 20, to fall significantly in 2004. Since 2005 the number of users has been gradually increasing up to 40 in 2007. In 2008 it fell slightly to 20 users per million (http://www.alexa.com/data/details/traffic_details/amina.com, 2008).

According to data provided by Alexa.com, the majority of Amina.com users accessed the site from Russia and Ukraine, although Austria, Latvia, Norway and France were significantly represented.

Alexa.com provides additional information on other websites most frequently visited by Amina.com users. According to the data, Amina.com users visit websites of human rights organisations focusing on human rights violations (particularly Human Rights Watch and Prague Watchdog); and websites with news, cultural or historical information on Chechnya, such as Kavkaz Center (www.kavkazcenter.com), Kavkaz.org (www.kavkaz.org), and Qoqaz.net (www.qoqaz.net). Furthermore, Amina.com users frequently visit the websites of regional newspapers like Russia Today (http://www.russiatoday.ru/). They also read Chechnya News (http://www.chechnyanews.com/) as well as the Russian government website (http://www.gov.ru/).

8 The traffic rank on Alexa.com is based on a combined measure of page views and users (reach).

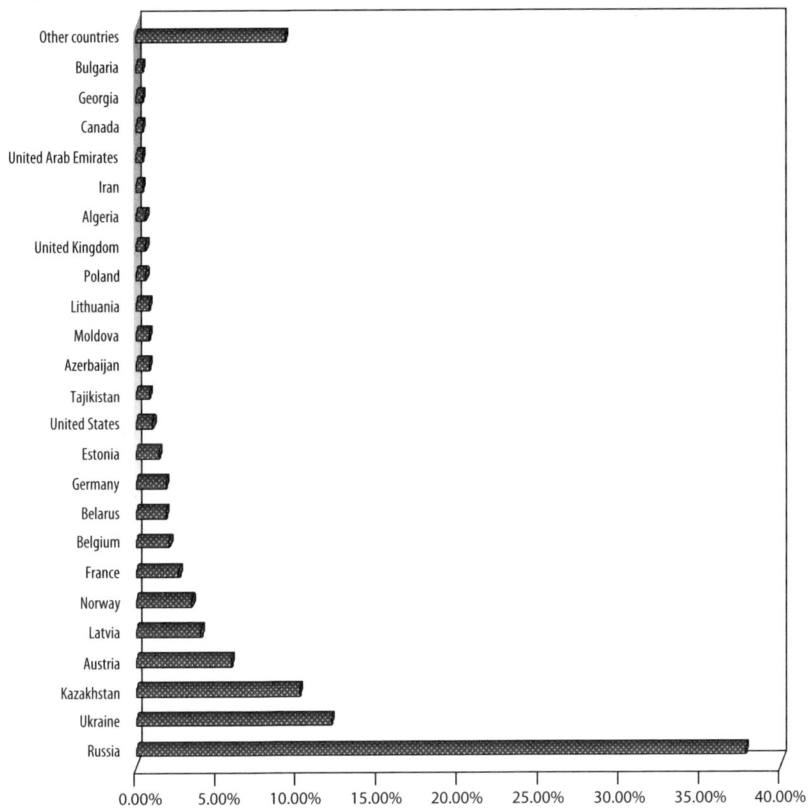

(based on information available at: http://www.alexa.com/data/details/traffic_details/amina.com, 2008)

Amina.com is primarily in Russian language, but also features Chechen and English. There are additional web pages in German (with 3,676 posts[9]), Italian (904 posts), French (308 posts), Dutch (292 posts), Turkish (97 posts), Georgian (90 posts), Lithuanian (80 posts), Norwegian (79 posts), Spanish (77 posts), Polish (55 posts), Hebrew (30 posts), the languages of Dagestan (23 posts), and Swedish (17 posts). It should be noted that Amina.com users often mix languages; when writing in Russian, Chechen words and phrases are often used.

According to users of Amina.com *Foreign languages* online discussion boards, the forums were established for the practice of foreign languages. In fact, this is

9 The term "post" relates to replies to a question given on the online forum. The numbers of posts enumerated in the paper refer to the time this paper was written (until 31.03.2008). It should be noted that the numbers fluctuate and increase every day.

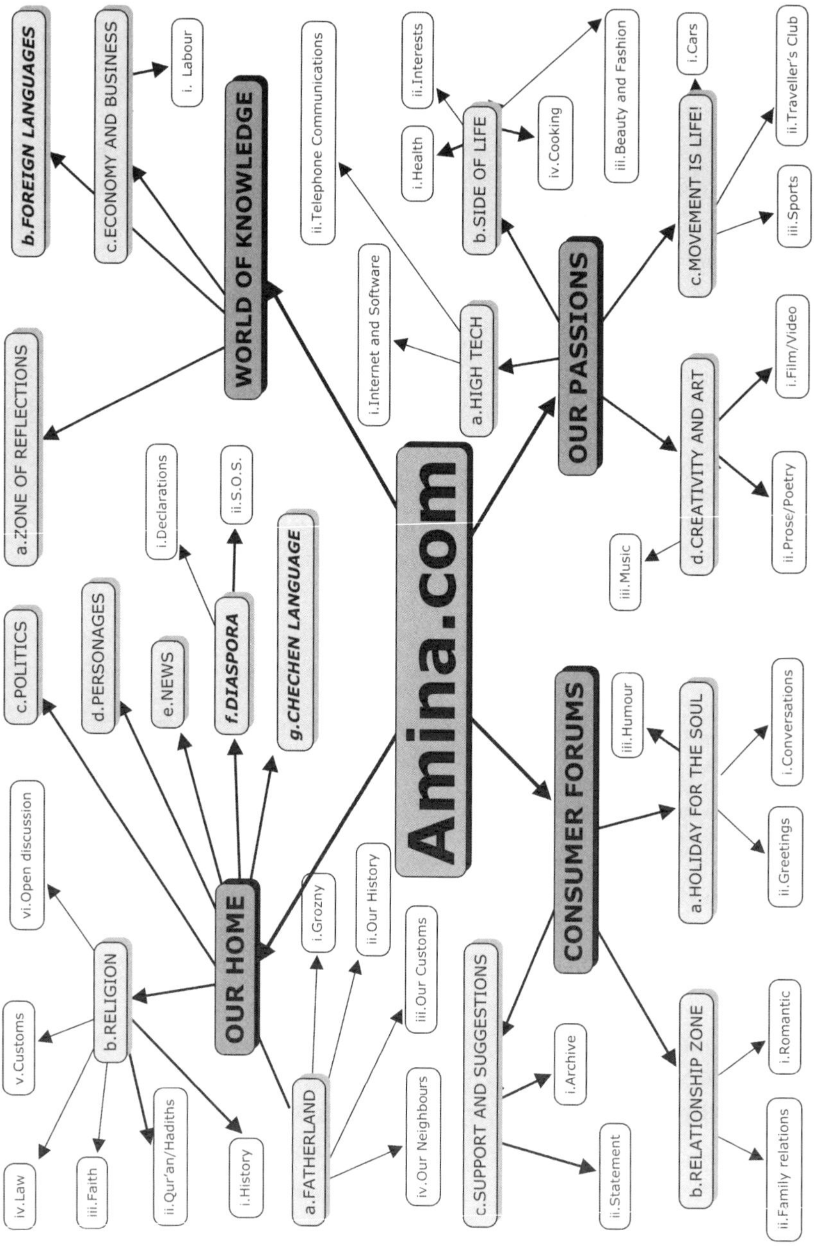

(Categories of topics discussed on http://www.selard.com/, 2007)

often an opportunity to begin online discussions with Chechens living in the particular countries in which the language they seek to practice is spoken. Another option of establishing relationships with Chechens living abroad is through the Diaspora thematic category.

The above topics fall into the previously discussed categories present on other Chechen websites, i.e. culture (Our Customs), religion, history (Fatherland, Personages), Caucasus and Chechnya (Grozny), politics and economy, language (Chechen language, Foreign languages), place of residence (Diaspora, News), and leisure (World of Knowledge, Our Passions, Consumer Forums).

When analysing Chechen social networks in Europe the category of *Diaspora* is of particular importance. In the Diaspora section, visitors are questioned about their national identity. The results are as follows: Chechen – 71%, "other" – 10%, Russian – 6.67%, Ingush – 3.03%, Tatar – 1.62%, Ukrainian – 1.62%, Dagestan – 1.82%, Jewish – 1.41%, Azeri – 1.21%, and Ossetian – 1.01%. The *Diaspora* section contains discussion boards dedicated to particular Chechen Diasporas, including European. The section contains discussions related to particular countries of residence as well as opinions on those places. Next, there is a group of additional topics like psychological problems of the Chechen experience, Chechen organisations, and discussions on reasons for migration. Finally, the Diaspora category constitutes a unique platform for establishing social networks based on *taip* identity; furthermore, Chechens look for their old friends here.

Chechens in the *Diaspora* section were asked to assess the country where they reside. 48.65% of the respondents expressed very favourable opinions on their place of residence, having no complaints; 13.51% "wish to relocate", and 37.84% perceive their new country as beautiful but wish to repatriate (http://www.selard.com/9818.html, 2008).

The Diaspora category is a valuable source of information on European Chechens. To illustrate this thesis I will refer to some information presented in one online discussion board in the group – a general topic *Chechens living in Europe*. In this discussion group, people discuss issues related to the integration process and express their opinions on both Europeans and fellow Chechens residing in Europe: "I have noticed that many people don't want to live in Europe and stay here only because they have no place to go, it is safer here and we have more opportunities" (http://www.selard.com/2181.html, 2006). Posters voice a will to sustain Chechen culture: "We live in Germany, but our Chechen mentality does not surrender. (...) Integration is individual for each person, for each family"

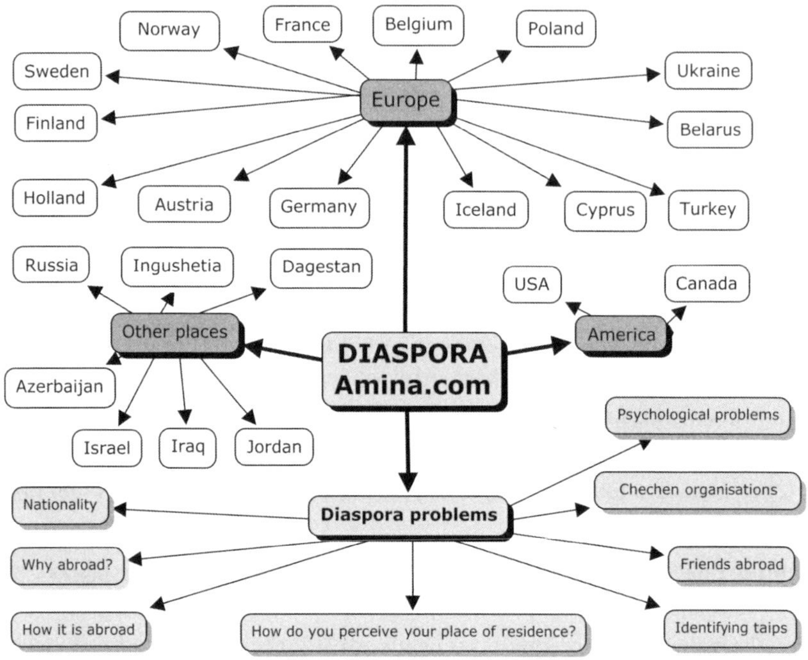

(Based on information placed at: http://www.selard.com/s3.html, 2007)

(http://www.selard.com/2181.html, 2006). Some posters stressed the negative attitude Europeans expressed toward Chechens, as well as differences in values between Chechens and Europeans:

"I was in a shock when I found out that I live among people unfamiliar to me, with a different mentality, with different concepts about life. I can understand them a bit, since their lives do not differ from Russian standards, but also, in a way, I cannot understand them. For me, till now it is not clear how it is possible to turn away from old parents because of past insults (...). I cannot understand how old parents can sell all they have earned for many years and then go travelling, saying: Let the children do what they want, this was earned by us" (http://www.selard.com/2181.html, 2006).

Posters frequently voice concern on integration policies and the services offered to refugees and asylum seekers. Also found on the boards are those expressing a longing for Chechnya, their desire to return to Chechnya, as well as their difficulties and frustration with the adaptation process:

"I could not adapt here, although I know the language and I have work, I have also citizenship, I envy those who could stay in their homeland" (http://www.selard.com/2181-p41.html, 2008). Others stressed the importance of the new social relations they have established and their desire to remain in their new country. To quote one representative statement:

"It's nice in Europe, I have already got used to it and it feels 'convenient'. One year is enough to adapt. But a whole life will be not enough to understand people here. I despise their outlook on life. They have no sanctity. Right now I do not want to come back, because I want to achieve something, I want to take advantage of the time I am here. (...) But I certainly want my children to know and love our homeland, the land of our fathers. And when I get old, I wish to come back" (http://www.selard.com/2181-p41.html, 2008).

Some people, particularly those living in Germany, expressed a will to return to Chechnya, though only under certain conditions. For example, one poster declared:

"I have a permanent residence in Germany, life is not bad here, well, parents work as doctors, I study. (...) I certainly want to return, but only when I see that my Chechen Republic prospers in Islam" (http://www.selard.com/2181.html, 2006).

Amina.com creates a unique opportunity for the establishment of social networks based on a Chechen culture and history, *taip* identification, current place of residence, and common interests. Nevertheless, it should be noted that there have been controversies related to Amina.com, namely a controversy surrounding the so-called "Council of Chechen Alims", who have accused the portal and its owner of presenting offensive pictures in the section "Chechen Photo Gallery" (Pohl 2005).

www.facebook.com

Facebook.com, a U.S.-based social utility service established in 1997, allows members to keep contact with friends, establish new relationships, as well as upload photos and videos. When using Facebook.com, a person first creates a profile (containing, for example, a photo and selected personal information). Also, one can search for friends who may already use Facebook.com, or find new friends. In addition, it is possible to establish or join some thematic groups. Facebook.com has more than 67 million active users (http://www.facebook.com/press/info.php?statistics, 2008). It is the 6th most-trafficked website in the world (http://www.alexa.com/data/details/traffic_details/facebook.com, 2007) and the 2nd most-trafficked social media site in the world (http://www.comscore.com, 2007). Daily reach per million for Facebook.com has been rapidly increasing since 2006[10]. In 2006, less than 10,000 people using the Internet were visiting Facebook.com, while since 2007 this number has been increasing up to 60,000 at the end of 2008 (http://www.alexa.com/data/details/traffic_details/facebook.com, 2008).

At the time the paper was written, Facebook.com contained 19 Chechen thematic groups[11]. Membership in these groups is primarily composed of persons of Chechen origin, however those interested in Chechen culture, history, or the Chechen political situation are also represented. Chechen groups are primarily in English, though numerous groups use Chechen, Russian, Arab, and Turkish. The majority of Chechen users of Facebook.com live in Turkey, Jordan, and the US, but also Russia. Other users come from UK, Australia, Canada, the Republic of South Africa and some other European countries, like Norway.

There are approximately 5,000 members signed into the groups, though the same people often join more than one group. The most numerous group gathers over 1,000 members. Variables describing the groups are: *Name* (e.g. "CheChens Noxchi Chechnya Noxcho", "Freedom for Chechens", "Justice for Chechnya", "Independence for Chechnya!", "Noxchi Mott"); *Type of a group* (e.g.: Common Interest – Beliefs & Causes, Common Interest – Languages, Common Interest – History, Common Interest – Current Events, Common Interest – Politics, Geography – Regions, Entertainment & Arts – Dance, Student Groups – Social Groups); *Contact information* (including an address of a person/organisation who established the forum); *Description* (a goal of the group); *Attached photos and videos*; *Posted Items* (post profiles, photos, photo albums, notes, News Feed stories, and external content); *Discussion Board* (a forum for conversation between group members; if the group is "closed" or "secret", only members can see the board);

10 As determined by data provided by Alexa.com, the majority of Facebook.com users accessed the site from the USA. The other users come from Canada, Colombia and the UK. I do not attach detailed data, since it is not possible to differentiate countries of residence of Chechens using Facebook.com.

11 The number of groups fluctuates almost every day. New groups are being established while others vanish. During 2007 the number of groups fluctuated between 15 and 25. Furthermore, some groups are established not only by Chechens, e.g. inhabitants from Caucasus, but also touch issues related to Chechnya.

Members' profiles; The Wall (a forum for group members to post comments publicly, i.e. visible for everyone).

One of the most numerous Chechen groups is *Justice for Chechnya*, found under the category *Common Interest – Beliefs & Causes*, it counts nearly a thousand members. The least numerous group is *Chechens 4 Ever,* under the category *Organisations – Community Organisations.*

The social networks among Chechen users of Facebook.com are based on *common culture and tradition*. Many groups discuss topics related to the continued destruction of Chechen national heritage at the hands of Russia. They stress their will to sustain their Chechen identity and the uniqueness of Chechen culture. "Chechen people are very different from the others. In addition, Chechens have a totally different language, culture, and traditions" (http://www.facebook.com/group.php?gid=6468000689, 2007). The common culture is especially visible through visual representations, particularly those expressing Chechen national symbols, such as the Chechen flag, maps of Chechnya, *the Lone Wolf,* and photos of famous Chechens. These symbols, present in almost every group, are frequently accompanied by discussions on their symbolism.

Chechens, in various groups, discussed Russian oppression, particularly the destruction of their culture and the slaughter of innocent people:

"Since they were colonized by the Russians in the eighteenth century, Chechens have suffered under a systematic campaign of discrimination and were forced to deny their cultural identity" (http://www.facebook.com/group.php?gid=2209157662, 2007).

A process of Russification was often recalled:

"During the rule of Joseph Stalin, Chechens were forbidden to speak their own language and a campaign of Russification began. In 1994, Russia invaded Chechnya in order to crush a growing independence movement. During the two-year-long conflict, Russia destroyed vast swaths of the country, levelled the capital city of Grozny, and killed tens of thousands of Chechen civilians" (http://www.facebook.com/group.php?gid=2218500390, 2007).

Also discussed was a painful awareness that the world has forgotten about the military conflict in the Caucasus:

"While the world's attention is focused on Palestine and Lebanon, the suffering of the Chechen people is often forgotten. This group serves as a reminder of their plight" (http://www.facebook.com/group.php?gid=2218500390, 2007).

There were frequent calls to action, calling on people to join the fight for

Chechen independence, "against the spilled blood of children that floods Chechnya, and for the people who are willing to fight back, against the Russians..." (http://www.facebook.com/group.php?gid=2231744016, 2007).

Posters often emphasized the pride of their Chechen origin: "The Chechen race is eager for this race! We will overpopulate the global race! We are the Proud Chechens of the World and we will win this race!!!" (http://www.facebook.com/group.php?gid=6331037046, 2007)

Posters frequently blessed Chechnya and those who fight for its liberation: "May Allah bless our brave worriers... I hope we will soon get our freedom" (http://www.facebook.com/group.php?gid=6468000689 , 2007).

This leads us to next category of topics, that is, topics covering *Caucasus*. There are groups calling for pan-Caucasian unity: "This group is meant to unite all the people of Caucasus (CIRCASSIANS, CHECHENS etc...) and keep them posted on the latest news and events going on in our homeland, God bless Kavkazia" (http://www.facebook.com/group.php?gid=2218500390, 2007).

Finally, a significant topic of discussion relates to *religion*. Islam was stressed as an important factor of Chechen identity. The role of religion as a bulwark against Russian oppression was frequently discussed: "Russian subjugation did not stop Islam from spreading. Religion became a form of passive resistance that had persisted since czarist times through the Soviet period" (http://www.facebook.com/group.php?gid=2230527412, 2007).

Religion is also a central issue for establishing Chechen transnational networks, as many Chechen national traditions, such as music and ceremonial dances, stem from their religious traditions.

Another group of topics present on Chechen Facebook.com groups is the *history* of the Chechen nation. Chechens repeatedly describe their views on their origins and their history: "The Chechens call themselves Nokhchi and, along with their cousins, the Ingush, are known as the Vainakh peoples, one of several ethnic groups collectively referred to as North Caucasian" (http://www.facebook.com/group.php?gid=2230527412, 2007). Posts placed in almost all forums recall the genocide of the Chechen people. One group, *Recognize the Chechen Genocide*, is dedicated exclusively to discussions on the planned massacre of the Chechen nation. Posters describe dramatic events of Chechen history, often attaching terrifying photos and short films depicting the ongoing bloodshed. "We shouldn't forget our history (...) We should forgive but shouldn't forget. Some Russian people came to CHECHNYA and killed children, men, women (...) what is the difference between Russian people and terrorists" (http://www.facebook.com/wall.php?id=6609217302, 2008).

Also discussed were current events related to Chechen history, such as the Beslan school siege: "Russia is using the Besland and Moscow siege (in which the Russian forces themselves stood for most of the civilian casualties, by the way) as an excuse for continuing the illegal and brutal acts in Chechnya (...)" (http://www.facebook.com/group.php?gid=2209157662, 2008).

Another concept evident in Chechen groups Facebook.com is *language*. There are separate groups dedicated particularly to the Chechen language. One such group, *Noxchi Mott*, has as its stated goal the promotion of the Chechen language; a goal broadly discussed in other discussion boards. In addition to providing basic information on the Chechen language, great attention is paid to learning the Chechen language, particularly in regard to the Chechen Diaspora. Posters voice enthusiasm about the Chechen language: "I love learning more and more about our language! :)" (http://www.facebook.com/group.php?gid=2229065350, 2008)

Finally, there are online discussion groups on *current events, the political situation, and leisure*. However, these topics appear tangentially, being found in groups dedicated to other issues such as Chechen culture or tradition.

As determined by empirical evidence, the categories of common culture, history, religion, language, issues related to Caucasus and leisure shape transnational Chechen networks on Facebook.com. Chechens dispersed all around the world share an interest in sustaining the Chechen identity as well as discussing common problems they have. Beyond the geographical borders Chechens construct transnational networks.

www.chechenyafree.ru

Chechnyafree.ru is a portal providing news from Chechnya, as well as Chechen culture, traditions, history, and religion. This Russian-based online forum, established in 2002, had 1,581 registered users in December 2007 who until that date had posted 47.651 messages. Chechnyafree.ru has a traffic rank of 185,287 hits in a three-month period (January to March 2008), with its number of users (reach) peaking at the end of 2004, from less than 10 users per million since 2002, up to 20. Since 2005 it has been maintaining the same level (about 10 users per million) (http://www.alexa.com/data/details/traffic_details/forum.chechnyafree.ru, 2008).

According to data provided by Alexa.com, the majority of Chechenyafree.ru users accessed the site from Russia and Norway, Austria, Ukraine, Kazakhstan, Belgium, and France. Detailed information is presented in the following chart:

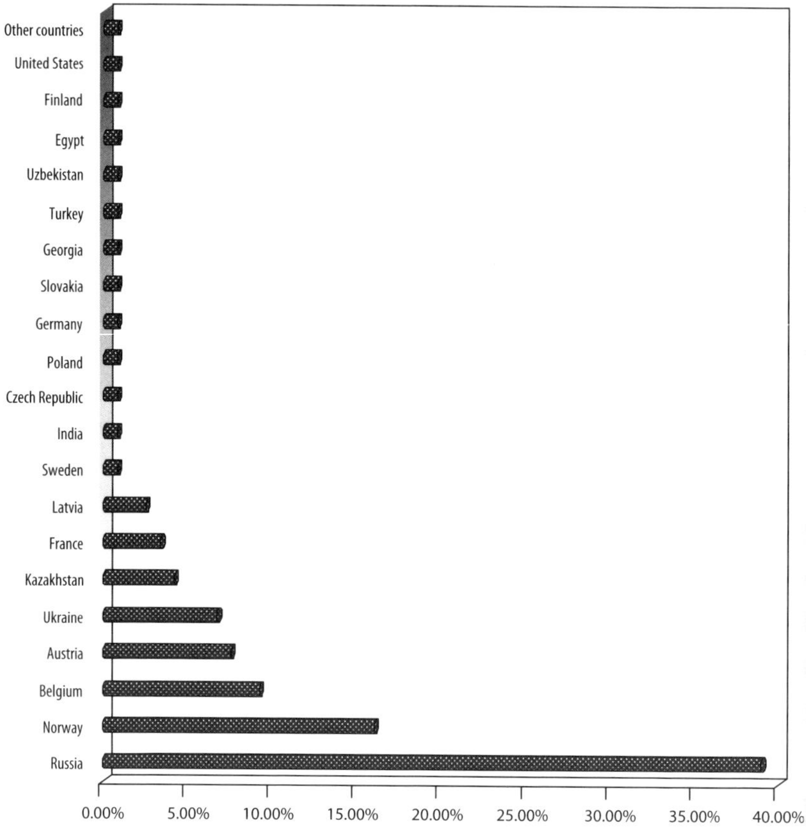

(Based on data available at: http://www.alexa.com/data/details/traffic_details/forum.chechnyafree.ru, 2008)

Alexa.com provides additional information concerning the websites most often visited by Chechenyafree.ru users. According to the data, Chechenyafree.ru users frequently visit other websites with news and information on Chechen and Caucasian culture and traditions, such as Chechen.org (http://chechen.org/), Chechnya.ru (http://chechnya.ru/), Chechenpress.com (http://www.chechenpress.com/), Kavkaz.strana.ru(http://www.strana.ru/), and Shali.tk (http://www.shali.tk/). Additionally, the website of the Russian government (http://www.gov.ru/) is frequently visited.

Chechenyafree.ru is in Russian language. Posts placed in the forum of Chechenyafree.ru are divided into the following categories:

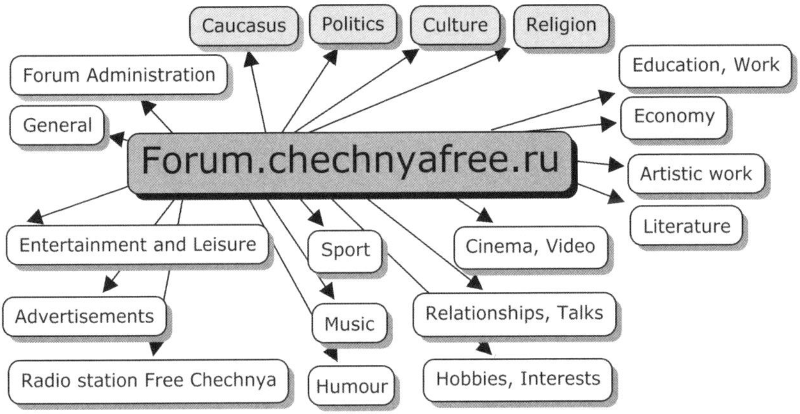

(Based on information placed at http://forum.chechnyafree.ru, 2007)

Each of the above categories is furthermore divided into groups of topics and various online discussion boards. Several categories are of particular interest, i.e. *Caucasus* (contains 678 posts spread out into 21 online discussion boards), *Politics* (74 online discussion boards, 3,255 posts), *Culture* (47 online discussion boards, 1,855 posts) and *Religion* (104 online discussion boards, 1,924 posts). Also significant is the category *Relationships, Talks,* since it is the most numerous group (it contains 9,822 posts). Other categories, e.g. *Education, Work* (198 posts), *Economy* (93 posts), *Artistic Work* (195 posts) and *Literature* (2,422 posts) are not unique for online Chechen forums (Chechens may discuss the issues also on other internet forums, not necessarily Chechnyafree.ru). The category *Caucasus* contains e.g. discussions on Chechen nationality, events crucial for Chechens, the situation in Ingushetia, Chechen business, Chechen personages, ethnic relations in Chechnya and also in the Chechen Diaspora, including America and Chechnya at Wikipedia. The latter is also present at Amina.com.

In the *Diaspora* section, Chechens describe the stories of their lives; they explain where they live and what they do there. The also discuss issues related to integration in a host society as well as their will to go back to Chechnya. The majority is satisfied with their life abroad. Users of the Diaspora online discussion board live in the UK, and England, Belgium, and Sweden in particular. They usually study or have already graduated. They frequently avoid the perspective of repatriation. Posters often express positive opinions on their life, but at the same time perceive Europeans as distant people.

The next category, *Politics*, contains the following topics: news and discussions on the current political situation in Chechnya and Russia in general, Russian international politics, elections in Chechnya, the memory of war victims in Grozny, the meaning of freedom, drug addiction, and also a discussion on Kavkaz Center. The latter contains some critical opinions on the reliability of the medium.

The most-discussed topic in the section *Culture* is: *Shall a Chechen girl marry a Chechen boy?,* with 261 posts. It was a man who started the discussion. He pointed out that while it is acceptable for a man to marry a non-Chechen girl, this is not allowed for a woman. The poster was criticized by both men and women. A Chechen girl remarked, "Any Chechen girl who respects herself, Chechen traditions, and above all the family, will never think of not marrying a Chechen man!" (http://forum.chechnyafree.ru/viewtopic.php?t=53, 2007)

Another broadly discussed topic was: *Can a Russian girl marry a Chechen boy* (207 posts). Again, girls frequently expressed negative opinions about exogamic marriages: "I am categorically against mixed marriages. It is always the same – sooner or later they break up; children suffer which should not be like that" (http://forum.chechnyafree.ru/viewtopic.php?t=11, 2007).

Negative opinions were justified with a need to preserve the Chechen nation. Men who took part in the discussion expressed more liberal opinions on exogamic marriages.

Another popular topic in the *Culture* category is *My city* (160 posts). Posters mainly recollect Grozny, attach photos of the city and comment on their current place of residence. Another popular group is dedicated to the *Caucasian nationality* (145 posts) and covers topics related to the perception of people of Caucasian origin, i.e. the problem of discrimination.

Finally, the category *Religion* contains online discussion forums about Koran, jihad and other issues related to the religious law (134 posts). Another significant group of topics evident in the category is about politics (141 posts); e.g. reasons of the war in the Chechen Republic (mainly economical reasons are pointed out). Another large online group covers the topic of conversion from and to Islam (101 posts). Posts placed in the forum usually express either negative or sceptic opinions on religious conversions, e.g.: "As a Muslim, I can accept that. As a Chechen – I cannot accept conversion. Who has changed faith, will change it again. I do not trust them. Belief comes with mother's milk" (http://forum.chechnyafree.ru/viewtopic.php?t=393, 2007). In the next large online discussion board (89 posts), people discuss the relation between religion and national identity, e.g.: "Different nations can have the same religion, but people who practise one religion (even without variations) can fight with each other" (http://forum.chechnyafree.ru/viewtopic.php?t=386, 2007). Another popular topic of discussion in the forum is Islam in the Middle East.

It should be noted that categories of topics described above constitute the broader concepts present on all Chechen internet forums analysed in the paper, i.e. *Culture, Religion, Chechen history, Caucasus in general, Politics and Economy, Language, Place of residence,* and *Leisure.* The concepts are present in different categories, e.g. *Culture* is discussed in the same category on Forum Chechnyafree.ru, but also in the Caucasus section and *Politics.* Topics related to the place of residence of the respondents can be found in the Diaspora section, but also in the language section. *Leisure* is a concept particularly developed on Chechnyafree.ru. It includes *Entertainment and Leisure, Cinema, Video, Sport, Artistic work, Humour,* and *Hobbies/Interests.*

The Forum Chechnyafree.ru is of particular interest for European Chechens. They built their transnational networks on the basis of national identity but also on experiences of their life in Europe. It should be stressed that users of the forum are usually educated and even if considering repatriation do not envisage it for the near future. Posters frequently complain about European welfare as well as the distant attitude people demonstrate in social relations.

Internet Websites, Kavkaz Center

In the last section I will discuss another factor constituting Chechen transnational networks, i.e. the opportunity to stay informed about the current situation in Chechnya when reading internet websites. As previously mentioned, users of online discussion boards also visit websites with news on Chechnya. A website frequently visited by users of Chechen internet forums is Kavkaz Center. It is an "international news agency covering events in the Islamic world, Chechnya and

Russia" (http://www.kavkazcenter.com/, 2007). It claims to be independent from the government of the Chechen Republic of Ichkeria (CRI) and declares not to represent any other country's viewpoint. Kavkaz Center made it its mission to report about "the war, the war crimes, the evidence of genocide on the part of the state aggressor against the entire population and the position of those defending against aggression – the Chechen mujahedin" (http://old.kavkazcenter.com/eng/about/, 2007).

The agency was established in Georgia. It has been online since 2002, but it was founded in 1999 by the CRI National Centre for Strategic Research and Political Technology (http://www.kavkazcenter.com/, 2007, http://www.alexa.com/data/details/related_links/kavkazcenter.com, 2007). The website is published in

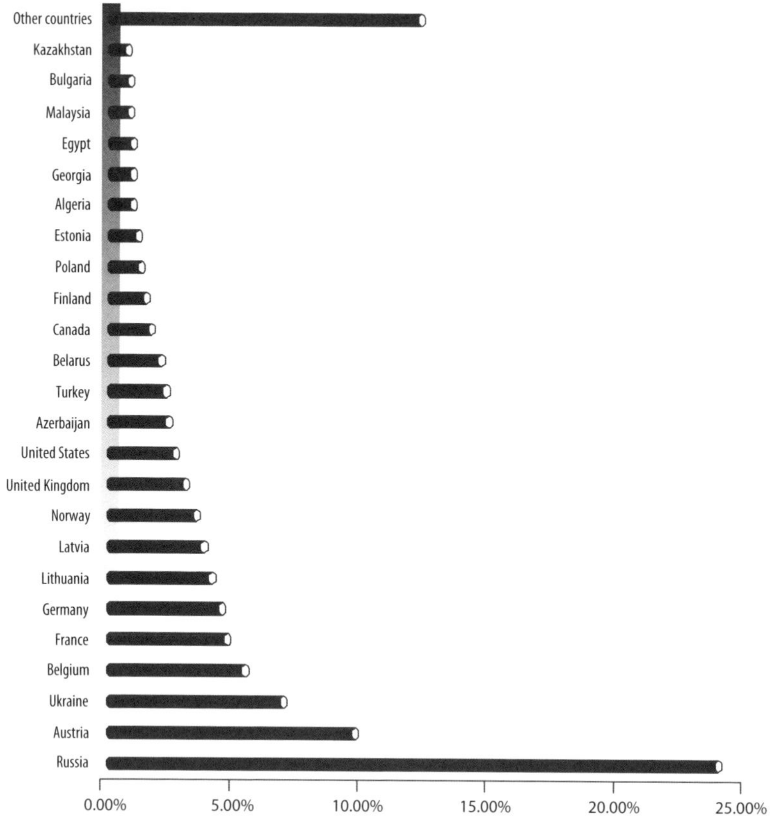

(Based on data available at: http://www.alexa.com/data/details/traffic_details/kavkazcenter.com , 2008)

five languages, English, Arabic, Ukrainian, Russian, and Turkish. Kavkaz Center has a traffic rank of 32,956 hits in a three-month period (January to March 2008). The agency had the highest number of users (reach) at the end of 2004, rising to 300 users per million, while between 2002 and 2003 it had registered less than 50 users. Between 2005 and 2007 the number of users slightly increased from less than 50 up to almost 80 users per million. At the end of 2005 and in the middle of the year 2006 the number of users jumped up to 180 per million. Since 2007 the number of users has slightly decreased to 20 per million (http://www.alexa.com/data/details/traffic_details/kavkazcenter.com, 2008).

Due to data provided by Alexa.com, the majority of Kavkaz Center users accessed the site from Russia, Austria, Ukraine, Belgium, France, Germany, Lithuania, Latvia, Norway, the UK, the USA, Azerbaijan, Turkey, and Belarus.

Kavkaz Center provides the following groups of information:

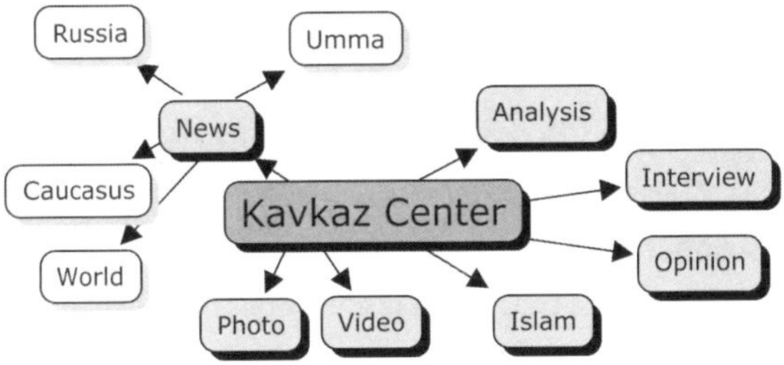

(Based on information placed at: http://www.kavkazcenter.com, 2007)

Kavkaz Center informs about current events in the world, in Russia and Caucasus. The news are related to Islam or the Caucasus Diaspora, e.g. in the section *World* Kavkaz Center placed information from Denmark: "Far-right lawmaker Geert Wilders posted a controversial anti-Qur'an documentary on a video-sharing website (...)" (http://www.kavkazcenter.com/eng/section.php?id=w , 2007). The section *Caucasus* contains information on mujahedin battles, armed clashes, and victims. The section *Umma* (i.e. worldwide community of Muslims) informs about events directly related to Islam, e.g. in the Middle East or Afghanistan. It disseminates information on Al Quaida and Taliban. Kavkaz Center posts letters or movies received from Islamic fighters. In the next section,

Analysis, critical articles about international policy related to Islam are placed; particular attention is paid to Russian, U.S. and European policy worldwide. There are also book reviews on the topic. The category *Interviews* featured discussions with prominent Muslim warriors or politicians from Caucasus or the Middle East. Also interviewed are European politicians who deal with the Chechen conflict. The personages are either personally interviewed by Kavkaz Center correspondents, or articles come from other agencies; e.g. Chechenews.com. Another section, *Opinions*, provides critical articles on globalisation, the war in Iraq, the Middle and Far East. The articles usually come from various newspapers, e.g. Daily Muslims or Middle East Online, but also from Associated Press or The Washington Post. *Photo* and *Video* sections contain pictures from the war in Chechnya and international events related to the military conflict, as well as other military conflicts concerning *umma*.

Kavkaz Center undoubtedly shapes Chechen transnational networks when providing information on the Chechen war and current events in Caucasus. Nevertheless, it should be noted that it is a controversial medium. It is criticised for supporting the Chechen independence movement and for an explicitly negative description of the Russians. Furthermore, because of these controversies, it was moved from the Lithuanian website to the Swedish one. According to Chechnya Weekly (2004), "Lithuania's State Security Department closed down Kavakaz Center in September under pressure from the Kremlin."

It is important to note that there is a number of other websites providing information on Chechnya, e.g. Chechenews (http://chechenews.com/). According to Alexa.com, Chechenews is located in Canada and is online since 2006. Chechenews has a traffic rank of 386,412 (as for March 2008). Chechenews users are primarily from Europe (27.8% readers reside in Norway and 16.7% in Belarus, 7.8% in Poland, 2.2% in Estonia, also 2.2% in Austria and 1.1 % in Finland). Chechenews is also read in the United States (15.6%), in Azerbaijan (12.2%) and Russia (11.1%). Other users come from the United Arab Emirates (3.3%). Chechenews provides information from Ichkeria, but also covers issues with a particular focus on Islam; it also features the sections: *Opinions*, *Law*, *Sport*, *Articles*, and *World News*. Furthermore, it broadcasts Chechen TV. Chechenews is in Russian language.

Another website providing information about Chechnya is Chechenpress.co.uk (http://www.chechenpress.co.uk/english/index.shtml). It is located in the UK, and it has a traffic rank of 3,867,024.

Also visited is Chechnyanews http://www.chechnyanews.com/) located on the Malaysian website. It provides news from Russia, and topics related to terror, human rights, refugees, and war crimes.

Finally, it is worth mentioning that in Europe there is a large number of both governmental and non-governmental organisations and associations dealing with Chechnya or the Chechen Diaspora. They often support the integration of the Chechen Diaspora into a host society. Chechens, when visiting the websites, are either provided with information on Chechnya, or on events related to the Chechen Diaspora (e.g. cultural festivals, movie shows or practical information related to their legal situation). When given information on the Chechen Diaspora, real, not virtual, transnational networks emerge. Examples of such European websites are listed below:

- http://www.tjetjenien.dk/index.html (Support Committee for Chechnya, located in Denmark)
- http://www.chechnya.fi/ (Finland-Chechnya society)
- http://www.tsjetsjenia.no/index.php?kategori=8 (State Committee for Chechnya, In Norway)
- http://www.savechechnya.org.uk (The Save Chechnya Campaign in the UK)
- http://chechnyaadvocacy.org/ (The Chechnya Advocacy Network (CAN), international organisation with agencies in Paris and Brussels)
- http://www.comite-tchetchenie.org/ (Chechen Committee in France)
- http://2007.worldchechnyaday.org/page/About_WCD (World Chechnya Day)
- http://www.wolnykaukaz.org/kaukaz/ (Free Caucasus Committee in Poland)
- http://www.kafkas.org.tr (Caucasus Foundation in Turkey)

Conclusions

Chechen online discussion boards and websites promote the emergence of social transnational networks. Chechens in Europe can find their family members or *taip* members when visiting Chechen online discussion boards. They can exchange their social capital, e.g. practical information related to finding a job or to the process of applying for refugee status, but they can also express opinions about subjects that matter to them, and stay informed on the current situation in Chechnya.

The topics they frequently discuss are related to Chechen culture, the Islamic religion, Chechen history, language, Caucasus, news from Chechnya and from countries in which they currently reside as well as various issues concerning economy, politics, and leisure. As determined by empirical data, Chechens appreciate the opportunity to sustain their national identity when visiting the internet forums and websites. The transnational networks' *content* reflects the meaning that particular actors convey to common values and everyday problems they share. Due to the technological development, a new quality of social relations has appeared, in virtual space though, but it influences reality, i.e. people's identity and actions related to their integration into a host society.

Bibliography

Author Unknown (2004): Separatist website finds a home in Sweden. In: Chechnya Weekly 5, 43. Retrieved January 4, 2008:
http://www.jamestown.org/chechnya_weekly/article.php?articleid=2371326.
Alexa.com (2008): http://www.alexa.com/data/details/traffic_details/forum.chechnyafree.ru. Retrieved: March 20, 2008.
Alexa.com (2008): http://www.alexa.com/data/details/traffic_details/forum.chechnyafree.ru. Retrieved: March 20, 2008.
Alexa.com (2008): http://www.alexa.com/data/details/traffic_details/amina.com. Retrieved: March 20, 2008.
Alexa.com (2008) http://www.alexa.com/data/details/traffic_details/facebook.com ,26. Retrieved: March 20, 2008.
Alexa.com (2008): http://www.alexa.com/data/details/traffic_details/kavkazcenter.com. Retrieved: February 3, 2008
Alexa.com (2008): http://www.alexa.com/data/details/traffic_details/kavkazcenter.com. Retrieved: February 3, 2008
Amina.com (2007): http://www.selard.com/s3.html. Retrieved: January 10, 2008.
Amina.com (2007): http://www.selard.com/9818.html . Retrieved January 15, 2008.
Amina.com (2006): http://www.selard.com/2181.html. Retrieved January 15, 2008.
Amina.com (2006): http://www.selard.com/2181.html. Retrieved January 15, 2008.
Amina.com (2006): http://www.selard.com/2181.html. Retrieved January 15, 2008.
Amina.com (2008): http://www.selard.com/2181-p41.html. Retrieved: March 20, 2008.
Amina.com (2008): http://www.selard.com/2181-p41.html. Retrieved: March 20, 2008.
Amina.com (2006): http://www.selard.com/2181.html. Retrieved: March 20, 2008.
Barnes, J. A. (1954): Class and Committees in a Norwegian Island Parish. In: Human Relations, 7, 39–58.
Bott, Elizabeth (1957): Family and Social Network. London/Tavistock.

Castels, Stephen (2003): Towards a Sociology of Forced Migration and Social Transformation. In: Sociology, 37, 1, 13–34.
Corbin, Juliet/Strauss, Anselm (2008): Basics of Qualitative Research. Los Angeles/ Singapore.
Chechen Forum Selard, http://www.selard.com/. Retrieved March 28, 2008
Chechnya News, http://www.chechnyanews.com/. Retrieved March 28, 2008
Facebook.com (2007): http://www.facebook.com/group.php?gid=6468000689. Retrieved: January 20, 2008.
Facebook.com (2007): http://www.facebook.com/group.php?gid=2209157662. Retrieved: January 20, 2008.
Facebook.com (2007): http://www.facebook.com/group.php?gid=2218500390. Retrieved: January 20, 2008.
Facebook.com (2007): http://www.facebook.com/group.php?gid=2218500390. Retrieved: January 20, 2008.
Facebook.com (2007): http://www.facebook.com/group.php?gid=2218500390. Retrieved: January 20, 2008.
Facebook.com (2007): http://www.facebook.com/group.php?gid=2231744016. Retrieved: January 20, 2008.
Facebook.com (2007): http://www.facebook.com/group.php?gid=6331037046. Retrieved: January 20, 2008.
Facebook.com (2007): http://www.facebook.com/group.php?gid=6468000689. Retrieved: January 20, 2008.
Facebook.com (2007): http://www.facebook.com/group.php?gid=2218500390. Retrieved: January 20, 2008.
Facebook.com (2007): http://www.facebook.com/group.php?gid=2230527412. Retrieved: January 20 2008.
Facebook.com (2007): http://www.facebook.com/group.php?gid=2246058387. Retrieved: January 20, 2008.
Facebook.com (2008): http://www.facebook.com/press/info.php?statistics. Retrieved: January 20, 2008.
Facebook.com (2007): http://www.facebook.com/group.php?gid=223052741. Retrieved: January 20, 2008.
Facebook.com (2007): http://www.facebook.com/wall.php?id=6609217302. Retrieved: January 20, 2008.
Facebook.com (2008): http://www.facebook.com/group.php?gid=2209157662. Retrieved: January 20, 2008.
Facebook.com (2008): http://www.facebook.com/group.php?gid=2229065350. Retrieved: January 20, 2008.
Forum.chechnyafree.ru (2007): http://forum.chechnyafree.ru. Retrieved: February 3, 2008.
Forum.chechnyafree.ru (2007): http://forum.chechnyafree.ru/viewtopic.php?t=53. Retrieved: February 3, 2008.
Forum.chechnyafree.ru (2007): http://forum.chechnyafree.ru/viewtopic.php?t=11. Retrieved: February 3, 2008.
Forum.chechnyafree.ru (2007): http://forum.chechnyafree.ru/viewtopic.php?t=393.

Retrieved: February 3, 2008.
Forum.chechnyafree.ru (2007): http://forum.chechnyafree.ru/viewtopic.php?t=386. Retrieved: February 3, 2008.
Forum.chechnyafree.ru (2007): http://www.kavkazcenter.com/. Retrieved: February 3, 2008.
Forum.chechnyafree.ru (2007): http://old.kavkazcenter.com/eng/about/. Retrieved: February 3, 2008.
Forum.chechnyafree.ru (2007): http://old.kavkazcenter.com/eng/about/. Retrieved: February 3, 2008.
Forum.chechnyafree.ru (2007): http://www.kavkazcenter.com/. Retrieved: February 3, 2008.
Forum.chechnyafree.ru (2007): http://www.alexa.com/data/details/related_links/kavkazcenter.com. Retrieved: February 3, 2008.
Kavkaz-Center: www.kavkazcenter.com. Retrieved March 28, 2008.
Kavkaz.org: www.kavkaz.org. Retrieved March 28, 2008.
MITCHELL, J. CLYDE (1969): Social Networks in Urban Situations. Analysis of Personal Relationships in Central African Towns. Manchester.
POHL, MICHAELA (2005): Amina.com under attack. Rift opens between Chechen leadership and its Diaspora. In: Chechnya Weekly, 6, 39. Retrieved: November 5, 2007: http://www.jamestown.org/publications_details.php?volume_id=409&issue_id=3500&article_id=2370374).
PORTES, ALEJANDRO (1996): Global villagers. The rise of transnational communities. In: The American Prospect, 25, 74–77.
PORTES, ALEJANDRO (1995): The economic sociology of immigration. In: Portes, Alejandro (ed.): Economic Sociology and the Sociology of Immigration. A Conceptual Overview. New York. 1–41.

PORTES, ALEJANDRO/ESCOBAR, CRISTINA/RADFORD, ALEXANDRIA WALTON (2007): Immigrant Transnational Organizations and Development. A Comparative Study. Princeton.
Russia Today: http://www.russiatoday.ru/. Retrieved March 28, 2008.
Russian Federation: http://www.gov.ru/. Retrieved March 28, 2008.
SASSEN, SASKIA (2000): New frontiers facing urban sociology at the millennium. In: British Journal of Sociology, 15, 1, 143–159.
SMITH, MICHAEL (1998): Transnational Localities. Community, Technology and the Politics of Membership within the Context of Mexico and U.S. Migration. In: Smith, Michael/ **GUARNIZO, LOUIS (EDS.):** Transnationalism from Below. New Brunswick, 197–238.
VERTOVEC, STEVEN (2001): Transnational social formations: towards conceptual cross fertilization. Paper presented at the Workshop on „Transnational Migration: Comparative Perspectives". Princeton.

Source Country Information through Recognized Refugees

NINO HARTL

The main problem regarding any information on the country of origin is the reliability of the source material. Numerous reports on the region of the Russian Federation/Chechen Republic amount to nothing more than generalized statements or deal exclusively with the political/human rights aspects in Chechnya. From these sources it is practically impossible to generate a clear picture of the social infrastructure.

After reviewing the various reports as well as the source material, one can agree upon the fact that the reconstruction of Chechnya is well underway, but it remains unclear when this redevelopment actually started. Furthermore, basic information regarding the costs of food, medical care, pharmaceutical products, as well as infrastructure, public services and their availability is missing. The question regarding the existence of social services is also left unanswered. But it is these kinds of questions that asylum authorities are most concerned about – be it for the sake of clarification regarding refoulement inquiries or for the validation of the authenticity of statements made during the asylum-seeking procedure.

The fact that Chechen refugees have now found a home in Austria presented the opportunity to embark on a unique European project: the acquisition of information by means of interviewing recognized refugees.

It was made clear from the beginning that, under no circumstances might political and/or human rights aspects be the subject matter of the project or the interviews, especially since it was impossible to neglect the personal experience of those being questioned. In any case, the Chechen Diaspora now domiciled in Austria offers an abundant source of information.

The project's goal was to attain a detailed picture of Chechnya's social infrastructure, thereby gaining insight into everyday life as well as the most important aspects of social life between 2005 and 2006.

In cooperation with the Austrian Integration Fund (Österreichischer Integrationsfonds) a total of 40 recognized refugees (23 women, 17 men) between the ages of 29 and 47 were interviewed. The selection criteria included:
- 25–50 years of age;
- equal numbers of women and men;
- provenance from the largest Chechen towns.

Those polled were natives of the following towns: Tolstoi Jurt, Grosny/Sakan Jurt, Grosny, Chassaw-Jurt, Schelkovskoi, Kalinovski, Snamenskoi, Novij Atagi, Argun, Grosny/Alchankaja, Urus Martan, Starye-Atagi, Kosomolsk, Gudermes, Naursk, and Barmut. The majority of the interviewees had left Chechnya in 2005.

The report was structured as follows:
- Basic foods and their supply
- Medical care and its availability
- State benefits and their availability
- Basic infrastructure
- Employment, wages, and job seeking possibilities
- Media
- Social structures
- Courts and police
- Other

One example topic would be pension payments and other state benefits. In the meantime it is known that pensions and other state benefits are being paid out again[1]. But how did the actual situation present itself in 2005/2006? Was an improvement already noticeable at that time? How were payments actually effected?

The interviews ascertained that the pensions (of the interviewees and/or their

1 Leyla Dzeitova, President of the Chechen-Ingush Non-Governmental Organisation VESTA. Minutes of her visit to the independent Federal Asylum Senate, 31 March 2008.

relatives) amounted to the following figures[2]:

Amount of Pension	< 1000 rouble	1000 – 2000 rouble	2000 – 3500 rouble	3500 – 5000 rouble	Don't know/N.A.
% of interviewees	26	26	13	9	26

Pensions are paid by the following authorities[3]:

Pension payment	Russian State Authority	Post Office	Don't Know / N.A.	Other
% of interviewees	43	37	18	2

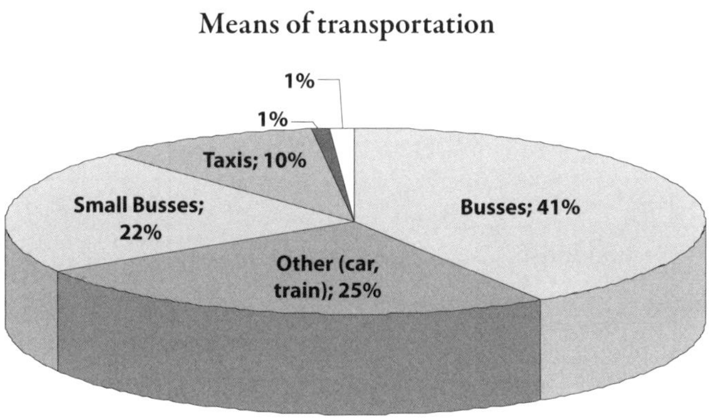

Additional examples of the methods of evaluation:

2 BAA/ÖIF (2008): Social Infrastructure in Chechnya, p. 33

3 BAA/ÖIF (2008): Social Infrastructure in Chechnya, p. 34

Means of transportation between towns and cities	**Specified means of transport**
Busses (large)	29
Other (car, train)	18
Small busses („Marschrutkas“)	16
Taxis	7
Hitchhiking	1
Don't know / N.A.	1

Which specialized medical doctors are available?

Medical Doctors	**Specified Doctors**
General Practitioner	12
Gynaecologist	9
All specialist fields available	9
Surgeon	8
Paediatrician	5
Dentist / Orthodontist	3
Cardiologist	2
Urologist	2
Traumatologist	2
Outpatient Departments	2
Therapists	1
Only First Aid	1
Orthopaedic	1
N.A.	16

Inevitably, any report compiled in this way will not meet the requirements of an updated classic country of origin documentation. This kind of a report does, however, offer a closer insight and understanding of social structures and gives a clear and detailed picture of the in situ situation that could not be conveyed by other forms of reporting. Aspects concerning questions of political and human rights have been sufficiently covered by other reports.

Authors

Robert Chenciner, Ph.D., Trevelyan Scholar, Pembroke College, University of Cambridge, MA; 1987- Senior Associate Member St Antony's College, University of Oxford; 1990- Honorary Member USSR/ Russian Academy of Sciences, Daghestan Scientific Centre. Anthropology, material culture and economic history books include Daghestan. Tradition and Survival (1997), Madder Red, a history of luxury and trade (2000), Tattooed Mountain Women and Spoon Boxes of Daghestan (2006). UK asylum expert on former Soviet states since 2000. OSCE observer in 4 FSS elections.

Franck Düvell, Ph.D., Social Scientist, since 2006 Senior Researcher at the Centre for Migration, Policy and Society (COMPAS), University of Oxford. From 2003/04 Jean Monnet Fellow at Robert-Schuman Centre for Advanced Studies, European University Institute (Florence), and from 1998–2003 Research Fellow at the University of Exeter. Lecturer in sociology, political science and geography at the University of Bremen, Germany. Among his publications: "Illegal Immigration in Europe" (Houndmills, 2006), "Migration. Boundaries of equality and justice" (Cambridge, 2003, with Bill Jordan), "Die Globalisierung des Migrationsregimes" (Berlin, 2003), and "Irregular Migration. Dilemmas of transnational mobility" (Cheltenham, 2002, with Bill Jordan).

Nino Hartl, Master degree in Law, University of Vienna. Currently in the Department of Legal Affairs and the Dublin Regulation at the Federal Asylum Office, Federal Ministry of the Interior, responsible for the Russian Federation in the Country of Origin Information Unit.

Martin Hofmann, Master degree in Political Science and Philosophy, University of Vienna. Programme Manager, Intergovernmental Dialogue and Research at the International Centre for Migration Policy Development (ICMPD) in Vienna since 2003. Lecturer at the Danube University Krems, Department for European Integration. Research Interests: Irregular Migration, Integration, Migration and the European Union.

Karolina Łukasiewicz, Master degree in Sociology, Jagiellonian University; Master degree in Applied Psychology, Jagiellonian University; Master degree in European Political Sociology, Dalarna University, Sweden. Ph.D. student in the Department of Social Anthropology, Institute of Sociology, Jagiellonian University.

Anna Maciejko, graduate in Social Policy from the Department of Journalism and Politics at the University of Warsaw; founding board member of the Polish Migration Forum, a non-governmental organisation, worked on refugee integration issues with the Department of Social Policy of the Mazovian Voivodship Office.

Martin Malek, 1991 Ph.D. in Political Science (University of Vienna). Since 1997 (civilian) researcher at the Institute for Peace Support and Conflict Management of the National Defence Academy (Vienna). Several internships in research institutes in Germany, Russia, Ukraine, and the U.S. Areas of expertise: State failing theories, theories of ethnic conflicts, security and military policy in the Commonwealth of Independent States (especially Russia, Ukraine, Armenia). Author of two books and some 250 publications in thirteen countries.

Emilia Małys, graduate of the law faculty of Wrocław University and the School for Human Rights of the Helsinki Foundation for Human Rights. 2002–2007 expert at the Office for Aliens on asylum procedures as well as Dublin procedures (family unification). Since 2007 senior expert in the Department of Migration of the Ministry of Labor and Social Policy.

Cerwyn Moore, Ph.D. from Nottingham Trent University in 2004, Master in International Relations at the University of Nottingham, Bachelor degree in International Relations from Staffordshire University. Taught at Nottingham Trent University from 2004–2006, since 2007 lecturing post in International Relations at the University of Birmingham. Research focus: political violence, particularly in Chechnya, and interpretive approaches to International Relations.

Zuzanna Olszewska, Master degree in Forced Migration from the Refugee Studies Centre at Oxford University, currently doctoral candidate in Social Anthropology at Oxford, working on Afghan refugees in Iran; founding member of the Polish Migration Forum; previously worked with the United Nations High Commissioner for Refugees in Warsaw on separated refugee children in Poland.

David Reichel, Master degree in Sociology, University of Vienna. Researcher at the International Centre for Migration Policy Development (ICMPD) in Vienna since 2007. Research Interests: Migration and Integration Statistics, Irregular Migration, Migration Sociology and Discrimination.

Alexander Schahbasi, Master degree in History, University of Graz and University of Jordan, research associate at the Chair of Civil Law at the Friedrich-Alexander University Erlangen-Nürnberg, head of the research team of the Austrian Integration Fund.

Alice Szczepanikova, Warwick Postgraduate Research Fellow in the Department of Sociology at the University of Warwick, United Kingdom. Research focus: gendered aspects of forced migration from the countries of the former Soviet Union to Europe. Also editor of the website Migration Online (www.migrationonline.cz) focusing on migration processes in Central and Eastern Europe. Publications about Chechens in Europe in the *Journal of Refugee Studies*; *Diasporas: Independent academic journal*; *Studi Emigrazione* and *Chechen Society Today*.

Edith Vasilyev, Master degree, graduated from the Federal Academy for Social Work as a qualified social worker, diploma studies in Spanish and Russian at the University of Vienna. Since 2004 with the Austrian Integration Fund (ÖIF): Assists recognized refugees as a social worker in the context of an integration programme, project management.